MATRIARCHS, GODDESSES, AND IMAGES OF GOD

Also by Susanne Heine and published by Augsburg

Women and Early Christianity

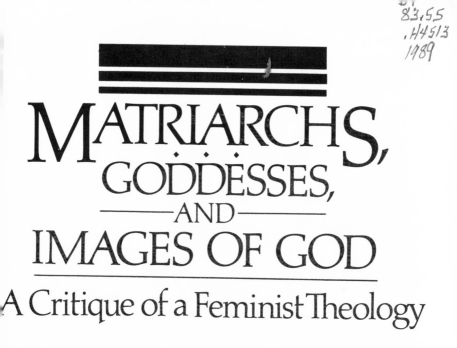

MATRIARCHS, GODDESSES, AND IMAGES OF GOD

A Critique of a Feminist Theology

SUSANNE·HEINE

Translated by

JOHN BOWDEN

AUGSBURG   MINNEAPOLIS

MATRIARCHS, GODDESSES, AND IMAGES OF GOD
A Critique of a Feminist Theology

First United States edition published 1989 by Augsburg, Minneapolis. First English-language edition published 1988 by SCM Press. Translated from the German edition with the approval of Verlag Vandenhoeck & Ruprecht, Göttingen.

Original German edition published 1987 under the title *WIEDERBELEBUNG DER GÖTTINNEN?* copyright © Verlag Vandenhoeck & Ruprecht. English translation copyright © 1988 John Bowden, published by SCM Press under the title *Christianity and the Goddesses*.

Library of Congress Cataloging-in-Publication Data

Heine, Susanne.
  [Wiederbelebung der Göttinnen? English]
  Matriarchs, goddesses, and images of God : a critique of a
feminist theology / Susanne Heine : translated by John Bowden.—
1st U.S. ed.
    p.   cm.
  Translation of: Wiederbelebung der Göttinnen?
  Sequel to: Women and early Christianity.
  Bibliography: p.
  Includes index.
  ISBN 0-8066-2421-3
  1. Feminist theology. 2. Women in Christianity. 3. Feminism—
Religious aspects—Christianity. 4. Woman (Christian theology)
I. Title.
BT83.55.H4513   1989
230'.088042—dc19   89-403
                                         CIP

The paper used in this publication meets the minimum requirements of American National Standard for Information Sciences—Permanence of Paper for Printed Library Materials, ANSI 7329.48-1984. ∞™

Manufactured in the U.S.A.   AF 9-2421
93   92   91   90   89   1   2   3   4   5   6   7   8   9   0

Contents

No Heart without a Head

1. Everyone is prophesying the end of the women's movement(s) and feminism. Men have long been sure that these movements had no future. When the struggle for equal rights for women theologians began in the Reformed churches in the 1960s, the church authorities comforted themselves with the thought that once 'they' got married and had children, the 'fashion' would soon die out. Now in that case the authorities were proved wrong, but the argument is still a topical one: marriage and children are seen as a means of discipline. It would be dishonest to deny that a good deal of feminist existence has already been shipwrecked in the haven of marriage.[1]

The aims had been many and varied, as many and varied as the 'battlefields' of the war between the sexes. There was and is a good deal to do: physical violence against women, the prevention of individual development by role-stereotyping, a rejection of the 'right to pleasure', legal discrimination as a result of the privatization of the family, the barrier to women in public and higher professional fields, less wages for the same work, and a wealth of prejudices like the view that women are incapable of thinking clearly and acting ethically. And a good deal has also been achieved, from a shift in consciousness to a change in real circumstances. Nevertheless 'total' achievement still escapes women. But – hand on heart – how could it have been achieved? Has 'total', 'perfect' achievement ever been realized in the history of the human race? Let me state quite simply first of all that this 'totality' is always involved in the tug-of-war between the quest for realization and eschatological hope, and is threatened by a 'Fascist' myth of salvation which seems ineradicable in its many guises (Chapters 3 and 4 of this book will return to that).[2] The fact that not everything has been achieved certainly does not mean that women are finished. But resignation soon ends ideals of perfection where these do not take reality into account.

The first slogan was 'sisterly solidarity', imagined as a world-embracing community of all women. One could have learned from the history of analogous attempts – from the Communist International to the Roman Una Sancta – that this aim is too lofty. Solidarity is not uniformity. The sisters began quarrelling; feminism and feminist theology developed very different positions. Does that mean that they are a failure? I would argue that that was the only possible way of avoiding a rigid dogmatism, drawing a boundary along a particular line which makes people blind to the concrete situation, the demand of the moment. So that, too, is not a convincing indication of the end that is prophesied.

Self-criticism broke out in women's own ranks. 'Have we overlooked something somewhere? Have we suppressed differ-ences, kept quiet about ambivalences? Overlooked ambiguities? Why did we get approval from the wrong side, why did the assent of our enemies surprise us?'[3] It became increasingly tedious to reflect on woman as woman or, as the art historian Alexandra Petzold put it in a humorous yet aggressive way: 'I've had a belly full of always reflecting only on the sacrificial nature of womanhood!'[4] In fact the debate is becoming increasingly matter-of-fact, is being carried on less in ideological terms, with a sense of humour and a critical methodology. Self-critical reflections and changes of course are not treachery to the cause or to the sisters. Self-criticism and detached cross-checking of one's own theses are regarded with good reason as an academic virtue, because they sharpen the arguments and make them more effective. The abandonment of 'tender thinking' (Hegel) which is reluctant to seek clarification through contradictions in the subject-matter seems to me to be a hopeful sign of progress. And why should there not be a vigorous struggle if it furthers knowledge? There can be no question of the end of feminism; on the contrary, the front is becoming broader and the arguments more differentiated; unnecessary irritants are being dropped, leaving more energy to concentrate on the cause, on the particular area under consideration. Academic conferences of women historians, women art historians, women philosophers are evidence to the public of the contribution of women to scholarship, since they leave on one side the fruitless and indoctrinating 'conversion' of the male part of humanity without of course avoiding necessary confrontations.

In the first volume of my historical criticism of a feminist theology, *Women and Early Christianity*, I have already indicated how much the development which I have sketched out here seems to me to be necessary. I do not know whether it can be seen as a coincidence that feminist theology in particular is still largely drifting in an ideological stream and regards self-criticism as a threat.[5] One may make very profound statements about the close relationship between theology/church and ideology, and also about the fact that the churches tend at best to take up existing trends, and hardly ever develop any innovations oneself. However... things need not remain like this, even if this has often been the case.

2. In the meantime feminism and feminist theology have also been accepted or recognized to some degree. But it would be too good to be true if such a recognition were always related to the matter in hand. Today women theologians can arrange services which eliminate all male elements in language and conceptuality: God becomes Goddess, Jesus Christ becomes Jesa Christa, the Holy Spirit is referred to as she. The question whether this can be the last word in feminist wisdom will be discussed in Chapters 1 and 5 of this book. Here my first concern is to point out soberly that such services no longer cause much of a stir. Is this progress? No. What may mean liberation for the feminist insider is mocked by outsiders or is welcomed in a paternal, patronizing way as a way in which women who are discriminated against by 'fate' can cleanse their souls: 'That's all right, if it helps them!'

In addition to this there are the 'progressive' circles who greedily take up anything that is 'modern' and a bit scandalous or stimulating: the second-hand avant-garde. Just a certain amount of recognition (not too much and not too little) encourages them to grasp the iron – which the moment they touch it proves to be cooling down. In the meantime there are enough theologians, men, who let feminism trickle down from the pulpit, and enough teachers of religion who appreciatively unfold the terrible history of patriarchy to the children of both sexes. But do we not believe that such fashionable feminism should also show a tooth or a claw, which could move someone, somewhere to real 'conversion'?

Everything is ambivalent, no cause is clear 'in itself', because there are always questions of the motivation behind the way in which it is taken up and communicated. In a way women can chalk up as progress the fact that misogyny no longer emerges in such an undisguised form. Here even the second-hand avant-garde performs a service. However, it would be a serious mistake to argue from that to the existence of an increasingly friendly attitude towards women based on conviction. I at any rate prefer clear opponents like the progressive feminists who only play their role so long as no flesh-and-blood woman crosses their path. One can associate this with experiences of antisemitism. Certainly on the whole it is socially tabu to show an inner antipathy to 'the Jews'. That keeps excesses in check, but nevertheless the ice remains thin and breaks easily; those who steer clear of contact with Jews in private circles and publicly dissociate themselves from them may have sufficiently 'respectable' excuses for so doing or disguise their attitude by explicit philosemitism. One of the successful tactics is 'to get oneself an advantageous position in relation to others by adopting a morally qualified verdict on the "Third Reich" '.[6] That also applies to the feminist demand for human rights for women: to follow fashion in endorsing it has advantages – not in all circles, but in many – but it constantly causes disappointments to those involved. By then it is usually too late; well disguised, someone has become established in one's own ranks who has been moved by quite different motives to seek friendship with women. And who could produce an irrefutable proof of the dishonesty of the motivation? So recognition can also be camouflage.

The pioneers of feminist theology with whom we shall be concerned in subsequent chapters have meanwhile put their stamp on at least one generation of women. Their arguments have acquired something like universal validity and are handed down as the 'assured results of feminist scholarship': we already have popular accounts of the material; schools and colleges disseminate it; and some university teaching lends it academic status. The sparrows are already piping it from the roofs of the temples of the goddesses: the God of Jews and Christians is guilty of patriarchalism and as an omnipotent father has humiliated and destroyed women for centuries. The accepted view here is that the theology of the patriarchy has disguised the fact that God is really mother, and has made us forget how well disposed to women were the early high cultures of humanity, in those days of the creator goddesses when in a primal state of holiness in a matriarchal epoch nature, woman, birth and rebirth developed unhindered. Males raging destructively and greedy for power (so the thesis continues) proved the downfall of a better world; since then the myths and images of former matriarchal spirituality have had to yield to what has sprung forth from the male head: reflection on monotheism and polytheism, on finite and infinite, on this world and the beyond, on nature and spirit, on good and evil.

Granted, there is a fascination in these theses of the reversal of reality as it can currently be experienced. But are they all true? Are not a whole mass of pious 'lies' concealed here, against which hardly anyone protests because they are so obvious? So this book will be concerned with a critical survey of feminist theories about God as mother, the goddess myth, matriarchies and androgynous myths, about Jesa Christa and finally about the question whether there is such a thing as a feminine science.

I write with a degree of scorn, and indeed sometimes with anger. The illogicality of some lines of argument can take one's breath away, and I get angrier and angrier because I see and also experience the degree to which women harm their legitimate intentions in this way. They make it easy for the opponents of their humane purposes to dissociate themselves, whether through mockery or by sympathetically recommending a psychiatrist. The most effective and most used-form of defence is ignorance.

Certainly, feminist theological literature has found a great response in feminist circles, but what Barbara Sichtermann calls 'approaching the lions' den', the 'argument put forward by the other side',[7] has so far not really taken place. Sigrid Schade, art historian in Berlin, aptly thinks that there can be no being-for-oneself in the representation of the sexes, even if this means a 'narcissistic insult'[8] to both sides. I would go on to add that if women and men cannot take this insult they will find themselves in the dead end of isolation. So it is not an argument but a misrepresentation when the attempt to get out of this dead end is described with a raised finger as 'going over to the opponent's camp'. Those who take this view must ask themselves whether it does not conceal a stubborn refusal to argue with anything which does not have the same kind of scent. What is evident in other disciplines, a capacity for cross-checking and methodological reflection, should also be noted and taken seriously by a feminist theology.

Not all forecasts of an end to, and stagnation in, the 'feminist cause' are really at an end; nor do all the forecasts of progress and recognition amount to serious recognition. But who or what prevents us from pursuing interests further, in a more sophisticated, more critical, more stubborn way?

3. More sophistication in thought and even greater exactness in dealing with methods and 'material' are a presupposition for further successful steps. The historical criticism of particular positions in feminist theology or criticism of types of historical reconstruction was the focus of my first book. It is in the nature of things that such criticism was not possible without systematic reflection. The thematic focus lay in the history of earliest Christianity from the perspective of women. In this second volume the focus must now be changed. We shall be involved in systematic criticism using the historical question: was it really like that? The subject-matter embraces historical periods which lie much further back in the past: the early high cultures and the period represented by the Old Testament. The further back a history lies, the scantier the evidence is from this past, and the more difficult the reconstruction. It will emerge that only systematic reflection makes plausible judgments possible.

The terms 'systematic' and 'system' do not have very happy associations. The ghost of Hegel's absolute system seems to be conjured up; is not reality trimmed back to the idea, instead of being perceived in its multiplicity? The suspicion of ideology arises, and Karl Marx raises his voice in warning us not to elevate particular circumstances to the status of spiritual essences for the benefit of the powerful. And finally have not the churches always lent to the personal conviction of faith the appearance of demonstrated and universally valid truth?

So I must offer a short explanation of what I mean by 'systematic' and how I shall be systematic in the following chapters. I shall begin from the overall sphere of reality in which each individual is and was at any time: the initially confusing multiplicity of phenomena, facts, motives, experiences. Each individual is a systematician who involuntarily attempts to bring order to that which thrusts itself upon him or her, to make sense of it. What thrusts itself upon the individual includes not only what comes 'from outside' but also what takes place 'within', one's sensibilities, the nature of one's perception, the mode of awareness of assimilating all this. 'Inward' and 'outward' cannot so easily be distinguished; it requires a degree of effort to do this. So the individual is the 'system', the 'whole' in which the totality of reality is represented.

If we separate the 'inward' from the 'outward', if by a process of abstraction from ourselves we leave out of account the fact that we are the ones who are acting from a particular motivation, it soon emerges that almost anything goes; everything is possible. Seen in this way history is a panopticon of unlimited possibility. People have already thought and done everything! So truth, understood as what seems to us to be right and valid, as what is so important to us that we motivate ourselves by it, does not lie in history itself but in our relationship to it. Systematic thinking therefore means mediating between tradition and our own present 'horizon of motivation'.[9] This is what the next five chapters are meant to suggest, and not more, since every human motivation is quite free: mediation cannot be forced, and that is confirmed not least by experience. True systematic thinking therefore means recognizing and acknowledging the freedom of the individual's system.[10]

System also means order; it is the opposite of muddle and confusion. Freedom of system is not identical with lack of system. My starting point is that everyone attempts to bring the manifold variety in the total sphere of reality into an overall context which is consistent for him or her. This does not rule out mistaken ideas and stalemates produced by contradictions. Feminist theology, too, is full of them. It would be a disaster if we shut our eyes to that, since otherwise legitimate intentions would be buried and there would be no communication.

Systematic thinking also means discovering complexes of meaning, for what is, is not meaningful simply by virtue of *the fact that it is*. Feminists immediately see that in connection with a patriarchal society. But if this statement is correct, must it not also be true of a matriarchal society? It does not need to be proved that meaning and not 'assured facts' keep people alive; that is to some degree evident. But that does not yet answer the question what meaning could consist of. A distinction of levels of meaning[11] – which is again systematic – seems evident. Human beings are a 'part' of nature and gain their significance from what is attractive to them, what gives pleasure, health, and what is useful to them for sustaining their physical and social life. But human beings are also spirit, and despite their justified utilitarian struggle cannot avoid the ethical demands of law and conscience. For what fits together well at the level of thought often results at the level of action in contradictions which cannot be resolved, and no matter what we decide leads to ambivalence and guilt, whereas forgiveness, atonement and love are clearly fulfilled only in hope and thus in faith. So the systematic ordering of contexts of meaning also discloses the insoluble dilemmas of human existence and warns us against forcing these into the procrustean bed of an absolute system which claims to purge reality of all dilemmas.

Without systematic reflection it is also easy to get entangled in avoidable dilemmas, simple contradictions, which lead a feminist theology that is insensitive to them into dangerous alliances with ideologies of the most varied kind: with antisemitism, with the libertinism of the so-called sexual revolution, with the anti-intellectualism of conservative social systems and with a fixation on reductionist theory of a scientific kind. It will be the task of the following chapters to substantiate this thesis.

4. I am critical of and, as I have already said, also often angry at the sisters who nevertheless have very much the same intentions as I do. But to have good intentions does not mean that one's efforts at communication will or must succeed. I want my criticism to help that communication which, where it is successful, reinforces intent. All the writers I quote have good insights; they criticize the ominous exclusion of personal motivation from current scientific theory; the enslavement of nature in humankind and around us; the many projections and shifts of a thought which

does not retain a concern for totality; the destructive forces which can be built up even by the most sublime claims of Christian faith. But the way in which they attempt to communicate these correct insights leads in precisely the opposite direction, and serves to reinforce those ideologies which are being attacked. Attempts at communication by assertions, moral imperatives and edifying speeches are no help against this undertow. Anyone who attacks those with heads and not hearts must not have a heart but no head. It is important to look at things in a sharper and more sophisticated way and in so doing bring them to a point. Some delight in aggression, which will sometimes strike readers of this book, serves the same purpose. However, the sisters whom I have quoted are not slow to apportion blame to both males and females.

So it has been important for me not to withhold judgments which run counter to the feminist argument but to incorporate them into what seems to me to be a necessary and honest counter-question. I hope that in this way I can show sufficiently clearly that as a result, while very often the means of communication collapses, the intention does not; indeed in this way the intention emerges more clearly.

In all this I am aware that no one can compel a readiness to leave the ways we have embarked on, to listen to arguments and to enter into discussion. That is the consequence of the freedom of the individual's system that I have described very briefly. But I gladly grant my hope, indeed my confidence, that there is such readiness for discussion.[12]

CHAPTER ONE

God the Father, God the Mother

The strict name of God

Blessed art thou,
O Lord our God and God of our fathers,
the great, mighty and revered God,
the most high God,
who bestowest lovingkindness,
creator of the universe...
O King, Helper, Saviour and Shield...
Thou, O Lord, art mighty for ever...
Thou art holy
and thy name is holy...
Cause us to return, O our Father, to thy Law.
Draw us near, O our King, unto thy service,
and bring us back in perfect repentance unto thy presence...
Bless us, O our Father,
with the light of thy countenance.[1]

'Lord', 'revered God', 'King', 'Shield', 'Father' – that is the way in which pious Jews still address their God in the Eighteen Benedictions: in the morning, in the evening and on the Sabbath. All these names appear in the Old Testament, and more besides: as warrior hero and leader of heavenly and earthly hosts God annihilates the enemies of Israel (Song of Miriam, Ex.15.1ff.; Song of Deborah, Judg.5.1ff.). He is Lord over all other gods and men, strong and terrible, king, supreme lawgiver and judge, a divine patriarch, who – as a feminist verdict has it – justifies all the evil deeds of the male patriarchs.

God is indeed also Father, although he does not have this name in the Old Testament anywhere so often as might be supposed from a knowledge of the New Testament. But God is a strict father: 'Know then in your heart that, as a man disciplines his son, the Lord your God disciplines you. So you shall keep the commandments of the Lord your God, by walking in his ways and by fearing him' (Deut.8.6).[2] 'For the Lord reproves him whom he loves, as a father the son in whom he delights' (Prov.3.12). As father God gives his people Israel, or even the individual, ethical instruction, the Torah, the 'Law of God'.

God is Father, because he has created humankind: 'Is not he your father, who created you, who made you and established you?' (Deut.32.6). There is also the very powerful conception of the child as a lump of clay that can be moulded in the hand of the one who begets him and rears him: 'Yet, O Lord, thou art our Father; we are the clay, and thou art our potter; we are all the work of thy hand' (Isa.64.8). Not all 'children' speak like this; many have turned from their Father, deny him and their origin. And God the Father suffers and feels insulted: 'Sons have I reared and brought up, but they have rebelled against me... Woe to sons who deal corruptly' (Isa.1.2-4). Injured love makes the Father angry: 'And I became as one who smote them on the back; I turned against them' (Hos.11.4). The jealousy of this God towards all other gods, 'fathers and mothers', in whom people could and have put their trust, is even now communicated to both Jewish and Christian children through the Ten Commandments.

Nevertheless, the strict God of the Old Testament is not a cruel God to his own people: 'The Lord is merciful and gracious, slow to anger and abiding in steadfast love... As a father pities his children, so the Lord pities those who fear him' (Ps.103.8,13).[3] Indeed, love virtually overwhelms the divine Father: 'For as often as I speak against him (= the people), I do remember him still. Therefore my heart yearns for him; I will surely have mercy on him...' (Jer.31.20). God the Father has taught his people to walk, taken them in his arms and drawn them to him with 'bands of love' (Hos.11.3-4). This is no blind love without criteria; just as

God is a father to orphans without rights who gives them justice (Ps.68.6), so God knows that people will always remain children and in need of forgiveness. For is there anyone who with the best will in the world does not sometimes fail others? Who among the mortals can say that he is perfect? No one escapes guilt. Anyone who does not recognize that is regarded as a stubborn sinner; judgment comes upon him. But anyone who has insight and turns in confidence to the Father may be certain of the love and mercy of his heavenly Father.

Thus this God has all the traits of the caring father who is strict but just to his children, especially his sons, in the family of the patriarchate. He brings his children up to obey his law, punishes them and rewards them, loves his children and feels offended if the children do not follow him, if they forsake him or even deny him. He can be furious with them, but he wants to win them back by having mercy on them and looking after them. He does not abandon his children, and they do not get away from him. All the authoritarian features of the paterfamilias, but also the humanly understandable and lovable ones, can also be found in God the Father.

The New Testament is striking first of all for the way in which the name Father is used for God much more frequently than in the Old Testament. Here it should be stressed that the address 'Abba' (Mark 1.36; Gal.4.6; Rom.8.15), the word that the small child burbles and which is best translated 'Papa', is the basis of a new, intimate relationship of trust in God which is free from anxiety: the Father God, who as Son is equal to human beings in everything (sin apart), who lays aside his exaltation and authority so as not to leave men and women alone even in their dying, creates a new relationship with God. Without doubt these features of the New Testament Father God are striking, and so the favourite parable of the Prodigal Son (Luke 15.11ff.) appears in every children's service or school curriculum. Nevertheless, we should not fail to notice that the names of God which attest his power, superiority and strength are still there: he is the Lord of heaven and earth, the Lord of all men and women, the king who establishes his rule, the judge of good and evil, and the Father who surrenders his utterly obedient Son Jesus to the minions of the law. The Old and New Testaments cannot be played off against one another. Almighty as he is, God can show his people his shining countenance and lovingly lead them on the way of life; but he can also hide himself, and can be experienced as the absent God: where was God when the tower of Siloam crashed down, burying people under it (Luke 13.4)? The dark, incomprehensible, indeed apparently destructive God, who does not lay aside his strangeness, does not disappear in the New Testament. Jesus does not reply to the question about the dead at Siloam with a statement on the problem of theodicy but puts a question in return: 'Do you think that they were more guilty than anyone else?' No one is innocent; there is no one who does not deserve to die at any time. And that means: do not ask, for God transcends your capacity for understanding. This God, the Father behind the Son who has come close to us, is also the God of the New Testament.

Such omnipotence removes God from human understanding; it transcends the power of the patriarchal kings, fathers and other rulers of the world. This has not prevented these rulers from continually deriving their power from the power of God, from transferring the distance between the utterly other God and humankind to the distance between them and their subjects. The parents are 'partners in procreation', we read in a rabbinic text from the sixth century of the Christian era.[4] This participation in the divine power of creation then gives the parents, and above all the father, almost divine authoritiy over the children. The Jewish historian of the first century of the Christian era, Flavius Josephus, interprets the narrative of the sacrifice of Isaac on Mount Moriah in the following way:

> Isaac, noble-minded as he was, being descended from such a father (= Abraham), took the news (that now he was to be sacrificed) well and said that it would not be worth his having been born were he not to obey what God and his Father had decided about him; indeed it would be wrong to refuse to obey even if his father alone had commanded.[5]

The hierarchy consisting of God – secular (or often spiritual) authority – *paterfamilias* still determines the social context in the Jewish-Christian circle of religion. The rulers of the world derive their power 'from above', and anyone who opposes them at the same time lays violent hands on the Holy One. The king as the

'Lord's anointed' or 'by the grace of God', the priest, the father
who 'presides' over his house are unassailable.

This 'theocratic short cut',[6] which has given its blessing to so
much abuse, inhumanity and violence in history has been criticized
by spiritual and political revolutionary movements since the
Enlightenment and has also continually been rejected, because of
its association with a vehement attack on Christianity and an
explicit atheism. Nevertheless, final success has still to come.
Anyone nowadays who takes part in the life of the Christian
community and its liturgical acts will encounter the biblical texts
which I have quoted being used in an unreflective way, in prayers
and hymns to the God of the 'theocratic short cut'. 'Women are
assigned the roles of the housewife, the widow and the mother,'
argues Katharina Knohl-Hohberg (who grew up in a Protestant
manse) in a witty critical article on 'Sexism in Hymns',[7] and she
goes on: as such they are 'constantly commended to the protection
of the male God, faithful to his earthly appendage in the form of
their husband: "He welcomes the orphans, fulfils the petition of
the widows and himself becomes their comfort and husband."'
Moreover in a respectable theocracy women are no longer
necessary at all. 'And though they take our life, goods, honour,
children, wife', goes the last verse of the great hymn for Refor-
mation Day, 'A Safe Stronghold our God is still'; it is hard to
understand the Lord Sabaoth, the Lord of Hosts, in this context
in a metaphorical sense, and 'the field', namely the battlefield,
which is mentioned here may still be misunderstood by some
fathers as the legitimate context of his actions.

Abused children

Thoughtful theological literature continually stresses that the
Father God and Lord God is not to be understood literally and
naively: God is not male and has no sex; names and properties
have 'only' symbolic significance. But what does 'only' mean
here? Symbols are very closely connected with reality. Women
who go to church must immediately get the impression that male
properties are at least more appropriate to God than female ones.[8]
In addition, there is the hiatus between theological reflection,
which has good intentions, and the means of communication

through pulpits and cathedras, which hardly stimulate such sophisticated thinking, but naively hand on what the language of the tradition offers. But naive communication cannot lead to reflective reception.

However, what makes the 'theocratic short cut' of this language of the male God so terrifyingly 'credible', false though it is, is the quite direct and personal experience which many women have of the other sex. This begins at the tenderest age.[9] My first encounter with a case of sexual abuse of children by close relatives is now well back in the past. In a confidential conversation at that time, an unmarried middle-aged woman told me that from the age of eight she had regularly been subjected to all kinds of sexual abuse by an uncle for almost twenty years. As a result she had not established any relationship with a man and had been undergoing psychotherapy for some time. She came from a good Christian home and for a long time had been involved in various positions and activities in the church and in the community. At the time I did not believe what she said and took it to be the expression of a suspect state of mind; her psychotherapy seemed to me to be more than justified. I am writing this because I am afraid that such experiences might seem just as incredible to others if they come up against them: the literature on this theme, which is the 'best-kept secret', but which is slowly but surely coming to light, shocked me over my reaction at the time. Meanwhile I have come to pay more careful attention to my surroundings and know that such experiences on the part of women are not extreme aberrations, nor are they limited to some 'lower level' of society.

I shall not be talking here of the sexual abuse of women generally. This theme, too, fills daily papers and professional studies. I am talking of the sexual abuse of girl children by their fathers and other close relatives like grandfathers, uncles and brothers. What form this takes can be discovered from the literature that I have mentioned. The sober statistics themselves speak volumes: the studies by Kavemann and Lohstöter (1983) for the Federal Republic of Germany calculate that on a conservative estimate there are a quarter of a million instances of sexual violence against girl children each year. 'How terribly common this is can be seen from the fact that on the basis of such figures it can be calculated that a girl is being sexually attacked in the

Federal Republic once every two to four minutes.'[10] Florence Rush
cites a statistic from 1981 for the USA of a million children; but
this statistic relates only to reported cases. The children themselves
keep quiet because they are afraid, because they love their fathers,
are dependent on them, need them as any child needs its parents,
because they often do not realize what is happening to them (or
only realize it much later), since they begin from the assumption
that nothing that the father does can be really bad. Members of
the family, including mothers, who know what is going on keep
quiet about it, for fear of their husbands and their violence or
because they are afraid that the family's reputation will be ruined
in the eyes of the neighbours. Thus in her calculations by means
of counselling groups which are not taken into account in criminal
statistics, Florence Rush arrives at the figure of twenty-five million
abused children a year. To my knowledge this problem is neither
perceived by nor discussed within the church: none of the counselling bodies mentioned in the literature is associated with a
church. If I am wrong here, I would very much like to know.

In view of such experiences, talk about the Father God and
God the Father as the representative of law and order, as the
one who loves, who has mercy on his children, becomes sheer
arrogance. What else can give rise to the cynical image of a father
who refers to the fact that he is a father while raping his daughter:
'Don't be afraid... I'm your father?'[11]

Nor do the other 'paternal' authorities offer to the girl to whom
violence is done in this and other ways the protection she needs.
Grown-ups in the circle of family and acquaintances often attempt
to deter the victim with a warning, with the 'moral' pressure not
to destroy the life of the father.[12] Legal protection is full of
loopholes; it is difficult for the children to communicate their
traumatic experiences in a courtroom; outside the intimate circle
of violence the fathers create trust and make a good impression;
in the case of a dependent child, who will distinguish what
happened 'willingly' from what was compelled? Who will
distinguish from outside what action is to be seen as fatherly
tenderness and what as sexual aggression? Who are the judges?
Have they perhaps too much understanding for those who are
accused because of what they themselves do? What we call the
powers of order in society, like e.g. the law, give no assurances

that justice will be done to the victims; training and educational institutions can themselves be actively and passively involved in the perpetration of violence. Teachers, too, are numbered among the 'closely connected' males who do violence to girls.[13] Educators, teachers and social workers often stand back when signs that help is needed reach them from those involved; they feel that this asks too much of them.[14] So where is the earthly authority of divine justice? For many women all that remains is suffering from their desperation and their hate. 'And if anyone else among you should dare to say or even only to think that I am a solitary case, abnormal, and your tender and voluntarily relationships were fundamentally different, then I would want to pour out all my heaped-up hatred, my disgust, my consequent paralysis on you, so that it deprived you of air and strangled you.'[15] Those are the words of a twenty-eight-year-old woman who does not have the strength to speak openly of what she has experienced.

Those who keep this field of the most brutal force in mind, or do not close their eyes to it (and to this should be added the force exerted on women by outsiders and by legitimate husbands,[16] the verbal violence, the institutional violence or sexual harrassment at work[17]), will know why feminists want to have nothing more to do with God as the father, the lord and king. However, one of the names of God gains new meaning for me against this background: that of the judge, who also seeks out the hidden sins of people and makes them perish in the flood. And who could fail to understand that the feeling of impotent wrath puts 'cursing psalms' on one's lips – a genre of biblical literature about which no one involved can be amazed (even if the immediate need for vengeance does not make any difference: e.g. Pss.5; 7; 36; 53; 58; 109).

The feminist criticism of the destructive male abuse of power continues in a comprehensive social critique far beyond the immediate negative personal experience: 'Since in Western tradition women are traditionally identified with nature and conversely nature is seen as an object of domination by humanity (the male), it is almost a truism to say that the mentality which regards nature as an object of domination calls for a symbol and attitudes which form the basis of the oppression of the woman by the man.' That is the way in which in 1975 Rosemary Ruether began her lecture in Vienna under the title 'Women, Ecology and Social Revolution' (she was giving it on the invitation of the then Archbishop of Vienna, Cardinal König). The exploitation of nature, the hypertrophy of technology, the balance of terror which threatens at any moment to get out of control, the 'ideal' of profit and power and the increasingly heedless work in chemistry and atomic energy and at the expense of living creatures (experiments with animals) – all that is one side of the attitude against which women protest as being sexist.[18] In view of that, is God still a 'safe stronghold'?

A God among gods

The misuse of God to legitimate human abuses causes women to be offended at God the Father. A feminist theology must take this state of affairs seriously, but it may not stop there. It has to go on to ask: how was this biblical Father God arrived at? What are the alternatives?

The phenomenological account I have given so far, simply listing the names for God as they appear in the texts, regardless of whether they are shaped by female or male concepts, must now be taken further by a historical-critical approach. The texts of the Old Testament do not all come from the time to which they relate. That is true above all of the early history before the formation of the state. The 'historians' of the times, who were never in fact concerned with historical facts but with the interpretation of the history of faith, collected together previous traditions to serve their particular interests,[19] and these texts, too, have often been worked over several times by later redactions. That makes a historical reconstruction extremely difficult, and the more difficult, the older the tradition is. Scholarship can initially work only with hypotheses which have greater or lesser degrees of probability and which equally prove subject to the interest of the person doing the reconstructing; they are also continually changed in favour of new hypotheses. Comparisons with other cultures and religions can be helpful to the degree that one begins from the basic thesis of parallelism. But who is to prove that the Old Testament is no different from its environment? So in such historical reconstructions we are somewhat groping in the dark. This must be taken into consideration in what follows.

If we adopt the chronology and the basic statements of the Old Testament books as we find them in the canon, without being too mistrustful of the authors, we get the following picture, the accepted opinion which influences both male and female theologians both through the literature they read and the teaching establishments which they attend. The ancestors of the Israelites were wandering shepherds who moved to and fro between cultivated land and steppe with their flocks of sheep and goats. So they were not sedentary and lived in groups of clans. This form of life is matched by their faith in a supreme tribal God who reveals himself to the supreme tribal leader, the patriarch, and is very closely connected with him. The leader of the clans is the founder of the cult. This God bears the name 'God of my Father' (Gen.31.5,29,42,etc.). Each tribe has its own tribal God; that distinguishes the forebears of Israel first of all from their polytheistic neighbours. When the tribes unite, they also bring together their particular deities. Similarly, the sequence of generations increases the number of gods and provides them with patriarchal names: 'God of Abraham, God of Isaac, God of Jacob' or 'God of the Fathers'. It was only a later tradition which fused these patriarchal deities into a single God and so put explicit monotheism, which in fact came much later, at the beginning of history. Moreover the name 'God of the fathers' is not the same thing as 'God the Father'.

The tribes which were not sedentary now pressed on to settle in cultivated land. This conclusion is drawn from the promise of land and people which permeates the patriarchal tradition. This process was slow and, contrary to the account from a later hand, did not take place by military means. In cultivated land the tribes now came up against a quite different form of religion. Imitating the bond between the farmers and the land and fertility, the many deities of the now sedentary people similarly settled at specific places, i.e. in cultic sanctuaries. Whereas the God of the fathers had joined the shepherds in their travelling, now it was necessary to make pilgrimages to the gods of the farming communities. With the settlement, the gods of the fathers also found an abode and associated themselves with the name of the supreme

Canaanite patriarchal God 'El'. Personal names and the names of cult places now have the addition '-el', e.g. Ishmael, Israel or the place Beth-el. We are now somewhere around the thirteenth century BC. The belief of the sedentary nomads is polytheistic. 'El', the father of the gods, is assimilated, but without paternalistic features being explicitly stated and developed. In the course of these developments the god 'Yahweh' also appears, similarly the god of a tribe who makes his contribution to the pantheon in connection with those of other settled tribes. The narrative of the exodus from Egypt derives from this tradition. Here too it was only much later that Yahweh was elevated to being the sole God of Israel.

When the Philistines, who invaded Palestine from over the Mediterranean, sought to drive out the settled tribes, these joined together and sought to centralize their defensive forces by establishing a kingdom in which the king was also the supreme general. The first king, Saul, came to grief in the battle against the Philistines; the second, David, managed not only to annihilate the invaders but also to combine the northern and southern tribes in a kingdom on an ancient Near Eastern model (c. 1000 BC). In support of his power politics aimed at union we have, for example, the establishment of a central cultic sanctuary in Jerusalem, the seat of the king and the personal possession of David. David's empire integrated not only a series of Canaanite city-states who as a result merely changed their supreme lord, but also their world of gods. In the temple of Jerusalem at the time of David and of Solomon, his son and successor, there was worship not only of the one God Yahweh but also of a wealth of gods and goddesses. On the model of the religious conceptions of other peoples (e.g. in Mesopotamia and Egypt) the king now becomes the son of God, or God becomes the father of the king.[20] Psalm 2 reproduces this tradition when it says in v.7: 'Thou art my son, this day (= the day of the accession to the throne) have I begotten thee.' Yahweh, later the only God, here emerges as the personal god of the Davidic royal house and legitimates it 'by God's grace'.

Yahweh, or the strategy of survival

Only at a time when the collapse of the kingdom both in the north[21] and later in the south was in prospect or as a result of the victories of the Assyrians over the north and the Babylonians over the south did polytheism collapse and the god Yahweh become the father of the people, associated with the hope for the return from exile and the dispersion to a new independent state. This never came about again,[22] and so Yahweh became the father of the pious individual. Though the Jews have always understood themselves as members of a community, as they still do, the personal relationship to God came into the foreground. History makes that understandable. So we can also see how the first and close tie of the child to its parent, to father *and* mother, is most appropriate for expressing the relationship between God and human beings as an inward one. The maternal features of God must not, however, delude us into forgetting that the time of God's 'becoming mother' is also the time of the sharpest polemic against polytheism and its female deities. How does this contrast come about?

Anyone who attempts to read the texts of the Old Testament 'simply' in this way 'as they stand' must at least be struck by the many duplications. A story is often told several times at different lengths and with divergent intentions. Thus different writers must have worked on the traditional material at their disposal in different ways. Mistrust is appropriate! These literary works largely come from a very late period. The exile in Babylon was the occasion for those who had been deported to survey the history of the people, to investigate the reasons for this radical failure of their existence as an independent state and to think about the future. When the Jewish exilic community under Persian rule and supervision was again able to return to Palestine, the rebuilding of the Jerusalem temple took place under quite new and different conditions from those in which it had arisen under Solomon. It is probable that two great complexes of writings came into being at this time: Deuteronomy and the Priestly Writing, both in priestly circles. The Babylonians had taken with them from Jerusalem only the upper classes around the court and the temple. The people of the land remained behind so that the land could continue to be tilled and did not become desolate. The Babylonians had taken over both government and administration. With the disappearance of the monarchy, however, the priesthood gained sole rule, so that after the exile a theocracy could develop.

Deuteronomy now came into being in priestly circles, presumably from Jerusalem, and displayed the characteristic features of a manifesto: 'One God, one people, one cult.'[23] Whereas Deuteronomy is still seeking to establish this demand, the Priestly Writing which came into being in the post-exilic period is based on it. From this standpoint the history of Israel is seen in a critical light, and above all the cult, since for the priest the cult ultimately occupies a central position: as the people and the rulers had constantly run after other deities, the penal judgment of Yahweh came to annihilate them. In particular the criticism of the kings, who fostered polytheism, lends itself to the claim of the priests to leadership, the claim that now they are the authority and the moral authority. The Torah and ethical instruction occupy a central place in the exile and post-exilic community.

The feminist reading of the texts describes this development dominantly from a moral perspective, as though 'rigid intolerance', 'unbearable obscurantism of election', 'a contemptuous lust for annihilation' were responsible for them as an expression of the defective psychological health[24] of the authors of these writings, whereas the variegated world of the polytheistic pantheon with its goddesses is seen as evidence of a healthy psyche. However, such posthumous psychological censures do not relate to the historical context, but simply shed some light on the relationship of the present to history.[25] If we look at history, then the attitude of those priests can also be understood as an admirable strategy of survival among the remnant of a people which had escaped the holocaust. The lost independence and the loss of the unity of the people which had came about some centuries before take on new contours in the independent belief of the one Jewish community in the one god Yahweh. This conviction allowed the Jews to survive yet more holocausts. By contrast the feminist generalization is not without its dangers, as a consequence of which the God of Jews is made responsible for the evil situation in which women find themselves in our civilization: only a small step separates such charges from antisemitism of a clerical or Fascist stamp, the contempt in which always proves to be hostile to women.[26]

This perspective of the Jewish community also shaped the tradition accordingly: old traditional material which contradicted the new faith retreats in the face of a monotheism which (it is claimed) already existed at the beginning of tribal life, and which still nevertheless glimmers through the many layers of the texts. At all events the new faith was not invented at a stroke or arbitrarily plucked from the hedgerow. Its roots lie deeper and go back further. The various tribal cults which later included the cults of the groups of people who had been integrated into the kingdom did not always coexist as peacefully as the conception of an assembly in the pantheon might suggest. One key to the cultic criticism of the 'alien religions' which can already be demonstrated before the time of the exile is cultic rivalry and thus rivalry within priestly circles. The background of cultic rivalry is constantly formed by tribal rivalries and political tensions. It is quite evident from the story of the golden calf (Ex.22), for example, that the levitical priests around Aaron followed Moses, the adherent of Yahweh, only after a power struggle over an alien cultic practice had come to an end, not without bloodshed.[27]

David might be mentioned as a second impressive example. After the capture of the Jebusite city of Jerusalem he set the Jebusite priesthood (the family of Zadok) at the top of the priestly hierarchy (Gen.14.18-20 legitimates the Zadokite tradition by projecting it backwards into the patriarchal period). This inevitably led to rivalry between the sons of Zadok and the Levites. In a reform of the cult around 400 years later King Josiah then wanted to help the Levites to prominence, but was not successful. The Zadokite priesthood prevailed and reduced the Levites to being auxiliary personnel at the temple in Jerusalem. In addition, against the background of political tensions there was cultic rivalry between the southern and northern kingdoms, between the royal house of David and Israel, which had been incorporated into his empire by his political ploys. The northern kingdom also had traditional sanctuaries to show, those which were unwilling to yield to the monopoly of the Jerusalem temple. After the death of King Solomon, Jeroboam I, the first king of the northern kingdom, which detached itself from the Davidic dynasty, promptly established two new cultic centres in Bethel and Dan with priests 'who were not Levites' and golden calves (I Kings 12.26f.). So there were more than just religious reasons why the priests from the time of the exile, who came from the southern kingdom, branded this as the 'sin of Jeroboam'. However, their taunt was not a particularly daring one since the northern kingdom had long since been razed to the ground; still, the golden calves of Jeroboam performed good service in legitimating their own position of pre-eminence.

There is evidence throughout history that secular and spiritual authorities, kings and priests, can become rivals. Israel is no exception here. Finally, prophecy also played a role in this trial of strength: the 'free', charismatic tradition against the priestly, but also against the dynastic establishment. As this 'establishment' could associate with a great variety of cults, the cultic criticism of the prophets was a logical conclusion; like that of Hosea before the catastrophe of the northern kingdom and Jeremiah before the collapse of the southern kingdom. Finally, a decisive role may have been played by the fact that many of the cults practised in Israel showed close parallels with the religion of the enemies of Israel (cf. e.g. I Kings 14.24; II Kings 16.7ff.). Might Israel have made common cause with the faith of its enemies who finally annihilated it?

The theology of the priests which became established in the exilic and post-exilic period could appeal in many respects to the prophetic tradition. It could understand itself as reform in the spirit of a proclamation whose interpretation of history had been proved right: the development of power, despotism, the accumulation of wealth in the hands of a small upper class, the exploitation of the poor, the development of the power and splendour of a polytheistic cult – all that had been an imitation of the enemy. The terrible outcome of this history had not been the result of either chance or a fatal catastrophe, nor had it been the ultimate will of God. The Jewish community could continue to survive because it understood events as the penal judgment of God and thus associated hope with a new beginning. Without this theology the Jews might possibly have disappeared from history: one more genocide. That they interpreted their history in this way is not necessarily to be derived from its course and conditions. It was their independent 'achievement'.

The theological texts of the late priests doubtless have a 'powerful' character: in the end they criticize a dominant tradition. Even good concepts need a certain pressure 'from above', since people do not always grasp the truth.[28] Any history is determined by many, even conflicting, themes. Thus themes come together here which at first sight are exclusive. As I have already said, God's 'becoming a mother' coincides with the struggle against feminine deities; the stress on the devastating power of the one God with the criticism of the powerful. Although the claim of the priests to authority may play a major role, we can equally see here an expression of the will to live and the faith of the Jewish community, which had survived with its former tribal god Yahweh. Therefore the priests themselves became adequately subject to criticism. We can read something about that right down to the New Testament.[29]

The motherhood of God

Many women leave the church in order to have done with Christianity and the church once and for all. Others leave the church in order – grotesque though it may sound – to be able to grapple with Christian belief again. After one of my lectures one woman member of the audience gave her not unusual reason for this. She wanted to make her own independent investigation of the sources of Christian faith: she read the Bible, studied commentaries and talked with women and with women theologians about her questions, but she no longer wanted to have anything to do with the patronizing and repressive talk of pastors and teachers of religion; this either gave her her old feeling of shameful subjection or made her so angry that she could no longer control her reactions. This woman came from an avowedly Christian home with an active religious practice. That is not to pass judgment on all pastors and theologians, but such reactions should make the church and its representatives think self-critically about themselves. According to the Christian understanding, the divine promise to Israel was no guarantee of a fulfilment.[30] But who says that the divine promise to the church is a guarantee that the gospel is not leaving her and seeking realization somewhere else?

There are other reactions from women who feel that the church has left them in the lurch. Some who have preserved at least a general religious interest seek other religions outside Christianity and think that they can see some realization of their femininity in the goddess cults of antiquity. (The next chapter will be dealing with these in detail.) Others who maintain their ties with the Christian tradition go in search of the feminine traits of the biblical God.[31] Here there is in fact something to be discovered which unfortunately has left hardly any mark on the liturgical practice of the church.

The strongest statements about the motherhood of God appear in Deutero-Isaiah, the later prophet of salvation in the exilic period (sixth century BC): 'Can a woman forget her sucking child, that she should have no compassion on the son of her womb?' And the prophet goes on to greater heights: even if a mother forgot her child: 'Even these may forget, but I will not forget you' (Isa.49.15-16). God calls his people together: 'Hearken to me O house of Jacob, all the remnant of the house of Israel, who have been borne by me from your birth, carried from the womb; even to your old age I am he, and to grey hairs I will carry you' (Isa.46.3-4). God says to the anonymous prophet whom we call Trito-Isaiah, from the period after the exile, who appears in Jerusalem in the Persian period (c.520 BC): 'As one whom his mother comforts, so I will comfort you' (Isa.66.13). In the book of Job God describes his creative activity with terms from the experiential world of the mother: 'Who shut in the sea with doors, when it burst forth from the womb; when I made clouds its garment, and thick darkness its swaddling band?' (Job 38.3-9). The action of mother and father can be limited to the idea of comprehensive parental functions: 'Has the rain a father, or who has begotten the drops of dew? From whose womb did the ice come forth, and who has given birth to the hoarfrost of heaven?' (Job 38.28-29).

The pious person snuggles confidently up to his God-Mother: 'But I have calmed and quieted my soul, like a child quieted at its mother's breast' (Ps.131.2). When the people murmur on their exodus from Egypt and long for the fleshpots of Egypt, Moses too gets weary of his sole responsibility: 'Did I conceive all this people?

Did I bring them forth that thou shouldst say to me, "Carry them in your bosom, as a nurse carries the sucking child, to the land which thou didst swear to give their fathers'" (Num.11.12)? Thus Moses reminds God of his maternal duties. But before his death Moses also admonishes the people: 'You were unmindful of the Rock that begot you, and you forgot the God who gave you birth' (Deut.32.18). Once again paternal and maternal features of God are combined in the'parenthood' of God.

God is like a mother bird which teaches her young to fly and takes them on its wings (Deut.32.11; Ex.19.4), like a hen who gathers her chickens under her wings (Matt.23.37; Ps.17.8; 91.4; 37.2 etc.). But the motherhood of God can also be directed aggressively against her own children if these turn away from the mother: 'I will fall upon them like a she-bear robbed of her cubs' (Hos.13.8). The mention of rebirth from the Spirit (especially in the Gospel of John, e.g.3.4-7) evokes maternal associations; the parables of Jesus among other things make use of the realities of a woman's life: the kingdom of God can be compared with yeast which a woman mixes with the flour until it is completely leavened; like a woman and her friends who search the house for a lost coin until she has found it, so God seeks out sinners for them to be converted (Luke 13.20-21; 15.8-10). Some feminist theologians also see in the female gender of words a reference to the feminine aspects of the biblical God. The Hebrew word for the Spirit of God is feminine, *ruach*, and the divine mercy which is constantly mentioned in the texts is also feminine, *racham*; moreover it can be translated in its original meaning 'mother's womb'.[32]

In order to bring out this femininity and maternal quality of God, women theologians and pastors also try to give a dominant place in liturgical texts to the feminine aspects of God. To this end Rachel Wahlberg has written a creed for women, which for the moment can already be regarded as a classical text of feminist theology:[33]

> I believe in God
> who created woman and man in the image of God,
> who created the world
> and entrusted the care of the earth
> to both sexes.

I believe in the totality
of the redeemer,
in whom there is neither Greek nor Jew
neither slave nor free, neither man nor woman,
for we are all one in redemption.

I believe in the Holy Spirit,
the feminine Spirit of God
who gave us life like a mother bird,
and bore us
and covers us
with her wings.

So we can certainly bring together some feminine features and formulate them as a counterbalance to a long tradition of one-sided stress on the masculinity of God. Nevertheless the question remains whether that is honest and meaningful. There is no doubt that male designations for the divine qualities and modes of action predominate in the biblical text. Accordingly the feminist concerns for a feminine image of God seem a little forced, especially where they use the feminine gender of a word for their arguments. The word 'Spirit', for example, has a variety of genders depending on the language. In German it is male, in Greek neuter, in Hebrew feminine; in English, of course, nouns have no gender at all. What does one achieve with this argument when one reflects that in German, for example, power, violence or greatness are all feminine although in feminine judgment they are very closely related to the character of the male? Nor is that the case only in German: in Hebrew not only is the sword feminine, but also *geburah*, male power.

Moreover it is dangerous and contrary to basic feminist interests when a division of the male and female properties of God gives a boost to the usual stereotyping of roles. In addition to childbearing, we find that loving care, oversight, clothing, feeding, the household are seen as 'typically' feminine;[34] justice, law, anger, punishment, power are seen as 'typically' masculine.

The maternal features of God to which some feminists refer belong to that part of the tradition which is opposed to goddess myths and cults: Hosea, Jeremiah, Deutero-Isaiah, Trito-Isaiah, Deuteronomy, the Priestly Writing. It is obvious what they want to say. Why do you need a mother goddess? Yahweh, the father, judge and warrior hero, can also give birth, breast-feed, care for and have mercy. Even if a mother left her child, God would never leave his people.

Anyone in search of the Old Testament God as mother will find indissolubly connected with this perspective the one God of heaven and earth and the strict father. That can also be seen in a positive light: male and female, separated here on earth, alien to one another or in conflict with one another, belong together in a totality. It is not God's fault that people have not always understood things like this, but instead use the power and masculinity of God as legitimation for the rule of men over men.

So in the tradition which we have in its final form the biblical God is far from being deserving of the name mother. His masculinity is never in question, nor is the fundamental repudiation of the female deities in the pantheon of the neighbouring peoples. It is striking that the name father for God as the expression of an inward relationship between God and people cannot be demonstrated until a very late period: it does not appear before the devastating attacks of the Assyrians against the northern kingdom of Israel and the Babylonians against the southern kingdom.[35] The name father for God in the context of the relationship between the faithful individual and his personal God appears even more rarely and much later. As I have already shown, in this way maternal and paternal elements are closely interwoven in some texts. If we leave aside birth and breast-feeding, there is nothing against understanding physical care, love, illness and mercy as a fatherly attitude towards children. And is not a mother's love also concerned to look strictly at a social life in accordance with the criterion of ethical maxims, fighting with children and for children if need be? Instead of our speaking of God the mother, in this tradition the concept of God must be seen, rather, in the more general aspect of the parent-child relationship. That the biblical God who has from of old been male also takes on maternal and, as we shall see later, other feminine features, shows rather that he is 'all in all' and can assimilate qualities or modes of conduct which are distributed between different divine figures in a polytheistic religion. The maternal side of this God, too, is at the service of the strict monotheism of Jewish faith, even if it was not beyond dispute at all times.

Impaired experiences of the mother

Let us try another experiment in thinking. Suppose that the biblical tradition had given us a goddess instead of a god, a mother in heaven instead of a father in heaven. Let us once again take up the remarks of many women who say that their unhappy experiences with their physical father got in the way of their access to a heavenly father, but that they could have trust in a heavenly mother. We would evidently not be human were all this impossible. In the course of the feminist revolution women have discovered their problems with their physical mothers, which are worked out less in open violence than through subterranean psychological pressure, yet prove just as great a burden in adult life. Mothers no long punish so much with their fists as with an indirect threat of withholding love or indicating that they have been insulted in a way which threatens their existence. Such mothers do send out not verbal but emotional signals: If you do that, you'll kill me. 'She hardly ever punished us,' wrote a woman about her mother. 'She had a worse method. If we had to do something and didn't want to do it, then she would say, "Then I'll do it myself."'[36] Daughters complain about being tied to mother's apron strings, about being treated like children, about being put down, about too few good words, about too few words at all. 'I never understood her (= the mother); for me she was an authority of whom I was afraid'; 'I could never touch her; that humiliated me a great deal'; 'She recognized me intellectually but she despised me as a person and a woman in the same way that she despised herself.' Daughters suffer from the fact that they feel responsible for their mothers, and already did as children; they feel as it were mothers of their mothers. They get on better with their fathers and feel accepted by them.[37] The reverse is also true. Anything, in fact, may be the case. Mothers also exercise emotional power over their sons, just as sons have to suffer violence in various forms from their fathers. The literature is full of examples.[38]

It is no coincidence that the books of Alice Miller, and especially her first, *The Drama of the Gifted Child and the Search for the True Self*, evoked a flood of enthusiasm, but many readers were so terrified by the recognition of repressed childhood torment that they could not go on reading them. Alice Miller offers for the phenomena which she describes the psychoanalytic theory of narcissistic disruption. Here is the emotionally uncertain mother who feels threatened by the original vitality of her child; who envies and hates the child for it and can only love the sensitive child once it has learned to renounce itself to the point of self-surrender and, through its own intuition, by anticipating the command, to fulfil the deep-seated needs of the mother. Thus the child lives with the false self of the mother; it has lost the real one. Out of weakness and uncertainty these mothers make their children pliable. True, mothers do not exercise violence, but in her practice as an analyst Alice Miller has also come across the sexual seduction of the small boy by its mother.[39] Feminists again make men and fathers responsible for damaging mothers – but which comes first, the chicken or the egg? What takes place in such instances is the vicious circle of the hurt hurter. Women with bad experiences of their fathers may be helped by the mother in heaven; women with bad experiences of their mothers may be helped by the father in heaven. Again it was in a conversation with women after a lecture that I heard one of them say: 'If God is a mother, I'm scared of the resurrection.'

Neither the phenomenological selection of feminine features of the biblical God nor the historical-critical quest for the place where these features arose, nor recourse to human experiences of parents, seem to me to take us further. If one reflects on the terrifying variety of possibilities of violence between parents and children, then the 'disembodied' and transcendent conception of God as the 'wholly other' which is so reviled by feminists takes on power to release us: 'Thank God' that God is different from us human beings!

You shall not make for yourself any image

Therefore as a fourth and last stage which can in fact help us out of many contradictions, systematic considerations about the question of God are necessary. I shall start from the statement that God *is* Father. What does this 'is' mean? The Jewish-Christian tradition has always excluded physical ideas of procreation.[40] The biblical God is not like Zeus, who occupied himself pre-eminently with begetting physical descendants and thus populated heaven and earth with demigods. The Christian confession of the virgin birth is simply meant to say that the conception of a physical procreation of Jesus by God is as out of the question as is his origin simply from a human being. The main reason why the phrase 'conceived by the Spirit (of God)'[41] keeps appearing in the biblical texts is to rule out biological associations: the word 'conceived' is never to be understood literally. Nor is the phrase 'God is father' to be reversed to become 'our (physical) father is God'. The effect of Judaism and Christianity is to portray God the creator as the 'wholly Other', as the one who is defined as not being a creature.

Feminists have labelled this sexless, transcendent, spiritualized, abstract God who is critical of myth a product of a male consciousness and made him responsible for any drop of blood which human beings have shed in their struggle against other human beings: males, theologians 'project' a 'divided spiritual principle, the product of the development of patriarchal consciousness, on to the cradle of human culture'. The woman who wrote this, Gerda Weiler,[42] sees this cradle as having been a matriarchal one. I shall be devoting a whole chapter to the problem of matriarchy. Here we are primarily interested in the relationship postulated between 'spiritual principle' and 'patriarchal consciousness'. 'The idea of "God as spirit" is abstract, and one can only abstract from what can be seen, which must have come first.' The demand "You shall make no image" injures people, leads them into neurosis. The human course towards worshipping God without images is not spiritual progress but development towards a schizophrenic - i.e. divided - mode of human existence. The psychologically healthy person remains fruitfully bound up with his or her world of images.'[43]

Without doubt images, symbols, perception are part of human life and their absence is felt as a deficiency: but they are only part of human reality and of themselves are a 'schizophrenic' product of division. Aristotle, though a male, like many philosophers was aware that human beings are concerned with being whole. He speaks of *three* forms of activity, all of which are needed for a meaningful life: *theoria* as an act of will and capacity for knowledge (science); *praxis* as the realization of ethically-based responsibility ('virtue') and *poiesis* as formative action which makes something perceptible.[44] Poiesis includes the manifold forms of art (rhetoric, the graphic arts), ritual actions, festivals, symbols in the religious and the secular spheres. A theatre performance is poiesis, but so too is going to the theatre; communities, states give themselves poietic symbols e.g. with emblems and banners; festivals express their occasion and meaning in symbolic form. Every faith seeks to depict itself in formative action; everything can 'become a parable' (Goethe) for it: stars, plants, animals and human beings through either their form (eye, hand, hair, etc.) or through their feelings (hunger, thirst, erotic desire, etc.). 'In practice faith creates for itself a "fixed" expression, since whatever is inward needs its outward form if it is to be effective in the world. This manifold external form is referred to with the term 'positivity' (the Latin translation of the word *poiesis*). This is not the opposite to negativity but denotes being put (*ponere* = put) into reality. In this sense positivity presupposes inwardness, just as the gift of a bunch of flowers presupposes the inner disposition. Where this inner life is missing in statements there is a dead positivity, form without soul... That which is inward (faith, love, hope) may not be separated from the external elements in which it is manifested and the external elements are completely misunderstood if they are looked at empirically, i.e. without taking account of their significance.[45] Positivity can become rigid in empty forms unless faith is alive. Any faith – polytheistic, Jewish, Christian – develops its poietic, positive expressions in a physical form: one is stronger in rites and dances, another in imagery or language (poetry, narrative). In every case it is true that the more powerful the faith, the more effective the form. Even before her or his capacity for knowledge, an individual is accompanied and shaped by the forms which surround him or her, determined by whether they are empty or powerful.[46] Like everything in human history, form is subject to change; forms can change their significance or the significance can seek new forms. The history of all religions is evidence of this.

All that is just one element in the Aristotelian triad that I have mentioned. The credibility of the expression in a physical form is lost if it is accompanied by modes of action which violate the ethical demand for humanity; and it is lost if insight goes on its own ways which are no longer communicated by other modes of activity. This last is probably to be diagnosed as the 'malady of our time'. That young people when growing up arrive 'at the age of reason' and thus abandon their faith as 'childishness' does not indicate a neglect of poiesis but a neglect of theory, the link between reason and faith.

Theory, too, the primarily detached reflection on God or the statement 'God is father', can also disclose a saving knowledge. If we take this course, it is striking that in biblical texts talk of God is accompanied by negations. God is father but does not beget; God reveals himself but remains invisible; God is life, but not affected by death; God acts in history, but is transcendent ('in heaven'); one may not make an image of him (in the literal and metaphorical sense): he is creator, not created himself, he is 'wholly other'. This *via negationis* dissociates God from all naive identifications with human reality or forms a critical demarcation over against them. Now there is an important reason for refusing to associate God with the 'dross of the finite' (Hegel). Only if God really remains transcendent can he be a critical factor over against humankind, i.e. that which can provide a decisive critique of all human attempts to appropriate power and rule over all living things. This theme runs through the Bible from the tower of Babel (Gen.11.1-9) to the way in which Jesus withstands temptation (Matt.4.1-11).

With the prohibition against images the biblical tradition also rejects all attempts to gain control of God as an 'object' that can be manipulated and to claim him for all possible interests. The intention behind stating all that God is *not* is to keep God free from the conditions of finitude, from 'contamination with the certainty of the senses', but also to prevent him from being imagined as the other-worldly being who 'crouches outside the world' (Hegel), from where he stirs up world history at whim, when he feels like it (*deus ex machina*).[47] Even if only in theory, such a world would be conceived of in as objective terms as this one and could not withstand the critical argument that it was a mere projection.[48] But God is not a 'thing' either to see or to touch or to imagine. All that would be 'bad metaphysics' (Hegel).[49] Were God an object, then objects would be interchangeable: what you set your heart on is your God, says Luther aptly in an explanation of the first commandment in the Greater Catechism. In that case what would be the difference between God and a good, fast automobile? The loss of either equally drives the 'owner' to despair. Only the confession of several gods would offer the chance of complaining about the loss to a heavenly rival. By contrast, the transcendent God of the Bible is the critical principle which is implemented in the same tradition in an ethical claim: You shall not dominate, kill, exploit... On the one hand feminists like Gerda Weiler, whom I have already mentioned, find quite vehement words for protesting against all possible forms of a claim to power, and on the other hand they accuse the biblical God of rigorist moralism which despises humanity. But does this God not pass the same verdict on the quest for power of people like Gerda Weiler?

The effort at analogy

So the *via negationis* draws a critical boundary line. God is not an object, he cannot be possessed; in this respect he refuses to legitimate human claims to Lordship. Therefore he is called the only (true) Lord, king, judge and father: for that reason, too, we read 'Call no one on earth your Father' (Matt.23.9).

But this talk of God is only a first, albeit necessary, one. If we remained here we would have to give up speaking of God 'positively', in the twofold sense of the word. This leads to the next systematic move. To say 'God is Father' is to use an analogy.[50] 'All statements of faith are analogies. In an analogy reflection is transferred from an object that can be perceived to another concept to which no perception corresponds directly.'[51] Talk of God *per analogiam* thus presupposes the *via negationis*: God is not identical to an 'objective', physical father; he is 'like' a father. The great eighteenth-century philosopher Immanuel Kant developed analogy very vividly. When he says that concepts without perception are empty, he touches on the problem of talk of God which limits itself to the *via negationis*; then in so doing he criticizes talk of God which he himself calls 'dogmatic anthropomorphism'.[52] But how can our reason associate what we see with what escapes our perception? Kant's answer is: '...if we limit our judgment merely to the *relation* which the world may have to a being, the concept of whom lies outside all knowledge of which we are capable inside the world...'[53]

Kant distinguishes three ways of gaining intuition without which a concept, even the concept of God, does not work: first through empiricism – an object can be shown, seen, perceived with the senses;[54] then through 'inner perception', i.e. the awareness of a dimension or a context (space, time, cause, etc.) to which no tangible object corresponds.[55] But in so far as he is God, God can neither be a thing nor a category within our consciousness, for this too would simply be human. So we are left with the third possibility: analogy. This does not compare thing with thing, that which can be experienced with that which can be experienced, nor even the earthly father with the heavenly father. Analogy is not an incomplete, incidental similarity between two objects 'but a perfect similarity of two relations between quite dissimilar things.'[56]

To make clear what is meant by this Kant uses an example which is also not alien to the Bible; when governed by inner laws, a city is imagined as a body with a soul; so by analogy Paul calls the Christian community a body the organs of which are meaningfully related and interact (Rom.12.4-5; I Cor.12.12-27). By contrast Kant speaks of a city which is despotically governed by the single will of the ruler by analogy with a hand-mill, the mechanics of which function soullessly by the power of the one who uses it: 'For there is certainly no likeness between a despotic state and a hand-mill, whereas there surely is between the rules of reflection upon both and their causality.'[57]

What do these considerations contribute to the question of God and his name, whether God be imagined as father or mother, male or female? That the analogies of the hand-mill and the state are not comparisons is immediately clear; but we are talking about God, so language can easily go wrong. However, the very first step of our systematic considerations should have warned us that God the Father has no more to do with a human father than a city with a hand-mill: there is nothing here that would allow a comparison. However, things are no better with God the mother.[58]

The analogy brings together neither objects nor persons but organic (or mechanical) functioning, the rule according to which something happens, in short a relationship to another relationship. What is involved here is how we can honestly talk of God at all. For 'by means of such an analogy,' Kant says, 'I can give a relational concept of things that are absolutely unknown to me. For example, as the promotion of the happiness of children... is related to parental love, so the well-being of the human species is related to the unknown in God which we call love; not as if it had the slightest similarity with any human inclination, but because we can posit its (namely God's) relation to the world as similar to that the things in the world have among themselves.'[59]

So on closer inspection the dispute over God the father or God the mother proves obsolete. Any name of God which is not understood as an analogy makes God an idol, and that means a tangible or imagined object; so while the father God has had evil consequences, the consequences of the mother God would be no better. However, the twofold step of the *via negationis* and the use of analogy has healthy consequences not only for honest talk of God but also for what people do.

So that 'God is father' means that he is not like earthly fathers, but his fatherhood 'corresponds in the highest sense to what the word means'.[60] Whenever we speak of God as father we go back to possible human experiences of fatherhood. Nevertheless God is not our father with his limitations, his guilt (and his crime). God's fatherhood transcends our experiences of fathers to the point that he is the embodiment of fatherhood, the 'perfect father in heaven' (in the theological tradition this way of speaking is called the *via eminentiae*). So God as Father is always more than all positive experiences of fathers and measures all negative experiences of fathers by the criterion of God's fatherhood.

But this means that this double step in thinking has very tangible consequences, in that God becomes the ally of all those who suffer under the arrogance of false fathers. Our fathers are not gods, and parental authority may not be derived from God as the supreme ruler, either in an apparently positive way (patriarchalism of love) or in a negative way (despotism). That is the inevitable conclusion of the *via negationis*. But our fathers are faced with the demand that they should be perfect like the Father in heaven: perfect, not powerful; perfect, not authoritarian. That earthly fathers cannot attain such perfection (otherwise they would indeed be gods) does not mean that they need not strive for it and that they can be excused from being criticized in the light of this claim.

If one does not think of God *per analogiam* but imagines him empirically or makes him a mere inner perception, one does not just confirm the criticism of religion; this virtually provokes the establishment of human and divine authority. That church doctrine and practice have largely refrained from such critical theoretical reflection and still do so even today is not to be seen simply as a result of the old, well-known concern for power. This often happens as a result merely of anti-intellectualism or laziness, a charge which is not directed against Christians generally. Not everyone is to be expected to engage in complex reflections about analogy, even if that were possible, but theologians, both male and female, who are involved in academic work, and as teachers of the church are responsible for communication, must be concerned with it. And even if not every 'pupil' sees what reflections underlie an attempt at communication, nevertheless these reflections are involved in communication and shape the form of talk of God which is not a short cut. Therefore hostility to thought and theory is to be opposed, for good reasons, which can be substantiated both biblically and dogmatically. We shall continually get into the situation, and not only when 'women' are the theme, of referring to a correct tradition while opposing another which we have recognized to be false. In the biblical texts, too, there are conflicting positions, which is why we need a closer examination of the kind that I have undertaken here, brief though it may have been. Those who allow themselves to be terrified by the father God and his earthly representatives are endorsing the false tradition. I take no offence at the father God because he is an invitation to our fathers to be perfect, and stands over against all fathers who lay claim to a godlike authority. A mother God would be the same standard for mothers; but I think that fathers still need it more.

In the fullness of images

Let us return once again to the personal experiences of individuals with their parents. Against the background of our theoretical considerations neither positive nor negative experiences of a father must establish or damage relationships with a father God. It is clear that positive experiences form the basis of the analogy. The one who is loved by a father can say, 'If my father... how much more my heavenly father.' Let me recall the prophet Deutero-Isaiah (Isa.49.15-16), who talks about a mother like this. Many biblical texts talk about God in this way, independently of the analogies of which they make use. The one who is dominated by a father can say: 'Though my father does not... at least my father in heaven does!' Is the repudiation of an earthly father to have so much power that it destroys any connection with the father God? Negative experiences can also lead to a longing and a hope for protection by the power of God which is superior to all human authorities. Conversation with women has shown me that that is possible, and that many women gain strength from offering resistance.

Father and mother are not the only analogies in talking of and to God. Not very often, but at decisive points in the Bible, God is the friend: God speaks with Moses face to face as with his friend (Ex.33.11); God can be called 'friend of my youth' (Jer.3.4); and in the New Testament it is said pointedly that Christians are not servants but friends of the Lord (John 15.15). Abraham is called a 'friend of God' (James 2.23) and Luke, the great story-teller, produces analogies in extended parables: God is like someone who does not reject his friend when he asks for a loaf at midnight (Luke 11.5ff.).

Eroticism also contributes to the formation of analogies. God is beloved, bridegroom, marriage partner. The Song of Songs, a collection of cultic love poetry, was accepted into the canon (after many difficulties, but it got there in the end) as an analogy for the relationship between God and people. Each side can complain about the faithlessness of the other (Isa.49.14; Jer.2.2). The analogy of the bride brings us to the New Testament, where the kingdom of God is compared to a wedding feast (Mark 2.19f.; Matt.22.1; 25.1). At the end of days this wedding will be celebrated in great splendour (Rev.19.9; 21.9,17). But all these analogies are in the dialectic of negation, 'God is not...', and the claim which transcends everything, 'God is always more than...' That can be done by anyone who has made the effort at analogy without being afraid of the many names and images of God which the tradition has brought together. It is precisely its wealth which makes it appropriate for protecting us from one-sided identifications.

If there were more care over theoretical discourse in the communications of the churches, then the relationship with God would not have to be set aside along with childhood faith. That does not exclude praxis and poiesis, but includes it, and there would not be such unnecessary polarizations as e.g. poiesis against theory.[61] Secondly, such considerations would enter into liturgical language, but not so as to produce a complete contrast, with God now being spoken of more by analogy with a mother. It is the wealth of analogies which colours the relationship with God and makes it varied. The use of the little word 'like' could indicate more than it usually does, that God can be spoken of only by way of analogy. And finally, as e.g. the Catholic dogmatic theologian Karl Rahner has always demanded,[62] talk using the *via negationis* should be a constant ingredient of any talk of God in order to counter objectifications and appropriations of God. In this way it would emerge that the equation 'God is male – only males may be priests – all believers are addressed as "brothers"' is not a consequence of talk about God but a by-product of the theocratic short cut; but where this legitimates the praxis of the church any talk of God remains incredible and an empty shell.

CHAPTER TWO

Eros of the Goddesses

Idols and whores

'They also built for themselves high places, and pillars, and Asherim on every high hill and under every green tree; and there were also "initiates"[1] in the land' (I Kings 14.23-24). This charge is made against Rehoboam, the son and successor of King Solomon in Judah. He was not the only one; hardly any king, whether in Judah or Israel, was regarded as being beyond reproach in this respect. Anyone like King Asa of Judah who destroyed these 'alien' cults was praised. He had expelled the 'initiates' from the land, removed all the idols and deprived his mother of the status of 'queen mother'[2] because she had had a statue erected to the goddess Asherah – in the Canaanite pantheon the wife of the supreme God El: 'And Asa cut down her image and burned it at the brook Kidron' (I Kings 15.11-13). Jehoshaphat son of Asa completed his father's work by exterminating the 'rest of the initiates'. And the great cultic reform of King Josiah which – according to the text – he implemented with reference to Deuteronomy consisted in orders to 'bring out of the temple of the Lord all the vessels made for Baal, for Asherah and for all the host of heaven' (II Kings 23.4ff.); he 'did away with' the idolatrous priests, pulled down the dwellings of the 'initiates' 'where the women wove hangings for the Asherah' (v.7) and also destroyed all the places of idols in the land: 'And he broke in pieces the pillars, and cut down the Asherim, and filled their places with the bones of men' (II Kings 23.14).

Monotheism was far from being something that could be taken for granted in pre-exilic Israel; we have already noted this in the previous chapter. Even the few passages I have cited show two things: first, how dominant the Canaanite cults must have been among the people of Israel and Judah, and secondly, that this domination is matched by the vehemence of the repudiation of these cults by the tradition of a later time.³ Those who handed it on were of the same stamp as prophets like Amos, Hosea or Jeremiah before them. Among the idols which fell victim to their verdict were in fact a series of significant goddesses. However, whether a return to them is in the interest of feminists remains to be seen.

In a symbolic action which is characteristic of him, the prophet Hosea marries a prostitute at God's bidding: 'For the land commits great harlotry by forsaking the Lord' (Hos.1.2). Hosea's hope that the prostitute Gomer may cease her 'courting' and return to her husband matches God's hope for the return of the people. Otherwise, says God, 'I will put an end to all her mirth, her feasts, her new moons, her sabbaths, and all her appointed feasts' (Hos.2.11). In the name of Yahweh Amos proclaims that it is not Baal the rain-god who has made the land blossom; to demonstrate that, Yahweh made everything wither. 'Nevertheless you did not return to me, says the Lord' (Amos 4.6). The people continued to be wicked, and both men and women took part in the apostasy: 'a man and his father go in to the same (cultic) maiden, so that my holy name is profaned' (Amos 2.7b). And to the prophet Jeremiah God says: 'Do you not see what they are doing in the cities of Judah and in the streets of Jerusalem? The children gather wood, the fathers kindle fire, and the women knead dough, to make cakes for the queen of heaven; and they pour out drink-offerings to other gods, to provoke me to anger' (Jer.7.17-18). For Jeremiah, too, the people has become an unfaithful, promiscuous wife; through him Yahweh says: 'I remember your devotion of your youth, your love as a bride, how you followed me in the wilderness, in a land not sown...' (Jer.2.2). '(But) she went up on every high hill and under every green tree, and there played the harlot' (Jer.3.6b).

These instances could be vastly increased. In the Old Testament there are four in particular of these 'strange' Canaanite gods and goddesses who evidently were not so strange. In order of the frequency of mentions of them they are Baal, Astarte (or their cultic figures, the Asherim), El and Anat. Astarte, Asherah or Asherath are presumably different names for the same goddess. What do we know in detail about the supreme representatives of a heaven of gods with which Yahweh was contrasted? El seems to be completely assimilated to the God of Israel and plays no role in the 'battle of the gods'; Baal and Astarte are often named together. The names of these gods, like that of Anat, also appear as compound elements in Israelite place-names and proper names, and this too suggests assimilation; temples are built to the gods, statues are erected (the image of the bull plays a major role); their worship takes place above all on hills and in high places. Again and again in this connection there is talk of harlotry, which has suggested the ritual practice of the sacred marriage and cultic prostitution.

Once again: why this repudiation of a religion which had shaped the people over centuries? Cultic rivalry is one of the themes which is depicted in detail in the battle between Yahweh and Baal on Mount Carmel (I Kings 18.16ff.). That the fostering of his cult is also connected with political dependence emerges, for example, from the conduct of King Ahaz of Judah; in a military confrontation with Syria, Edom and Israel, Ahaz summons the help of the Assyrian king Tiglath-pileser, which enables him to win. As an expression of his thanks he has an altar erected in Jerusalem on the model of the altar that he had seen in Damascus (II Kings 16.7ff.).

I have already spoken of the interest and theological conceptions of the prophetic and priestly traditions. Feminists, however, see another motive as being decisive, namely the struggle of a patriarchal culture against a more original matriarchal culture which was characterized by myths, rites and a social practice in which women played a significant, if not dominant role. Only in a return to the roots of this culture does this feminist position see an opportunity for women in our day also to achieve self-awareness with a view to liberation from patriarchal slavery. Against the god Yahweh, 'the patriarchal, authoritarian principle of tutelage',[4] the goddess myths are not only investigated but also revived and, along with their symbols, utilized in a new ritual practice. In a modernized moon liturgy, for example, women sing and dance to 'lady moon' as 'our sister', 'our mother', 'our nocturnal beloved'.[5] These women are leaving all the present high religions; they no longer expect anything from the God of Christians and Jews. They are returning to an old buried tradition in which women still counted for something and could enjoy life.[6]

A barren myth

Heide Göttner-Abendroth in particular has collected and analysed the goddess myths as the expression of a matriarchal culture with the help of material from J.J.Bachofen, who researched into the matriarchate. In the following description I shall restrict myself primarily to the geographical area of Syria-Palestine and the myths of the Syro-Phoenicians because these are most significant for the Old Testament. The discovery made by a peasant in the bay of Minet-el-Beda, handed down by the Greek geographers as 'white haven', in Asia Minor, has since 1929 led to the systematic excavation of the tell of Ras Shamra, a little way inland. This soon proved to be the remains of the Phoenician coastal city of Ugarit. A number of archives and libraries which were found there contained a wealth of Ugaritic cuneiform texts: they give a good deal of information about mythological conceptions which, while not unconnected in their origins with Mesopotamia and Egypt, nevertheless have a form of their own. There are figures of female deities[7] as early as the strata of excavations from the fifth pre-Christian millennium; the texts themselves come from a later time, presumably from the fourteenth century BC, though we cannot rule out the possibility that they also contain earlier elements. The heyday of Ugarit was in the period between 1600 and 1300 BC; about 1200 the harbour was destroyed by invading Sea Peoples and not inhabited again after that.

The texts found there, the so-called Ras Shamra texts, are a quite illuminating source of myths which rivalled faith in Yahweh, and it is amazing that Göttner-Abendroth evidently has not tackled them in detail. She relies on selections made by earlier scholars and sees the myths of the goddess Anat and the god Baal as the expression of a developed matriarchal culture:[8] Anat, the 'queen of the hills', is the sister consort of Baal, her 'hero', a god who is subordinate to her. Imitating the rhythm of the seasons, Baal gets into the grasp of Mot, the god of death, and dies. Anat, loving and aggressive, fights against Mot for the release of Baal; she skins Mot, draws him through a mill and scatters the flesh over the fields. Mot does not die – after all he is the God of death – but he gives up Baal; spring comes over the land, it rains, and grass and seed spring up. The fertility of the land and also of human beings depends on Anat and her victorious struggle. Baal is mortal, Anat is not, so she is the dominant goddess – that is Göttner-Abendroth's final conclusion.

If we check these remarks against the source texts it proves that Göttner-Abendroth suppresses an essential element which does not fall within the range of her interest: neither Anat nor even Baal are at the head of the pantheon, but El and his divine consort Asherat.[9] El is the 'senior god',[10] creator of all that is made, father of humankind, also called 'the bull', friendly and gracious.[11] She, Asherat, bearer of the gods (seventy gods and goddesses have emerged from her), queen of the sea, appears in a clearly secondary role. If her husband, for example, refuses a request, she is called on as a mediatrix.[12] What is possibly a liturgical text depicts the coupling of El with her and a second goddess called Rchm, perhaps Asherah's maid,[13] in unmistakable clarity. The goddesses bear the two 'lovely gods' who are entertained with bread and wine – probably again a reference to the association of copulation, birth and the fertility of the land.

Anat and Baal are also children of the supreme divine couple. A large part of the texts deals with children being rivals of their parents. Baal, not Anat, wants to be ruler over all and have his own house. Anat supports him here. El is not yet as powerless as he is made out to be by some feminists and other scholars to whom they refer,[14] since he has to give his permission. It is Anat who seeks to wring this permission out of him through threats of death. When El refuses, Asherat is asked to intervene with the supreme God or to move him with gifts. First of all Asherat shows her fury that El has not been given any gifts: he has to be approached in the first place. But Asherat is more afraid of Anat than of El. So Asherat goes to her own spouse, who shows surprise at the visit, serves her a meal and announces that he then wants to lie with her (do male gods, too, want only one thing?). Asherat, not particularly interested, brings the conversation round to Baal's wish. El becomes cynical. 'If Asherat is a maid, let her lay bricks, then a house will arise for Baal like the other gods and a dwelling place like the sons of Asherat have.'[15] So El is not in favour; he leaves this matter to his 'subordinates'. How far there is cultic rivalry here of the kind what we have already seen from the Old Testament is no longer evident. But what interests us, namely the dominant position of the goddesses in the pantheon, cannot be attested from the Ras Shamra texts. The feminist selection is contradicted by the overall context of the sayings.[16]

The goddess Anat is without doubt the most impressive figure. She fights, wades in the blood of her opponents, is not 'sated with her killing; the heads she has cut off reach up to her waist'. 'She is filled with joy as she plunges her knees in the blood of heroes.'[17] It does not emerge very clearly from the context what has made Anat so angry. Since it is in connection with this that Baal expresses for the first time his wish to strengthen his power by building his own sanctuary, the cultic rivalry already mentioned might be seen as a motive. This may have been preceded by a neglect of the Baal-Anat cult which Anat avenges with a bloody annihilation of the apostates, also for the sake of Baal's honour.[18] At all events Anat acts just like Yahweh, at least when it comes to annihilating her enemies. Why is Yahweh then accused of violence by feminists and not Anat? At any rate it is a sign of progress that Yahweh does not wade with joy in the blood of his enemies.

After Anat has cleansed herself from the blood, Baal sends messengers to Anat and addresses her: 'Come to me from the battlefield, shed harmony on the earth, pour peace into the heart of the earth, much love into the heart of the fields.'[19] Gerda Weiler quotes another translation of this section and chooses a line from it as the title of her book ('I reject wars in the land'): 'The message of Baal, the word of the exalted one among the heroes: "I reject wars in the land, lay holy love on the earth, pour peace into the midst of the field, into your garden, under the pomegranate tree let us celebrate the sacred marriage."'[20] Those who presuppose a rite behind this text, which is suggested by the fact that myth usually has a setting in cultic life, translate yet again: 'Come into the land of wars! Set pots in the earth, pour a saving sacrifice in the midst of the land, set up vessels in the midst of the field.'[21] Thus the translations diverge considerably, since it is evidently uncertain whether Baal is talking about himself or addressing an invitation to Anat. In the one case Baal rather than Anat would be the one concerned with peace, in the other case Anat would be summoned to make good what she had done in her rage. Whatever the case, there is no disputing the bloody prelude to the scene, and feminists who stress their particular feminine gift for peace should at all events not refer to Anat. The title of Gerda Weiler's book conjures up inappropriate associations.

Since Anat and Baal, like Asherat and El, are gods of fertility, and war is identified with drought, and love and peace with growth and flourishing, Anat's battle may also be connected with this. Anat is always angry when she has to save Baal; then she couples with him, for only together do they create fertility. So Anat longs for Baal 'like the heart of the mother sheep for its lamb';[22] they celebrate their love feast in a meadow, taking the form of cattle, so that Anat bears a calf (cf. the cult of the golden bull or calf).[23] This form of religion is therefore aptly called a fertility cult or vegetation cult:[24] human children, young animals, corn and fruit are to grow. What happens in 'heaven', the expulsion of the gods, their defeats and victories, determines life and death. All eroticism is in the service of fertility. And again a conflict with feminist interests is clear; anyone who is on guard against reducing women to fertility and motherhood can hardly lay claim to the goddess myths. Anat certainly fights, but she fights in order to make all living things fertile. A lack of fertility at that time was probably the worst thing that could happen to a woman. We can see that from the Old Testament. As Sarah does not get any children, she sends her husband Abraham to the maid (Gen.16.1ff.); when Rachel sees that her womb remains closed her husband Jacob has to get children for her through the maid Bilhah (Gen.30.1ff.). The husbands do what their wives tell them, for descendants are of more value than the personal relationship between man and woman. The objection that in that case people could not have experienced anything like a personal loving relationship does not stand up to what the texts say. It is explicitly said that Jacob loved

Rachel and not her sister Leah, for whom he had to 'make' children at the bidding of his father-in-law; Elkanah attempts to comfort his childless wife Hannah, whom he loves more than his wife Peninnah, who is blessed with fertility, by showing her his love: 'Am I not worth more to you than ten sons?' (I Sam.1.1ff.)? But such comfort is no substitute. For Hannah, as for the others, the husband remains the means of their fertility.

All this shows how remote is the interest of women of four thousand years ago from what moves women today. Feminists who again revive the myths and rites from this period therefore overlook what was decisive at that time. They do not pray to the goddesses for fertility, yet this is the cornerstone of the submerged world of the feminine deities, and the myth, thus robbed of its intention, becomes barren in both the literal and the metaphorical sense. What has it to offer us in a period and civilization for which fertility has become a burden, if not a curse? If the women of those days rose up again, from a time when fertility was overshadowed by the early deaths of mothers and children, and heard our debates over contraception and abortion, our world would seem as strange to them as on close inspection theirs must appear to us. The selection of themes by feminists, when they depict e.g. Anat as mistress of life and death, when they depict the one set over her mortal hero, the gracious, warlike one who takes the initiative in love, exclusively 'proves' their interest. This is what women want to be today; they want to break the tradition of male destructive domination of their body and their soul. They are right. It is high time for that. But the arguments must be different; the arguments derived from the goddess myths can all too easily be turned against those who use them.

Sacred marriage

Nowadays when we talk about fertility and motherhood the associations are not particularly erotic: mothers differ from other women who are still in search of someone by whom to have children by virtue of their care and respectability. 'I love my husband and the children – if only there didn't have to be sex.'[25] This remark, which one often hears, sums up an attitude which is also shared by men: they do not expect from a wife and mother what they buy from prostitutes. By contrast the Ugaritic mother goddesses are far removed from such a split. Birth appears as the unproblematical consequence of a powerful eroticism which is vividly described: El's member is as long as the ocean; as hot as coals of fire on which the bird roasts is the desire of the god and his two wives; Anat transforms herself into a fleet bird when desire drives her to her beloved; for Baal she becomes a cow when he mounts her mightily like a bull.[26] But the aggressive deadly side of erotic desire also becomes clear: El wants to annihilate his rival Baal; he commands a serving woman to go into the steppes to couple with the gods of the field to give birth to ravening animals. Baal will be enflamed with desire for them and will be devoured by them. That is what happens and the consequence is a seven-year drought.[27] There are no problems of relationship or ethical problems. Eros develops when, where and to whom it may happen.

If we start by assuming that myth and cult belong together, then it is natural to assume a corresponding 'erotic liturgy' in which the assembled cult community enacts the myth. Three different practices are the topic of debate here: the sacred marriage, cultic prostitution and ritual defloration – themes which are disputed by historians. There is evidence for and against, and there are arguments for and against. The earlier the textual evidence the less clear the information that we gain; this is understandable, since a practice familiar to everyone did not have to be explained and at that time there was no historiography in the form of objective history writing. The clearest evidence comes from Mesopotamia, which was not without influence on Syro-Phoenicia, in connection with the Inanna-Ishtar cult: both these goddesses display marked parallels with Anat in function and character. However, to hear of Ishtar that 120 men could not exhaust her,[28] or to find a cultic image depicting a naked pair on a bed[29] tells us nothing about actual practice. This evidence can also relate to the myth. The warning against marrying a woman from the cultic personnel of Ishtar because she 'has' so many men[30] speaks a clearer language. The texts certainly provide evidence that the sacred marriage was celebrated at the turn of the year or in May/June, but they presuppose detailed knowledge about the particular form of the festival. Only in the centuries around the beginning of our era do these sources become clearer and more detailed, because they are written by people who adopt a detached and polemical attitude to everything, including the texts of the Old Testament. Sources of this kind include Herodotus, the Greek historian of the fourth century BC; Strabo, the historian and geographer from the first century BC; and the satirist Lucian from the second century AD. But it is precisely the critical attitude of these writers that raises doubts about the authenticity of the erotic cultic actions to which they bear witness. Opinions here are also divided among feminists. Some regard all this as a calumny and defend themselves against the prejudice that what they suppose to be times of feminine domination in heaven and on earth *ipso facto* go along with an ethical nadir, so that it is right to assume all the perversions that powers of imagination can conjure up.[31] Others, like Gerda Weiler, abandon themselves to fantasies of the opposite kind and become enthusiastic: 'For man and woman, love and sensual enjoyment are a holy experience. They transcend themselves, are caught up into divine ecstasy and become part of the creative cosmic force of life.'[32]

When it comes to historical reconstruction, only a few pieces of a puzzle can be put together, as it were islands in a total picture which is hidden from us: perhaps in Mesopotamia, Syro-Phoenicia and Palestine there was the practice of a sacred marriage in which intercourse between the priestess and the king represented the eros of the gods, and perhaps there was also cultic prostitution. There are no instances in Egypt, for example, or only at the time of the Ptolemies, when the goddesses of the religious circles I have mentioned were already native to the land. Perhaps the praxis differed from place to place, and later began to be combined with cultic and profane prostitution, so that the original religious significance degenerated into temple business, a development which has taken place everywhere, as it still does, where religion is associated with money. Polemic may have distorted many things a good deal. However, feminist critics must be allowed to be in the right over one thing: the cultic practice of eros was a sacral activity, not simply immoral, as it could appear in a superficial way. Eros and life derive from a source of power in which the old cultures looked on the divine numen.[33]

As I have said, historical reconstruction allows only conjectures:
here again systematic reflection on eros can take us an important
step further. The power of eros is not attested or refuted by
historical facts but by reflection on the significance of eros. The
Ras Shamra texts are not just about fertility. Taken literally they
reveal almost the whole spectrum of different desires, including
reprehensible ones: Anat and Baal manifestly practise incest;
some scholars do not rule out the possibility that sometimes Anat
also shared the bed of her father El with her mother Asherat:[34]
Scenes of wild coupling are accompanied by poetically skilful
descriptions of the desire felt, but it is not just the desire for
pleasure which dominates the scene: this alternates with desire
for power, delight in power and killing. In great excitement and
with arrogant hymnic words Baal tells Anat his plan to build
himself his own sanctuary: 'I will build a dwelling of the gods
such as heaven has not known, something which has not been
made known to men, ...to delight me at the summit of my power.'[35]

Anat unmistakeably expresses her delight in killing; while she
slaughters she rejoices, her liver swells, she laughs with all her
heart, feels pleasure and only ceases when she is 'sated'.[36] The
gods of the Ugaritic pantheon feel and act completely outside any
ethical disposition and moral order. Personal relations between
human beings which lead to love, fidelity and tender care seem
alien to them (even as feelings towards their children). But again
they are not un-persons, otherwise they would not be bound
together by such vigorous passion. However, this passion is the
decisive element in their relationships, if not the only one, and a
refusal unleashes bloody vengeance. When Anat looks on the bow
of the demigod and hunter Aqhat this passionate desire takes hold
of her to such a degree that one can rightly assume that the bow
is a part representing the whole and that what is desired is Aqhat
himself. In her pleasure she writhes like a serpent. She offers
Aqhat gifts and eternal life, but he rejects them: this bow is not
for a woman. Anat's vengeance is cruel and basic. Anat changes
herself and her servant into birds of prey and puts the servant in
her bosom, from where he hacks Aqhat to pieces. The erotic
metaphor is clear.[37]

If myth simply depicts social reality, as many people, including
feminists, assume, then a society in which such myths are current

would be in a bad position. That this is in no way the case is shown by the non-mythological texts of the Syro-Phoenicians or indeed those of their neighbours. As in Israel, the good king is the one who is like a 'father, mother and brother' to the people,[38] who defends the rights of the widows, the orphans and the poor, who ensures prosperity and public security:[39] marriage, divorce, inheritance leave even more room for individual arrangements than is possible nowadays. Thus for example a Ugaritic citizen in his will leaves all his property exclusively to his widow; his two sons are not taken into account, but are merely enjoined to obey their mother.[40] Incest, homosexuality, bestiality are forbidden and are punished.[41] There is also no frivolity about the relationship of these people to their gods. The votive inscriptions indicate the inner devotion with which the gods are invoked for deliverance from distress and which is offered to them as thanksgiving for help and protection.[42] At that time there was corruption and crime as in any human society; the texts also bear witness to that: we are not superior to them in that respect. But in that case how do such 'unrespectable' myths come into being in a society of people concerned for respectability?

Like the myths of all nature religions, the Ugaritic myths too are a reproduction and at the same time a personification of the natural life-cycle of becoming, passing away and becoming again. The myth postulates a world in the beyond in which eros and fertility, the conditions for preserving life, appear as divine persons who have an influence on the continuing existence of all life in this world. But here the myth takes no account of the limitations that are necessary for human social life, i.e. ethical commands and prohibitions. 'Exaggerated' in this sense, it endorses in a crude way what human beings experience in life-creating eros. The myth thus lives on the opposite side to the social reality of humanity: had men and women acted like those gods and goddesses, they would have destroyed the basis of human society. Plato already criticized the myths of the old gods in this direction: acts of violence, injustice and much cruelty determined the life of those gods, not beauty and goodness.[43] The myths which Plato had in mind had the actions of the gods controlled by *ananke*, blind destiny. The fertility myths of Ugarit indicate the mystery of nature which constantly emerges anew. Ethics, which human beings cannot dispense with, do not appear there. Precisely for that reason the myths of Ugarit are not a reflection of social reality.

For that reason the question whether the myths were matched by a real physical re-enactment of sexual intercourse can also be left open. For if it took place, this intercourse would belong in the sphere of cultic practice, to what with Aristotle we have called poiesis, and not to everyday life. That is the decisive argument against the charge of immorality raised by the polemic of all periods and used not least to demonstrate one's own moral superiority. For the same reason the myths of the nature religions cannot be used to hymn the praises of free love either.

The following experiment in thought should show how absurd it would be to put everyday practice and ideas of faith – in quite general terms – in a linear, representative context. Suppose that Christianity was one of the religions covered with the dust of centuries and its liturgical texts were dug up. The eucharistic liturgy would offer enough bloody associations to provide evidence for a corresponding practice if one were to take the texts literally. That such considerations are not utterly absurd is demonstrated by the pagan polemic against the Christians in the first century which accused the Christians of consuming the blood of sacrificed children.[44] In anti-Jewish ritual murder legends among Christians this theme undergoes a shameful revival. As the inscriptions of the people of Ugarit from 3500 years ago show, people were very well able to make a distinction in principle between myth and reality, but polemic tended to blacken opponents by attributing to them a considerable degree of 'primitiveness'. No religion was and is free of such seductions, whether it be pagan, Christian or Jewish. That Jewish prophetic and priestly traditions sometimes also engage in inappropriate and distorting polemic is neither their special characteristic nor does it justify a sweeping verdict on 'the Jews'. However, further comments should indicate how justified is Jewish criticism of a faith which in myth elevates the power of nature, fertility and eros to the status of a supernatural mystery and in so doing excludes the ethical question from matters of faith.

With fertility, eros stands at the centre of the Ugaritic myths. If we are not to get on a false track very natural to our own age, a first distinction must be made here. When we speak of eroticism we usually mean sexuality in a reduced biological and scientific sense. Seen in this way the sex life of animals is no different from that of human beings. Present-day 'enlightenment literature' is therefore mainly concerned with the biological function of sexuality, or with the empirical and statistical investigation of the act of intercourse.[45] According to this model a variety of techniques in love-making should shape human relationships in a satisfactory way.[46] Now there are no objections to these various techniques of love-making, but there are objections to the identification of sex and eros. It is part of the 'nature' of human beings not just to be natural in the biological sense. Eros is not mere natural love, and what may even be 'free love' should be able to elevate itself above physical determination.

In this context too it is worth looking at Plato. In the *Symposium*, Diotima, the wise woman from Mantinea, is teaching Socrates about eros. Eros, passion, is a powerful demon; it greedily desires him to possess what he needs. Eros seizes people, drives them on, makes them active and inventive in achieving the goal of their desire. Eros creates that enthusiasm for the sake of which people are capable of suffering much, if not everything.[47] Plato speaks of the divine madness from which the greatest goods derive for humanity. The person impelled by eros is not in control of himself; he is torn apart, he simply wants immortality, whether it is through begetting and procreation in the beauty of the body or of the soul.[48] For Plato, the erotic passion which is kindled by the beautiful body and leads to sexual union is only the lowest stage, one which is to be overcome. In looking on the beautiful the soul can and should 'recall' the idea of the beautiful, which for Plato is at the same time the Good,[49] and rise to the pure vision of these ideas.[50]

As is the fate of those who think dialectically, Plato has often been understood in a very one-sided way. What has become a commonplace as 'Platonic love' originally did not mean sour renunciation but a greater passion. Plato in no way rejects sensuality, but he does not reduce eros to it. Eros also drives a person on, even when he is in control of his reason, indeed still more when that is the case. For Plato, such all-embracing eros is not impossible even between man and women, though it is rare.

What social experiences underlie this side of the Platonic theory of love need to be discussed separately. Here I should at least point out that it is Diotima who knows about the mysteries of eros and communicates them to the ignorant Socrates by means of the Socratic method. The reversal of the usual roles is itself an erotic figure in which the equality in the play of eros is expressed.

Plato is not a mythologizer, though he too sometimes makes use of mythical forms of expression in a metaphorical sense;[51] just as he criticizes the divine myths of his time, so he would have been sceptical about the Ugaritic myths had they been known to him. Moreover in his doctrine of eros Plato ultimately aims at the idea of the good and in this is not to be compared with the myths of the gods and goddesses in the Ugaritic pantheon. However, what Plato says about the nature of eros is significant in this connection. To this corresponds the experience of eros as a power which seizes people, raises them above the level of the everyday, snatches them into heaven and casts them down into hell, a power to which human beings are surrendered. The attractive power of eros is not human in the sense of being merely natural; it is not at human disposal. Concerned for life and immortality, eros is also felt in the Ugaritic myths to be a divine power and is personified in the eros of the goddesses: sacred eros.[52] The unlimited life-creating power of the gods develops into unbounded, life-begetting eros.

The violence of eros

The language and imagery of eros are as varied and as ambivalent as the experience itself: frenzy, intoxication, feeling the ground go under one's feet, falling head over heels, experiencing the 'little death'. This popular phraseology characterizes the ecstasy that is bound up with eros: a going out of bounds which seeks the abyss and wants nothing but extinction from the object of its desire. It is from this going beyond the bounds that eros gets its energy, its pleasure. It transcends the bounds of the I, the uniqueness of the person, the limitations of social order and convention, the bounds of modesty. The breaking of the tabus with which society seeks to ban eros leads to that tension which eros needs to develop its desires, from which it finally at the same time brings redemption: the more shameless the transgression, the more violent and

'liberating' the enjoyment. Eros follows its inherent power inquisi-
tively, indeed as though possessed; it is not afraid of anything,
attacks whatever gets in the way and is goaded on further by it.
Its course is accompanied by combinations like 'conceal-discover',
'deceive-surprise', 'inflict-suffer'; pain and redemption cannot be
distinguished in its squandering of all its power.[53] Anat, the most
erotic of all goddesses, is familiar with all this.

The French 'theoretician of eros', Georges Bataille, seeks to
make a 'passionate appeal' with his analyses and literary forms
of love; '... opening the eyes to what happens, looking what is in
the face',[54] sacred and at the same time diabolical eros, the
repression of which wreaks a bitter vengeance. The fertility
religions, which are at least to the same degree religions of eros,
can do us precisely this service, but the feminist researchers into
the goddess myths do not want to make use of it.

Thus for example Gerda Weiler[55] regards the biblical Song of
Solomon as the cultic text for the celebration of the sacred
marriage, in the actual celebration of which not only king and
priestess but the whole cultic community was involved. In it she
sees the expression of the 'riches and maturity of a loving
relationship' 'in which people with equal rights – not embarrassed
by any rigid morality – may express their feelings freely'. This
language, which is not 'mere' language, says a good deal about
the interests of the author herself: 'mature' love, people 'with
equal rights', 'free' expression of feelings – those are our problems,
which are a very long way from the world of the goddesses.
Moreover Gerda Weiler finds herself in accord with a man, a
theologian following in the steps of Karl Barth, namely Helmut
Gollwitzer; he too sees present-day conceptions of love fulfilled
in the Song of Songs; he thinks that the 'non-interchangeable
once-for-all thou' is spoken of and given form here, an eroticism
which does not free the other from care and burdens (even if there
is nothing about that in the text, as Gollwitzer himself concedes);
and before the reader is aware of it, eros has become human again
and the Song of Songs is an example of 'unselfish mercy'.[56]

Barbara Sichtermann, while not being a myth scholar herself,
is nevertheless equally concerned for femininity. Among other
things she has done us the service of once again bringing out the
power and ambivalences of eros.[57] She sub-titles one of her articles

'An attempt to cross a boundary': 'Just as rape attacks not only the peace but also the physical integrity of a woman, and is therefore an ordinary crime of violence like any serious violation of the body, so sexuality certainly does not end up in a simple harmony of bodies, an exchange of affirmations. It seems to me that there has been an implicit agreement here which was over-hasty: a fiction of chocolate-box sexuality, in which two smiling faces and four open arms come together in contentment. As long as the feminist protest against trivializing an act of violation relies on the fiction of a peaceful feminist sexuality... the borderline between violation of the body and sexuality remains obscure. But this borderline is what it is all about.'[58] Like Bataille, Sichtermann also warns against closing one's eyes to the power of eros and the eros of power, 'driving passion out of ecstasy' and turning against males the 'flattering imputations' according to which feminine eros is more harmonious and more humane than male.[59] 'If the feminist movement wants to maintain its radical character it must stop being an accomplice in the domestication of sexuality.'[60]

Eros is vitality, and vitality is in a sense always 'bad', simply because all living beings seek to assert themselves, and some often get into conflict with others without any intention of being bad. Eros is self-assertion, and if one includes biological purpose, namely having offspring, it is self-affirmation in the service of the new, other life. So love is 'bad' to the degree that it storms heaven and tries to build the tower of Babel. But it cannot dwell in it, and must continually return to the preserve of the human community. This basic antagonism permeates the figure of eros in all its forms: it is high and lowly, life-giving and fatal, at the same time both sacred and reprehensible. Erotic literature has often expressed this ambivalence and the proximity to death in an intolerably cruel way.[61] And even if we do not want to take note of that, the fact remains that in every human being there slumbers this abyss, rejoicing to the heights, which violated souls[62] must feel even more strongly. This truth of eros, always continuing also to be evil as a vitality which breaks the bounds, remains one of the truths in Genesis 3, in which we are told that death came into the world with desire.

Moreover the almost martial power of eros, which is related to war, is that which can withstand war. In her foreword to

Aristophanes' *Lysistrata* Barbara Sichtermann has a refreshing
argument about the proximity and rivalry of eros and war. The
rebellion of Lysistrata's women and ultimately also of their
husbands is not determined by a 'capacity for peace as the result
of an insight into the ethical superiority of love', but by a 'readiness
for peace motivated by sensual desire'.[63] The women want to end
the war because they want their husbands and the men ultimately
end the war because they want their wives. Beyond question,
'Love finds a better presupposition in peace; it needs the undivided
attention of men and women, it co-exists badly with the clank of
weapons and the fear of death. But that does not mean that it is
itself peaceful.'[64] The 'martial settings of love' for which death is
the analogue of going beyond the bounds compete with the very
real death on the battlefield.[65] Eros bears weapons!

But the power of love is also matched by the love of power, the
undoubtedly terrifying insight that power, destruction and indeed
killing can give pleasure. The structure of obedience, political
'necessity', a concern for defence are not enough to make plausible
the enthusiasm with which human beings wage wars. In the last
resort the 'healthy everyday morality that an embrace is better
than a wound in the chest'[66] has so far not been able to rob the
delight in war of its violence, as war is not 'free of desire', and
love, since it is bound up with eros, is not toothless.[67] 'Must we
repress and ban any aggression (in the narrower sense), as the
peace movement suggests, so as at least not to succumb to the
fatal, or is there another way: that of confirming eros as a
marksman and at the same time avoiding the apocalyptic arms-
race on a large scale?'[68] The powerful eros can emerge as the
opponent of the eros of indwelling power. Political language can
make use of an erotic and obscene vocabulary, in order to
demonstrate the power of real weapons: 'Perhaps we can agree
that lying breast to breast is more stimulating than bayonets.'[69]

Eros shoots his arrow into a willing breast, not covered by our
hands, straight into a longing heart. Anyone who will not perceive
that, who puts up resistance, incites eros even more and provokes
the fatal struggle. Anyone who avoids the charming warplay of
love and laughingly with gentle words dismisses the power which
is slumbering in it loses his or her vitality: living corpses are
called 'zombies' or 'vampires'. Or eros reaches for even stronger,

criminal attractions. In April 1986 Raphael, aged three, died in Vienna after being maltreated by his mother's boy-friend. Mother and boy-friend were copulating alongside the child just as he was breathing his last. It was said to have been an overwhelming erotic experience; the murderer said in his own defence that they had never had such powerful feelings as at this time.[70] Is this an incarnation of de Sade's vision or Gilles de Rais' 'resurrection'?[71] Is it unfettered love or the revenge of Anat denied?

It is high time to deal with possible misunderstandings. Neither Bataille nor Sichtermann conjures up the desires of perverse eroticism. They are not in favour of war and crime. On the contrary: they want to draw attention to the abysses on which people build their respectable dwellings, so that they do not fall blindly into them. 'One of the most important values of sexual organization,' writes Bataille, 'is connected with the struggle to find a place for the tumult of the act of love in an order which embraces the totality of human life. This order is based on the tender friendship between man and woman and the way in which they are bound together by their children. Nothing is more important for us than to give the sexual act a place on the basis of the social structure.'[72] Granted, Bataille is at the same time pessimistic whether that will ever prove possible, and perhaps the traumatic experiences in his life have contributed to this.[73] Sichtermann makes a clearer and more matter-of-fact distinction than Bataille between the ritual praxis of eros as 'play', 'pattern', and the direct brutal force which ultimately overcomes even eros.[74]

The goddess myths at least teach us to take account of the power of eros. Where they are connected with rites, myths too are poiesis. They draw attention to the danger of Janus-headed eros; as we have seen, the social implementation of them has nevertheless been constrained by human ordinances. So in essence it is not so great a matter whether a complementary ritual poietic praxis, e.g. of the sacred marriage, corresponded to the sacred marriage. As a rite, as liturgy detached from everyday life, the physical enactment of a sacred marriage, no matter between whom, would be a permitted crossing of boundaries under the protective patronage of the gods, under the protection of the holy; it would be a first but nevertheless not completely harmless step towards the exclusion of force from 'normal' life. In everyday social life all kinds of other rules are regarded as a protection for society, so that families do not break up, or abandon children, and life and peace are not destroyed. The last resort of erotic wisdom is not an either-or but the capacity to distinguish when and where what forms of love correspond to what is possible at any time, what is desired or tolerable. Making such decisions is one of the most difficult things; there are no recipe books. Mistakes are inevitable, and that too is part of the reality of human existence. Catastrophes, exaltations are often needed to regain insights which seemed lost. The myths of people of four thousand years ago are unsuitable candidates for revival; but the powers which these myths conjure up still drive us on just as much and need to be thought about and given form in the present.

The discipline and indiscipline of agape

Christianity has always been suspected of being antipathetic to the body; but this charge is rejected by the practice of charitable love for which there is evidence from the beginnings to the present day (that there are always also those in a national church who do not take this seriously is another matter). So while Christianity has never been antipathetic to the body, the $64,000 question of its relationship to eros introduces confusion. Those who understand anything of eros do not hesitate: 'Part of the difficult legacy which the Christian West has handed down to the modern world is that it had the same word for philanthropy and sex: love.'[75] The God of the Christians, the *summum bonum*, the 'supreme good', and the goodness of human beings as the suppression of all physical desires even to the last corner of the heart are regularly seen in combination. So just as God himself, in contrast to the pagan gods, is free of all impurity, stain and guilt, so too men and women must free themselves from these things. 'Christianity never gave up the hope of one day leading this world of egotistic discontinuity back to the kingdom of continuity, illuminated by love.'[76] The consequence was that eros became profane, was banished from the realms of the holy and handed over to the 'impure' world.[77] In this sense profanization in no way means reification; the attempt to define eros purely in terms of the procreation of children closes people's eyes to the fact that the tension between shame and exaltation which characterizes love cannot be done away with. But if it has more of a share in the impure world, anyone who crosses the boundary towards it must necessarily lose his or her relationship with God. That is how Bataille sees the Christian position. But in admiring this as something exalted, as a fascinating dream, which he declares to be impossible to realize, he is maintaining the banishment of eros, which is the cause of his torments.

How could things have got in this state? The Judaism of the time of the exile and then Christianity opened up a new battlefield: agape, the caring, merciful love which seeks the well-being of the neighbour, took the field against eros. It was a gladiatorial struggle, for although agape has no weapons, it is armed with the arguments for humanity, and the net which it casts is no less dangerous to the attacker. Anyone who keeps the violence of eros in mind will already be well aware of what is involved. As human beings man and wife are equal, equally in need of food, clothing, housing, bodily care and tender love. What is true of them is all the more true of their helpless children. They are to be inviolate, hidden in the paternal and maternal hand of God, unharmed by evil words, sharp weapons and – unbounded desire: no human being is a mere means to an end.[78] Love does not show preference, is not exclusive, does not just see what is charming and successful in human beings, but sees them whole: with their limitations, their failure, their finitude. It is not that Christians have had all kinds of illusions about human passions. Because they were aware of them and their destructive powers they pronounced a ban on eros and sought to realize something of 'heaven on earth' in their communities. It soon transpired that this was not so easy, and so with good reason Paul conceded marriage as a means of protection against incontinence, as a means of keeping the fire in the torch of love small and under control.

Christian churches still take the view that eros, sensual love, desire, may not be separated from the marriage relationship which is seen as spiritual love and fertility. In particular the Roman Catholic church here refers to nature as being given and willed by God in this way and not in any other.[79] Here procreation is regarded as a divine purpose, but passion is to be controlled and subjected to reason. But what does 'nature' mean in this context? Why is biological functioning, apart from passion, called natural and the passionate desire for another person distinguished from what is supposed to be natural to the same extent as reason is? It is a feature of 'nature' or, better, of human nature that it cannot just be purely natural, as abstract biological thinking would suggest to us. Recourse to biological procreation is all too artificial for human beings, whose nature it is to be able to desire, think and will; it is in fact the result of a particular kind of reflection which focuses on what is empirically given and in so doing leaves all motivation out of account, whether this comes from eros, agape or reason. This kind of understanding of nature[80] is unnatural to human beings and is no different from the understanding of nature among those who seek salvation in the 'sexual revolution'. A remarkable parallel!

On the other hand, if it is human nature not to be able to be natural in a reduced sense, then eros, passionate love, and agape, caring love, are part of specifically human 'nature'. Eros desires the beautiful female form; agape is directed towards the needy, helpless, suffering physical form (thus e.g. the love of parents in the care of children). But though eros and agape would seem at first sight to be combined in this way, they do not go together. As Plato too already sees, eros seeks the beautiful and shuns the hateful, including the helpless, since he wants to resist something that resists him. Agape, household duties, seeing to the progress of the family and the upbringing of children were and are therefore by experience the most effective means of driving out love. What then remains is biological sex, pleasureless 'increase of the people of God', marital duty.

If this ends up in a war between eros and agape, the victory of agape seems to guarantee a more humane, less destructive form of life together. Agape is capable of stabilizing social conditions, not eros, but it can also misuse its focus on the weaker ones for constructing hierarchies. In this sense the strategy of love in the Christian tradition was very successful and did not always bring the desired peace between human beings, between men and women, into the souls of believers. I have already spoken at length of what happens when eros drives out agape. But what happens when agape develops destructive powers?

The struggle for eros has long been associated with the battle against a 'rigid' Christian morality. For de Sade eros could not but be blasphemous;[81] Bataille drove out with a revolver the priest who wanted to administer the sacrament to his lifetime companion who was fatally ill with tuberculosis;[82] Sichtermann, who is one of the 1968 generation, and Weiler, at one time a 'teacher specializing in religion', lament the decline of paganism. Here are four worlds which would not be comparable did they not have a common motive; the conviction that the Christian banishment of eros has not brought any blessing (to put it euphemistically). But I hear outraged voices from church circles already asking: can a pervert, a man plagued with erotic obsessions, a 'left-wing' woman and a 'deserter' be credible witnesses? Do they not all belong in that profane world of those impure who may have nothing to do with a pure Christ? Anyone who thinks like this plays into the hands of the figures I have just mentioned. One does not need to share their attitude to hear their arguments. Essentially two complaints are produced against Christianity by its critics, who take the opportunity to complain at the same time about the loss of the pagan world.

1. Although agape champions humanity and order, it, too, can display destructive powers by robbing people of their vitality. Anyone who takes the demands of the Sermon on the Mount literally or even misunderstands it as a training programme may perhaps, after long battles, be successful in conquering even the most inward promptings of self-preservation, hatred, envy, sensual desire; but he will emerge from this battle a shadow of himself and surround himself with dead bodies if he compels others to take this course. Eros can tear people apart as a wild animal attacks its prey; agape can throttle people, make them lose their nerve. Celsus, the Voltaire of the second century AD,[83] is a forerunner of Nietzsche in mocking the bloodless, miserable, gloomy Christians. For example, the renunciation of violence required from the Christian side might be seen not as a refusal to exercise vital forces but simply as incompetence, weakness. Many accounts of experiences in Catholic monasteries and Protestant manses are evidence that Christian socialization is often out to break people.[84] It would be unfair to doubt the honesty of such confessions.

2. Agape does not always prove victorious over eros, and the battle does not always take place in open country. Eros can go underground and from there engage in an even more effective and unassailable partisan activity. Eros shoots not only at a breast that is ready for his arrow but also at the backs of those who are running away from him. 'The assumption of a connection between the destructive and the constructive forces and needs of human beings is indeed disconcerting. Wherever we can separate the two clearly, we feel better, but we pay for this well-being with a violent denial, in the shadow of which the tabooed ties prove all the closer.'[85] The consequences of such a denial are bad enough: the proverbial Christian hypocrisy indicates self-deception that a superhuman claim can be met. Fantasies develop to veil things. Over conflicts there hangs like a sword of Damocles the noble claim of agape, ready to execute immediately anyone who seeks a realistic course and therefore does not avoid the dialectic of love. Politics, understood in the broadest sense as a balance of interests, needs 'the threat, the pressure and the intelligence of diplomacy', 'courage to take the offensive and the wisdom of balance';[86] for many Christians such words already have a whiff of the betrayal of purity, of the pure gospel. And so the supposedly complete discipline of love is often followed by the shadow of a tacit indiscipline. There are the secret orgies in the quiet room, even in the priest's cell, and the open, double morality blessed by the church. As long as eros uses his weapons in the dark, he enjoys the hospitality of the Christian home, but where he comes to light, he provokes indignation (and the remarriage of divorced couples would shatter even the basic foundations of the Roman Catholic world edifice). Marriage counsellors tell stories of how long Christian couples torment one another; the legally manipulated prohibition against divorce is no help to them if they are looking for possible ways of living.

Where do we go with eros, who makes himself so difficult to conquer or to drive out? The tradition offers only one 'solution', which is most ominous for women. Eros is given a sphere, the man. He is allowed eroticism as a privilege: before marriage, in marriage and outside marriage. Popular opinion says that a man needs that: 'he' is more sensual than 'she'; 'he' does not need any tenderness, and by nature comes more quickly to the point, always 'wants only one thing'. 'She', on the other hand, needs tenderness, not pleasure; her sensibilities are more balanced because by nature they are orientated on agape. Thus eros and agape are divided between the sexes. It is therefore hardly surprising if the battle between the two forms of love continues as a battle between the sexes. But such a battle does not count among the figures of eros, in which both are involved, in which man and woman alternate in aggression and surrender to gain 'profit' from both. The woman robbed of eros, 'castrated' and thus at the same time exalted to high heaven, who cannot put up any resistance, must goad the man's eros to the point of the most brutally realistic use of violence. The 'warlike scenes of love'[87] are in this way detached from real, death-dealing war. Weakness makes eros aggressive because no boundaries are set to it, and stimulates it to escalate its intrinsic need to go beyond bounds – by rape, bodily attack, incest, child abuse and any other similar breaches of tabu. Conversely it is also no good for men to be made incapable of passive surrender; that is shown by that form of prostitution which offers the skills of the 'strict schoolmistress' in successful advertisements. How else are we to understand such excesses? Only those who cannot see through the strategy of eros undertake absurd attributions of guilt: is not 'woman' an attraction towards the works of darkness? There is a grain of truth here, but the attraction lies not in the woman but in the 'heightened' impotence which is attributed to her in her role, an impotence that provokes eros. And 'the man' is not just the innocent victim; a lack of insight is the basis of all these damnable errors. Here is one more argument for reflection, for the much reviled use of the head if light is to be shed on the blind interplay.

It is not specifically Christian women who believe in their allegedly 'natural' gentleness and readiness for peace. Committed feminists who want nothing to do with Christianity have long advocated this disastrous course. They too should be told: 'The more strongly one sex seeks to dictate its conditions to the other on the field of sexuality – instead of seeing that there is only one set of conditions which applies to both sexes – the more alien will pleasure be to us and therefore the more ready the ground will be for violence without pleasure.'[88] Men have always been able to put across the 'warlike scenes of love' when they employ raw violence on women, so that they are allowed the verdict of extenuating circumstances. But we women contribute to this 'if instead of redefining the borderline between violence and pleasure... we deny the existence or the justification of those figures...'[89]

Towards an 'erotic' theology

I do not want to avoid the question of the relationship between eros and Christianity, of the theory of the destructive victory of agape over its greatest enemy. It would be wrong to suppose that the Christians were the first to discover agape. The problem of the different forms of love is considered in many traditions. First of all it is necessary to make yet further distinctions. To begin with I was speaking of eros and agape in connection with human nature: desire and loving care as the motive forces of life. The argument that the power of eros must be limited by the regulation of community life already brings us to the next level of human reality; we are not tied to nature as to the 'peg of the moment' (Nietzsche) in the same way as are animals; we are liberated, conscious, responsible and thus ethically qualified to act, in some circumstanes even against our nature. At this level agape is no longer just natural care and concern (e.g. love of parents) but will, obligation, seeking the well-being of the other in all kinds of physical and mental distress; it is ethics as a question of conscience. And anyone who has no conscience comes up against the order of justice as a compelling law, because human society is only livable in when law and order seek to guarantee humanity. At all times the ethical dimension of agape was the presupposition for human social life and at the same time always endangered it. There was and still is agreement among a wide variety of critics of the Christian tradition that bounds must be set to eros. Fear of chaos as a result of eros has proved justified, since among Christians as among pagans there is a lapse into obscene practices.[90]

Without doubt in Jewish-Christian religious circles the emphasis has long since shifted in favour of agape. Here it plays the decisive role in the 'drama' of love. With agape a consciousness of humanity has grown which is also struggling for recognition in a secular world. Losing or surrendering such a consciousness in favour of devouring eros cannot be in the feminist interest either, which is on the defensive when women are seen as the mere objects of desire.

At the same time the danger of the Christian tradition of human agape emerges when the power of erotic desire which is also innate in humankind is suppressed. Nature and spirit are not alternatives for human beings, though attempts have constantly been made in Christian tradition, too, to resolve the tense relationship in favour of one side or the other. In that case the ecstatics or the 'enthusiasts'[91] and the 'Platonists' among Christians fight one another, seeking to kill off their bodily nature for the love of God. However, these two ways are not the only controversial strands in the complex web of the material of Christian faith. There is a third way which cannot be taken without involving conflict with the two others. This, taking up the conceptuality that I have been using so far, might be called an 'erotic' theology. One example of this kind of theological thought is Martin Luther. He develops his theology among other things in opposition to Erasmus of Rotterdam, an opposition which is not without predecessors nor without subsequent influence. To put things in a pointed way one could describe Erasmus's theological thinking as an agapaistic concept, and that of Luther as erotic;[92] however, this is to exaggerate the contrast, because Luther's theology cannot be said to be hostile to agape but is distinguished by the dialectical combination of the two forms of love. Nevertheless I use the term 'erotic' in order to express the transcending of agapaistic one-sidedness, though that does not mean that Luther now lapses into the opposite, into a reduced erotic understanding of love.

Agape, loving care and concern, which all human beings are equally in need of, finds its most comprehensive expression in the Jewish-Christian command to love one's neighbour. Agape is quite simply the good. All good, Erasmus says, comes from the goodness of God. Where the Bible contains ethical instructions it is clear and good, however much in it remains dark and confused; the latter, says Erasmus, we can forget. Now man or woman is born as a 'neutral' being, neither good nor evil. We learn evil from evil people so a Christian education from the cradle onwards must

lead us to act out of agape. Just as all good comes from God, so
all evil comes from human beings, from offending against the
commandment of agape. It is the baser promptings of the flesh,
the body, that lead people to offend in this way. So human beings
are divided: 'below' they are cattle, but 'above', in their spirits,
they are divine beings. Thus the good, implanted in human nature,
at all events lies in the 'upper' part, in reason. It leaves the person
free to decide for the good and thus against the flesh. Now if
individuals make use of this freedom and successfully combat the
baser parts of their nature – here Luther is only superficially a
good Platonist – they are fused with God, the good, and become
like God. Now this fusing is one of the characteristics of agape;
I fuse myself with the wholly good, people are fused into a
comprehensive community under the sign of a *respublica Christ-
iana*, man and woman are fused into humankind (Erasmus is well
known for his stress on the equality of the sexes), and finally
humankind is fused with God in perfect love. All contradictions
and alien features which are in me, between me and the other,
between man and woman, between God and humankind, are
removed. The way to do this is indicated by love with its powerful
imperative 'You shall', or, as my grandmother used to recite, 'You
can if you will, so will if you should.' Erasmus concedes that this
way is difficult, but it still holds out the prospect of success. In
this concept agape is the queen of heaven who ultimately covers
all things with her white robe of all-embracing selflessness – in
the literal sense.

This notion exercises fascination, since it seems to fulfil the
wish for an end to the war between the sexes as well; moreover
it has been powerful in history and is frequently identified with
Christianity (in the singular). The longed-for perfection has,
however, never been achieved: that was also one of the arguments
that Luther used against Erasmus, not in peaceful academic
dialogue but with the vehemence of an angry man. Luther does
not dispute that agape is simply the good, but he does dispute that
human beings are capable of deciding for the good so simply.
They do not have complete control of themselves, of their bodies
or their wills or their reason. That is their 'nature'. We may think
that we want to be good, but that is far from meaning that we
really do will to be and even farther from our actually being able

to be good. The passions which conflict with the good are everywhere: in body, soul and spirit.

For Luther, evil is not simply an ethical failing but a power: the dark, ultimately incomprehensible side of reality. Just as the dark passages of the Bible are part of salvation history, so dark sides are part of human nature. And God? He too has his dark side; he works through good and evil, he is unbounded, as nothing is above him and nothing is like him. Would he be God otherwise? God is life, power, he must go on working, he seems creative and destructive, but the destructive side is 'transcended' in redemption since he practises goodness, grace, agape; the ethical instruction emanating from this is not, however, given to fuse God and humankind in one. It is no coincidence that agape emerges in the form of a demand. Like Erasmus, Luther attacks all enthusiasm and sets against it the claim of love. But he does not do that in the hope of being able to eliminate the dark side of humanity which is vital but also evil, life-creating but also destructive. The 'Thou shalt' is evidently directed against something which is in conflict with it; it is a declaration of war. Luther does not use the term eros, but the way in which he depicts the human inability to do good corresponds to the nature of eros that I have already described. Luther's explanation goes like this. The love command has two functions. First it is meant to prevent people from doing evil to their neighbours – agape limits eros. Secondly, it demonstrates that it is not agape but eros with the Janus head that dwells deep within them, not concern for the well-being of others, but desire in the all-embracing sense directed towards the self.

But human eros may not be killed off, since at the same time it is the experience of limitation: vitality comes to an end, the desire of love and the desire of knowledge do not attain their goal, for all the trouble of education. Thus thrown back on themselves, human beings remain lonely and desperate. They cannot reconcile themselves with themselves, with society, with the other sex, or with God. Their hope is redemption, the life-giving power of God, the love of God which elects and graces all at the same time. Erotic analogies accompany Luther's talk of God, which he draws from the Bible and not, like Erasmus, from Platonic philosophy: God is the other, the alien one, with whom one cannot be fused.

Precisely for that reason, not despite it, there comes into being the longing for reconciliation, for being one with him. But God also desires human beings and seeks to come close to them. Human beings are concerned to please God by seeking to fulfil his will, but in so doing they cannot gain control of him. God remains who he is. God gives people presents to show them his love, he saves them from danger and the threat of death, but they too remain who they are and tend to take such things as much for granted as the fulfilment of marital duties. If God fails to give one of his gifts, human beings become aggressive and try to sue for what they think that they should have; if human beings fail to think of God they feel the side of God that is turned away: the history of God's love with humankind is full of the figures of eros.

If God and man want to come together they have to go through 'death'. God dies on the cross and is raised to life; the erotic figure 'through death to life' also determines human experiince. As Luther puts it: 'When God makes alive he does that by killing, when he makes righteous he does that by making guilty, when he brings to heaven he does that by taking down to hell.'[93] Love, life, pain, death, sin bind eros and agape together in great tension; they overcome each other in their destructive power by confirming each other's independence. The language of redemption continues the erotic analogies.[94] In the eucharist the blood of the God made man is drunk and the body of the God made man is consumed – the physical union of God and man takes place. But God does not become 'merely' human nor do human beings become 'really' God, any more than man and woman dissolve themselves in union. They remain alien to one another and that maintains their relationship; in their longing they continue to resist one another.

This theology, too, is a decisive strand in Christian tradition. It can appeal to biblical writings and has also had an influence since the church fathers. It is an 'erotic' theology to the degree that it does not deny the experience of eros, either human eros in all its ambivalence, or the eros of God who elects and rejects, comes near yet remains alien. But here human eros is neither divinized nor diabolized, and the dialectic of love retains its tension. This theology should be rediscovered before Christianity is reduced to a cliché against which it is easy to fight in the name of the old myths. For now is the time to get rid of an old habit.

Just as there is no 'man' or 'woman' in the singular, so there is no such thing as 'Christianity'; the wealth of traditions is far too great for that. However, the discerning of the spirits is also appropriate here.

The lesson of Anat

These considerations have taken us a long way from the immediately 'natural' experience of the erotic and set us on the course of analogies which was already indicated in the first chapter. The use of analogies prevents the short cut – this time not theocratic but naturalistic – and a loss of relationship to reality. God's love is not human eros, so human eros is not divine. That is the basic criticism to be made of nature religions and their advocates like Bataille, though we can learn a good deal from them. By contrast God's love is always 'more' than human love (and human agape); it is the embodiment of vitality and life, indeed life itself (and the embodiment of graciousness and care). So faith in the living God offers a critique of the human forms of love and thus criticizes all eros euphoria as it is also to be found among feminists: a reduction to the vital powers of eros does not produce any redemption from all the evils of this world, as the 'sexual revolution' à la Ernest Bornemann would lead us to believe,[95] any more than does the denial of eros. That is the lesson of Anat: the kinship of life and death cannot be dissolved, either by the worshippers of life or by those who want to kill it off. In this sense the old myths are wiser than many of those who take them over today, but they do not disclose any nostalgic view.

It is as appropriate to say that eros is part of humanity as a vital force as it is to say that eros is destructive: in other words that its effect is to destroy life. This contradiction cannot be removed 'in a simple way',[96] although attempts are constantly made in this direction. Some people try to close their eyes to the destruction; others try to preserve people from destruction by breaking their life force. But just to say that they belong together does not help much either. Certainly both 'sides' are part of the 'wholeness' of humanity, but the way in which they are connected remains nebulous, or the moral imperative is used: 'You shall be whole!' How little fruit is borne or can be borne by the slogan also used by feminists about the sexuality integrated into the 'totality' of human nature may be illuminated by the controversy between Erasmus and Luther. The combination in the 'contradictory' statement can, however, be clarified by the basic dialectic of human existence, the dialectic of nature and spirit, being bound up in a given and being free as a result for conscious action. Nature stands 'beyond' good and evil, but action falls within the scope of ethical responsibility. Human beings would have to forego their individuality, their awareness, their capacity for motivation, their historicity to take part in the goodness of nature. As that is not possible, human beings also have to be responsible towards nature. Now if one denies the independence of nature or regards it as a power which is alien from, or indeed hostile to, mere humanity, the result is those forms of violation of nature 'within' and 'outside' humanity of the kind which feminists today also rightly attack. The feminist position seeks to restore one side of the dialectic, but that is too little, since it can no more tolerate the question of the dialectic itself than it can tolerate the position of those against whom it fights.

The revival of the goddesses and with them of the nature religions represents the negation of the individual, of consciousness, of freedom in thought and action, and thus of human personality; and the claim that this is not deliberate does not do away with the logic of this intellectual practice. I shall return to the dialectic of eros and agape later. In contrast to the Christian theology represented by Erasmus, in which agape conquers the vital power of eros, one learns from the nature religions, Georges Bataille, Barbara Sichtermann and so on the lesson that human beings also remain nature. That is the basis for my assent, especially as they do not all have the blue-eyed innocence of Ernst Bornemann and other representatives of the plea for human liberation with a view to mere natural sexuality, which is thought of as being pure and good (I am not excluding feminists like Gerda Weiler). The last step to a dialectical pattern of thought has still to be be taken. Dialectic means that the one, eros, not only conflicts with the other, agape, so that each limits the other, but that the one is transcended in the other and that therefore the two cannot get on without each other. To end this chapter I should say something more about what I mean by this.

Eros is not agape. Eros seeks to gain, agape to give itself away; eros seeks its own pleasure, agape the well-being of the other; eros helps towards self-discovery, agape towards unselfishness; eros is powerful, agape renounces power, sacrifices itself to the point of giving up the life that eros seeks to gain. On closer inspection, however, it proves that this assignation of properties does not happen quite like that. To some degree eros also gives itself away, is also directed towards the other, surrenders itself; and to some degree agape also wants to gain by preserving life, approaching it passionately and showing teeth to the powerful who play with the lives of others. There is passionate agape and tender eros. Nevertheless they are not the same; nevertheless their anatagonism remains and anyone who seeks to remove it triggers off the destructive powers of both. Only with one another (though that does not mean in harmony) or against one another (though that is not as an alternative) can both develop. It is part of the distinctiveness of dialectical talk that as long as statements are made in terms of content they seem vague, crazy, absurdly contradictory. The 'reciprocal transcendence' nevertheless emerges at the level of speech and thus for reality, in so far as one recognizes the basic relationship of speech to reality and does not see in it a sign which has merely been agreed arbitrarily.

If we begin from the fact that the manifold forms of human existence are fundamentally involved in the dialectic of nature and spirit, and that the one is transcended in the other, we can also understand that such dialectics are apt ways of expressing the 'great dialectic' of the relationship between God and man by way of analogies: God is the embodiment of life, thrilling and determinative; God is the embodiment of agapaistic love, yielding and sacrificing himself; God is distant and alien, near and familiar. But to recall Kant: God and humanity can never 'come together', not even by means of dialectic, as can e.g. eros and agape for human beings. However, as an analogy, as a definition of the nature and mode of relationship, the dialectical relationship between eros and agape can open our mouths to utter what is inexpressible.

CHAPTER THREE

Matriarchy: The Lost Paradise

The $64,000 dollar question for feminists

'The assertion that there was a matriarchy in early history or equality of the sexes in prehistoric times was particularly attractive to the feminist movement of the nineteenth century, since in the name of science it provided evidence that the oppression of women was historical and not biological.'[1] This comment by Marie-Luise Janssen-Jurreit characterizes not only the interest of that time but also an extremely topical interest in the historical reconstruction of matriarchal cultures. It has occupied the women's movement since the end of the 1960s and in feminist theology is associated with criticism of the one-sidedly male conception of God in Jewish-Christian monotheism.

But that is not all. The conviction that the the matriarchy once existed in history has taken on programmatic character. Anyone who doubts that there were matriarchies or who while acknowledging their existence depreciates them as a lower stage of human history, and finally anyone who thinks that there is no historical proof of a fully matriarchal culture incurs the feminist 'anathema'. Heide Göttner-Abendroth sees such people as ideologists or victims of the patriarchy, who do not belong to the community of those who believe in the matriarchate. The confession of faith runs: 'Without qualification I would describe the earliest religions of humanity as matriarchal.'[2]

An unqualified assertion like this should withstand critical examination. Therefore we must now consider the question whether there were such matriarchal cultures and religions, the plausibility of the methodology of the reconstruction, and the consequences that follow for women from all this.

Heide Göttner-Abendroth received the greatest response to her theory of matriarchy in the German-speaking world; Gerda Weiler also refers to it when she goes in search of traces of matriarchy in the Old Testament. And above all Elizabeth Gould Davis made an impression in the Anglo-American world with her book *The First Sex*.[3] Before them Josephine Schreier, who was born in Vienna in 1899 and died in the United States in 1962, was concerned with the theme in a very distinctive way; her posthumous work *Goddesses*[4] was reissued in Germany in 1978. In the meantime the hypotheses of matriarchy have often been brought together in summary fashion and have found their way into popularizing literature and even into school books,[5] which means that they are handed on as the assured results of scholarship. Would it then be too much to regard the question of their recognition as the $64,000 dollar question?

However different their positions may be in detail, the starting point of all the authors is that before the beginning of patriarchal history writing, i.e. before about 3000 BC, the whole world had been stamped by a matriarchal period. Göttner-Abendroth, for example, goes on to divide this period into the time of the simple matriarchy, that of the developed matriarchy and finally that of the world-wide matriarchy.[6]

Agriculture, from simple gardens to technically developed agriculture (artificial irrigation), formed the economic basis. Matrilinearity, i.e. nomenclature and inheritance by the female line, and matrifocality, the mother's dwelling as the centre of the formation of the tribes, characterized the family structure. Monogamy is said to have been unknown, and the polygamy of both sexes to have been the rule. Thus Göttner-Abendroth praises the great sexual tolerance and gives as its basis the lack of awareness of the role of the male in the production of the child. If at all, the mother as head of the tribe assigned functions and status in the tribe not to the father of her children but to her son or her brother. This structure is also said to have been preserved in the formation of types of state.

In the religious sphere the tribal mother is said to represent the mother goddess. All the myths were focussed on female deities; there were no male deities, for the hero who accompanies the goddess is, in contrast to her, mortal and plays a subordinate role in the cultic drama. The mother goddess combines femininity and earth, from which all living beings proceed. For example Richard Fester sees the foetal position in which burials were made as evidence that the dead were given back to the womb of the earth in the form of the embryo, in order to return from there.[7] So death is at the same time rebirth. From the dark womb the human being breaks out into the light of life. Night and moon are therefore the religious symbols of the matriarchy. In this interpretation the horns of the bull represent the two crescents of the moon. In images and sculptures of bulls the full moon often appears between the horns. Chronological calculation followed the lunar year, so the year has thirteen months; the night was the preferred time for councils, the administration of the law and cultic actions. Acording to Göttner-Abendroth the moon goddess of the developed matriarchy is threefold: virgin, beloved/mother and old woman. In the cult, priestesses perform the rites which imitate the rhythm of the seasons: initiation festivals in the spring, the 'sacred marriage' in the summer, the death and resurrection of the hero in the autumn and winter.

The individual themes in this panorama of a matriarchal period are derived from the myths of very different cultures and times; the question remains how far they can honestly be made into the desired picture, the picture of the matriarchy as a historical fact which is capable of being described.

It is generally agreed that matriarchies would have been notable for their especial readiness for peace. Wars were not waged, and warlike arts and the production of weapons were not practised. Therefore the matriarchal cultures would have been defenceless against the attacks of warlike pastoral peoples. Without giving further information Göttner-Abendroth speaks of a transition from matriarchal to patriarchal society which took place over a long period and was dominated by a struggle between the two cultures.[8] This 'patriarchal revolution' is often identified in the

Mediterranean world (in my further remarks I shall limit myself to this area) with the great Indo-Germanic migration (2500-1700 BC).

Opinions differ on the question how the matriarchy could collapse and what reasons may have led to the institution of male rule. Whereas Gerda Weiler simply uses the immorality intrinsic to the male sex as an argument, claiming that the last traces of matriarchy in Old Testament history were expunged in the exilic period, Elizabeth Davis gives a number of reasons: the role of man in the creation of a child by begetting it was first discovered by women. They attempted in vain to conceal this knowledge from men. When the latter discovered it, the woman was robbed of her superiority as the sole giver of life. From that point on men were able to attach conditions to their life-giving 'favour'. The women became dependent.[9] Or men who remained only loosely connected with the polygamous matriarchy went around the settlements hunting and plundering. These outcast, functionless men formed bands and made themselves independent of women through 'pederasty'. Skilled in weapons and by nature brutal, removed from the moralizing influence of women, they attacked the peaceful matriarchies and seized power for themselves. Davis decorates her account with vivid details: the raw flesh eaten by the wild hunters was perhaps a decisive factor in the overthrow – meat eaters are characterized by their larger sexual organs, 'and this development may have proved irresistible to women'.[10]

Josephine Schreier uses more sophisticated arguments to explain the transition from the matriarchy to the patriarchy. She refers to Freud's theory of identification, according to which people imitate one another. Freud sees this as the most original form of communication among human beings, so that it also plays a decisive role in the development of children. Anyone who takes another person as a model is seeking to develop the ego along the apparent lines of that model.[11] This structure of imitation makes sense only if the model seems superior to the one who imitates it. Freud cited this form of communication with reference to the relationship of the son to his father. Schreier modifies the model to the relationship between man and woman: those men in the matriarchy who sought to identify with powerful women were preferred. To be the ideal model is ultimately a flattering role.

'Only those men were elevated to kingship who had made this identification.'[12] As an example Schreier gives the couvade, the imitation of the process of birth by the father. To this realm too belongs the custom which can be demonstrated among many peoples of men wearing women's clothes and false breasts when performing public functions. However, again according to Freud, identification leads to rivalry: the one who imitates seeks to take the place of his ideal.[13] The men of the matriarchy who were supported by the women finally succeeded in doing that.

Hope from history

It is no coincidence that opinions on the origin of the patriarchy differ. For this is where authors have to explain how the earlier state which has been discovered, is believed in and hoped for turns into that for which there is undoubted historical evidence, that which can still be experienced today, in other words – to put it in more simple terms – they have to indicate what distinguished and should distinguish the earlier situation from that of today.

Josephine Schreier writes that what historical data can be regarded as relevant depends on the 'theories' by which one is guided. If we substitute the word 'interest' for 'theory', we can see what Schreier means: she follows a decided interest, draws a corresponding line through history, as she herself acknowledges,[14] and seeks to carry the reader with her. Only at the end of her book does she become more concrete. In respect of her legal position the woman has made gains in modern society: 'But her social position continues to be uncertain, threatened and attacked by the modern supporters of the patriarchy. The psychological need to eliminate and depose the mother' is something that Schreier finds in the literature of the leading psychologists, from Freud and Jung to the American therapists whom she came to know through her exile in the United States.[15] Josephine Schreier sets her reconstruction of early matriarchal history over against this demotion of the mother, indeed of the feminine.

Elizabeth Davis who, like Josephine Schreier, might be called an 'amateur scholar',[16] seeks to attack the 'myth of feminine inferiority' in her book. An earth-shaking reconsideration of a past repressed history is aimed at reawakening in the women of our century 'their ancient dignity and pride'. No one, Davis writes bitterly, has so far taken 'God's curse' from Eve.[17] Davis's aim is to bring about a 'matriarchal counter-revolution' against the patriarchal revolution which has exterminated matriarchal culture. She ends her book with gripping, almost apocalyptic words: 'The era of the cult of masculinity is now approaching its end. Its last days will be illuminated by the flare-up of such a comprehensive violence and despair as the world has never seen. People of good will seek help on all sides for their declining society, but in vain. Any social reform imposed on our sick society has only value as a bandage for a gaping and putrefying wound. Only a complete destruction of society can heal this fatal disease. Only the fall of the three-thousand-year-old beast of male materialism will save humankind.'[18] One does not get the impression that in Davis's view the chances of rescue are good.

Against such hopelessness Göttner-Abendroth sets the conviction that the lost paradise of the matriarchies can be regained. Societies under the domination of women can be a 'utopian guideline' by virtue of their religious character.[19] She thinks that we must not lapse into antagonism and absolutize the feminine principle in order to use it against the masculine principle. She is concerned only for the integration of both principles, and she is convinced that women can succeed in doing that now, even to the point of restoring the matriarchy. By 'precise knowledge of the historical forms' of matriarchal cultures and analyses of contemporary patriarchal forms of life and society it would be possible to translate the utopia into strategies for action.[20] But she does not tell us what these might look like.

Gerda Weiler builds above all on the work of Heide Göttner-Abendroth. She is concerned to regain the matriarchal person who can investigate the nature of things, who does not dominate nature but adapts to it, 'in order to bring about the rebirth of each day every morning and the revival of the whole creation every year by life and action, by loving surrender and cultic sanctification'.[21] She seeks a return to the tolerant world-view of the mothers,[22] to a 'natural order', which is 'morally compelling' without law.[23] Weiler also sees the destruction of the patriarchy as the only possible way of healing this world: 'Humankind needs the reintegration of the male into a matriarchal environment in order to regain wholeness.'[24]

In such outlines we can see quite clearly the hopes that women associate with the reconstruction of matriarchies. Such present hopes, which cast out their anchor into history, are the only explanation of the great attraction which matriarchal theories have enjoyed. Interest here is directed not by scientific detachment but by involvement in the unhealthy state of the world and the relationship between the sexes. In this interest one senses an experience of suffering, a hatred that can be sympathized with, and an understandable longing for another world which is better for women than our own. And if our further examination of the historical reconstruction of matriarchies also shows that the facts – which are still scanty – are not clear and the methods doubtful, that does not mean that these personal signals are being missed or may be underestimated.

Nevertheless, anyone who shares such an interest in principle, if not in all the details, should not be disturbed by a critical examination of the methods or the identification of interest and method. Göttner-Abendroth begins from the claim that the research into matriarchy carried on by males is prejudiced. So as a first stage she gives herself the task of 'assembling the prejudices of scholars',[25] in the form of a catalogue of sins. For Göttner-Abendroth, unprejudiced scholarship does not mean studying the sources thoroughly in order to go on to form a verdict but rather adopting their position and accepting matriarchy as a given. So Göttner-Abendroth can arrive at the 'unqualified' description which I have already cited of the early religions as matriarchal, although she stresses that she wants to regard the results of previous scholarship with 'ideological-critical caution'.

Now everyone who starts from a hypothesis should be unprejudiced. Any scholarship must work with hypotheses in which the interest of the scholar is articulated. Method, however, by virtue of its etymology, denotes the way, the procedure by which the hypothesis can be verified, or, if the approach does not work, must be falsified. That again serves to alter the hypothesis, so that one is compelled either to drop it altogether or to modify it.

However, as I have already said, Göttner-Abendroth is stuck in a circular argument: the presentation of the feminist interest as already a verified hypothesis must suggest that this interest has already been objectively demonstrated. But in this way she avoids any criticism, since the critic necessarily incurs the verdict of being incapable of objectivity; even more, he incurs a moral disqualification. By his criticism he demonstrates his prejudice. To put it plainly: anyone who does not show the right feminist interest does not have any scientific qualities. This line of argument, which is ideological in the negative sense, is well known from the totalitarian systems of both 'right' and 'left'. Anyone who does not toe the party line is no good as a scholar. I am not suggesting that the content of any of the statements made by Göttner-Abendroth amounts to any such ideology. But I do want to say that she is obviously unaware that the formal structure of her argumentation does match such intellectual and social totalitarian systems.

Science as a token of love

Here two levels are brought together, subjective interest and the methodological approach of matter-of-fact objectivity, an activity which for the period of the examination leaves subjective interest aside. If such an examination does not take place, any historical material is bound to confirm the interest. Such circular arguments are familiar from psychology. Thus for example psychoanalysts take into account the resistance of the patient. Resistance means that the patient refuses, of course unconsciously, to acknowledge the less flattering reasons for a disturbance. If therapists go on to evaluate this refusal as proof of the neurotic character of their patients, they will regard the therapy as all the more necesary. But if they do this, at the same time they will have evaded the critical question addressed to them and their interpretation of the disturbance of their patients. The conclusion is that the stronger the resistance, the stronger is the neurosis. The person of the therapist is thus of no account. What is overlooked is that the patient could rightly resist the diagnosis which is offered because it does not speak to his or her problem and is possibly even the expression of a problem felt by the therapist.[26] The models of disruptions in communication produced by Paul Watzlawick could be helpful here: his starting point is that people communicate on levels of both content and relationship. One example of the level of content is agreeing to visit a relative; an example of the level of relationship is that everyone wants to be noticed, valued, loved by the other person. Conflicts arise when these two levels are mixed; if someone does not want to visit the relative, the relative regards this as evidence of a lack of love and may even insist that the visit takes place as planned to compel a token of love, or withdraws in a sulk to complain about the lovelessness of the world or to plan revenge. Watzlawick reduces this confusion in communication to the apt statement: 'If you loved me, you would not contradict me.'[27]

Let us apply this model to Göttner-Abendroth's 'method'. If we separate the level of content (= matriarchate) from the level of relationship (= feminist interest) then she is saying 'by means of the flowers', or rather by her firm assumption of the matriarchate: if you love me you must agree with me; if you, woman, want to be in solidarity with me, you must share my firm assumption; if you, man, do not want to be included among the inhuman patriarchs, you must share my firm assumption. So Göttner-Abendroth communicates on the level of relationships, and the level of content is only the means to the end. In this perspective I could understand her: at the level of relationship she wants attention, solidarity and a humane attitude to women. I share this interest without qualification. But that applies regardless of the question whether I accept the hypothesis of matriarchy without critical examination. The critical examination, no matter what its outcome, does not diminish my solidarity. Conversely, I may not allow my solidarity to be forced or put to the test by being compelled to adopt the matriarchal hypothesis. Nor is Göttner-Abendroth's procedure a 'method' for argument with the other side, with those (men, but also women) who as a result of the same confusion call for support for her contrary interest or in fact set out to make a detailed examination of the matriarchal hypotheses. One can avoid the emotional pressure on the level of relationship; one can exercise counter-pressure or feign solidarity. On the level of content Göttner-Abendroth is open to attack and refutation.

The snares of causal logic

Whereas Davis and Weiler have a very similar approach, Josephine Schreier uses a clearer language. She too mentions a presupposition. However, this is not her theory but the readiness of the reader to be open and unprejudiced, primarily to pay heed to her interest.[28] She compares the enterprise of a historical reconstruction to the activity of a detective. An event is to be explained by a selection of relevant data and theories. Only one explanation, she thinks, can be the right one, and she demonstrates which model of explanation she takes to be correct, that of psychology: '...if we seek to understand human actions, we return to motives which cause people to act in a particular way.'[29] But Schreier does not see action as being either arbitrary or fortuitous. For her, action as something achieved is the consequence of a causal logic: 'In such conclusions we use general theories which associate certain conditions and processes with their causes. If we know that a certain state generally arises from a particular cause, we will be inclined to assume that in a given case such a cause also happened in the past, although we cannot establish directly that it in fact happened'.[30] Schreier makes use of the psychological theories of Sigmund Freud to this effect.

Schreier builds a bridge to the past by assuming that certain causes always lead people at any period to definite and thus similar reactions. I have already mentioned one example which is central for Schreier: people use as models others who are more powerful, who seem to them to be ideals; they want to become like the ideal they aim at and thus come to rival it. The consequence is a struggle for pre-eminence, for the position of the ideal figure. Such a pattern of attraction and reaction can be observed or confirmed through critical self-examination, and so, the conclusion goes, this attitude is necessarily part of the potential for all human behaviour, no matter when a person may have lived. Necessity is the basis of the causal logic which is characteristic of this pattern of attraction and reaction in the form of an 'if-then': if people are oppressed, they resist; if people have a sedentary life, the social position of women improves, as these are given stability of location by their ties to their children; if men come to know that they beget children, they exploit this power; women look after children, and so they are life-affirming; men wage wars, so they destroy life; all embryos in the womb are first feminine (XX chromosomes), so the woman is 'the first',[31] and so on.

This model of explanation is characteristic of the so-called individual or real sciences,[32] which nowadays are more dominant than the systematic sciences; indeed by a simple error they are regarded as science *par excellence*, even by feminists. The fascination and popularity of this model of science lies in its simple thought-structure.

(*a*) The object of this kind of science is anything empirical and thus observable. For example, the biologist observes butterflies, the physicist observes free fall, the sociologist and the psychologist observe modes of human behaviour. Even Freudian identification is included among the empirical sciences in that we can observe the phenomenon of imitation among ourselves and others. In the framework of this model what cannot be observed is 'speculation' in the derogatory sense.

(*b*) As a next stage an explanation is then sought for the material gained by observation. Why do some butterflies have eyes on their wings? Why do objects fall according to particular rules? Why do people practise particular rites? Why do people imitate one another?

(*c*)The explanation follows in accordance with the rules of causal logic, in other words according to the model of cause and effect. Here one empirical datum is illuminated by another: butterflies have eyes on their wings to ward off enemies; the gravity of the earth brings about free fall; people conjured up beings whom they thought to be supernatural out of fear of lightning and storms; people imitate great models in order to free themselves from a subordinate position. The goal of causal logic is a general and objectively valid statement.

(*d*) The logic of cause and effect is necessarily reversible. Any cause has a particular effect; any effect has a corresponding cause. This is what leads to the manipulation which is much criticized today. If e.g. anxiety drives people to conjure up supernatural beings, then making people deliberately anxious is a certain way of driving them to believe in God or in the church. The experience that times of crisis lead people to ask about religion then confirms the rule of causal logic. The sequence 'if... then' can be reversed to become 'then... if'.

What this model of thought does not note or deliberately omits is the human capacity for self-motivation: in other words, in his or her action a person can in principle avoid causal logic. Individuals can detach themselves, reflect on what they observe and act differently as the result of a deliberate decision, i.e. independently, from a motive other than that offered by causal logic. They need not become anxious when others want to make them anxious; they need not conjure up supernatural beings out of anxiety; they need not imitate models. A scientific method which can be used for natural phenomena becomes dangerous when applied to human beings and their motivation, since it deprives them of the possibility of deliberately opposing such compulsions. Any moral imperative, for example, would be *a priori* meaningless unless we could do other than follow some laws of causal logic.

The polemic against scientific theorizing, associated with the appeal for humane responsibility, is a recurrent theme in feminist positions. With admirable sensitivity many of these women call science anti-human, and indeed it is anti-human to define actions in terms of the mechanisms of causal logic and as a result to deny any freedom in motivation. But so far I can find no argument to this effect in feminist literature. This leads to two decisive mistakes. First, science continues to retain the model of the individual or real sciences, as though, for example, ethics were inaccessible to any scientific reflection. As a result the systematic sciences like philosophy or theology are dismissed as sheer speculation, a judgment which puts the feminist position in an unholy alliance with the real sciences.[33] Secondly, the arguments of the matriarchal scholars also amount to precisely what they criticize in science, according to the same model of causal logic, and as a result they get hopelessly confused.

Elizabeth Davis gives us one example of this. She thinks that as a result of their physical powers (the Brunnhilde saga is a recollection of this) the women in matriarchal cultures 'tested' their wooers: 'the sexual selection of a "superior father" by the woman...'[34] As a result of that the small and weak men would have been eliminated, and this too would have helped the women to gain greater physical strength as the result of better heredity. But the men, too, would have achieved increased physical superiority as a result of this 'selective breeding' (the term is mine, chosen for its allusion) and this would have enabled them to seize power from the women. In patriarchal cultures the men now made the choice and were inclined to marry 'the most sorry example of the women's world and make her the mother of the generation'.[35] The consequences for heredity would be obvious. Therefore according to Davis selective breeding on the basis of feminine choice should be reintroduced so that feminine influence should contribute towards the development of a worthy male sex.[36]

If we analyse this argument, the following pattern emerges. Davis says that for reasons of causal logic women can always only choose strong men, and men can only choose weak women. But is and was that necessarily so? Here an evolutionary theme is transferred to the sphere of human motivation. Further, the consequence of 'selective breeding' is strong women, but why men so much stronger that they bring the women under their domination? As a next step the argument from physical strength and a desire for power identifies a biological characteristic with an ethical attitude. When men produce such biologistic arguments, women rightly get annoyed. Moreover, is it ethically defensible to eliminate weak men? Is it not much more in line with an ethical attitude to allow weak women to participate in marriage and motherhood, even if that means that no heroes will be brought into the world? Does not such an argument also offer complete justification for eliminating weak women, handicapped people or primitive races? Davis concludes that if selective breeding by women were reintroduced today, a more worthy male sex could come into being. But how could that come about if one of the roots of the patriarchy lies in that very selective breeding by women which through its selection allowed men to become monsters? The degree to which Davis is rooted in the model of the individual sciences that she too repudiates is finally shown by her naive idea that one could transfer an if-then relationship (selective breeding by women 'makes' better men), once 'proved', from then to now, not to me or to you. But how would it happen again? By the 'conversion of the male sex',[37] which is biologically fixated on a desire for power? By a referendum? By the decrees of the authorities (did we not have that 'recently')?

Without arguing in detail as Davis does, Göttner-Abendroth also thinks that strategies for action could follow from an analysis of social conditions. But from where do we get the motivation for that? From the facts, which in any case go their foreordained way in a causal succession? How can the power of facts break through other than by humane interest? Thus the problem focuses on the question how an ethical motivation can be communicated. The matriarchy scholars do not write about that. Gerda Weiler is at least consistent in that she makes an accusation against humanity by taunting those who violate the humane.

One of the most ominous arguments which blindly takes over the logic of the individual sciences goes like this. If the woman was the 'first' from both a biological and a historical point of view, and therefore – so the argument goes – has to be the first again, as first cause she herself is responsible for all that follows, and is thus also responsible for the rise of the patriarchate. That follows as a result of this thinking, but feminist literature also has other examples of this kind of conclusion, without the writers seeming to find any special problems in them. Thus according to Schreier the process of the identification of men with women was provoked by their powerful capabilities.[38] Schreier then moves from psychology to biology. Past primal experiences will have left behind 'traces in the brain' and these will have been inherited by subsequent generations.[39] According to Davis, the selective breeding of women and the 'fact' that women were influenced by the large sexual organs of the wild hordes of meat-eating men contributed to the patriarchal revolution.[40]

How do such comments fit in with a feminist interest? Women have been told for centuries that they are guilty of everything and indeed provoke the guilt of men. Let me begin by assuming that feminists would not seriously agree with this. In that case, however, such fatal consequences can only follow from thinking in the categories of causal logic, categories which are intrinsic to that pattern of science which is so hated by feminists and so diabolized by them. But if that is the case, none of us has a chance of altering ourselves or our reality, and all moral appeals, with which even feminists are not sparing, are a contradiction in terms.

It is also interesting that the psychological and sociological arguments in the authors I have mentioned ultimately end up in biologism: inherited traces in the brain and chromosomes are our destiny. What can redeem us from this – and that is the only possibility in this model – is the next evolutionary step which for example Gerda Weiler believes to be close:[41] as it were a 'natural imminent eschatological expectation'.

On the level of method, matriarchal scholarship is characterized by hopeless confusion: the material level and the relational level (interest) are confused, as are arguments from causal logic and moral appeal; the demand for freedom from prejudice is matched by a cultivation of prejudices and, finally, attempts at historical reconstruction emerge in the form of edifying discourse, when the sisters, as I showed in the previous chapter, end up in enthusiasm. Those who call themselves matriarchal scholars have simply taken all this further. They have not invented it, but taken it over – from men, whom they accuse of being evil patriarchs.

Bachofen's liberation of the woman

Foremost among the men in matriarchal scholarship on whom feminists rely are J.J.Bachofen ('so the old Basel patrician is still very much alive'),[42] Robert Graves, L.H.Morgan, W.Schmidt and R.Briffault.[43] In an unmistakable way Bachofen contrasted 'paternity' as a development of the spirit, of individualism, of superiority over nature, of Promethean life, with a 'deeper', lower stage of motherhood which he saw as being bound to matter, unconscious regularity, 'eternal tutelage in an aging body'.[44] Nevertheless the feminists I have mentioned rely particularly on Bachofen's work in making their reconstructions of the matriarchy. There is hardly any critical discussion. Obviously they do not share Bachofen's interest in glorifying the superiority of the male, but they do not seem to see through the patterns of thought by means of which he seeks to justify his interest.

In Davis there is a modest swipe at Robert Graves: it is 'typically male ratiocination' to interpret the myth of the great Lydian queen Omphale, and Hercules who is subject to her, as a 'sex object', as a fearful example of the anxiety of men at the unbridled power of women.[45] Some chapters later Davis herself writes that as a result of the long period of feminine superiority the man built up an 'ongoing antipathy to women in his sub-consciousness', and for this explanation of the origin of the patriarchy refers to Bachofen:[46] the rule of women was the cause of the subsequent rule of men. Those are the modest gleanings of (contradictory) critical cross-questioning of matriarchal scholars. It follows that feminist matriarchal scholarship[47] uses the secondary literature of male scholars as a source. Moreover the authors refer to one another on a tertiary level (thus e.g. Gerda Weiler to Göttner-Abendroth). That cannot be good.

Popularizing literature has a positive summary of the feminist attitude to Bachofen: 'he remains the first witness to a history of the woman which only becomes of interest again a century later'.[48] But as neither Bachofen nor the other authors approached the primary sources dispassionately, scholarly interest and source material cannot be so easily separated even with them, especially as Bachofen and Graves in particular vehemently reject the ideal of objectivity among the historical scholars of their time. With this male literature as a source the feminist matriarchal scholars also take over its questionable method or doubtful results.

In connection with feminist matriarchal scholarship I have already spoken of a circular argument which comes about through the identification of interest and area of research: 'Because only what corresponds to my interests can be true.' This circular argument also appears in Bachofen, but it arises out of another interest, opposed to that of the feminists. Like the women who refer to him, Bachofen, too, innocently deceiving himself, thinks that he can leave aside prejudice in the viewing and ordering of historical material. He claims for himself the capacity of the scholar 'completely to dispense with the ideas of his time, the views with which these fill his spirit, and to put himself at the centre of a completely different thought-world'.[49] However, according to Bachofen the facts produced remain isolated from one another and incomprehensible in their multiplicity and pluri-formity unless they are attached to the 'basic idea'.[50] But when associated with the basic idea they assume the 'character of inner necessity'.[51]

Bachofen takes more than a thousand pages to 'prove' this basic idea: 'The battle between matter and the ancestral spirit permeates

not only the life of the individual, but that of our whole race...
Victory and defeat come in succession and call for constantly
renewed watchfulness, constantly new struggling.'[52] This battle
between matter and spirit, between feminine earthly nature and
masculine spiritual nature, runs through the history of humanity
like a scarlet thread. Bachofen rejects any suggestion which seeks
to designate the 'basic idea' as 'subjective experience', as a
'subjective law of thought'.[53] He is concerned with an 'objective'
basic law of human nature which alone can bring order into the
confusing multiplicity of historical phenomena.

Bachofen betrays the basic idea he has in mind to the attentive
reader, though only in short, not very striking, incidental
comments. He shows himself to be a natural philosopher who has
learned from Aristotle and Plato. The classical, ancient ontology
is his patron. This thought begins from the question of the
significance of that which is by nature. Any natural entity comes
into being as unique and individual. Nevertheless such an entity
develops in accordance with formative principles which are
arranged in each individual in an appropriate way. Thus for
example the seed of a plant bears the nature of the plant within
itself, the developed form of which shows the nature which is
invisible in the seed. To use Aristotle's terms, the *ousia*, i.e.
being as a supratemporal idea, becomes real in the *morphe*, the
individual, transitory form. This form is of a material nature; the
formative essence cannot be encountered as matter. To get from
the phenomenon of the natural entity to the formative idea, the
form of the entity must be transcended.

Completely in accordance with this ontological thinking Aristotle now describes 'the woman' as material and the man as the
formative idea. Bachofen refers to this. The feminine principle is
compared to wood and the male principle to the carpenter
who shapes the wood: 'Thus just as the carpenter, although an
individual, can make many tables, but the wood always provides
material for just one table, so too a man can fertilize many women,
but the material always has only enough to bear one fruit. The
movement of life begins with the influence of the male power on
the female material.'[54] With Aristotle, Bachofen concludes from
this that the male sex is more suited to lead and the female to
follow.[55]

The first thing that strikes the eye is the form of the entity. Only when one transcends this does one come to recognize the formative idea. Therefore perception of the form precedes recognition of the formative idea. Bachofen takes over this conclusion. So it is now quite clear why the material-feminine must be there before the formative-masculine. Bachofen is transferring a philosophical idea into history. As long as people had not recognized the formative role of the male seed, the feminine matter was first dominant in the form of the 'breeding ground', as he calls sexual promiscuity; then with the awareness of the procreative force of the male, the order of marriage, the matriarchy, began to establish itself, until finally the masculine, as an idea of all the forms, expressed itself by the subjection of the feminine and the material. Just as the perception of the form precedes the knowledge of the spiritual, so the woman as the material-maternal element preceded in history the male as the spirit-begetting idea. Therefore for Bachofen matriarchal culture and gynaecocracy, the rule of women, must have preceded paternity. So the history of human-kind must have begun with a general stage of matriarchal culture extending all over the world. For Bachofen, too, it is the case that the idea gives history its form, yet without even making the most superficial examination of the structure of his thought, since then feminists – with few exceptions – have spoken of matriarchal culture as an assured result of historical research! However, Bachofen does not present neutral material, which one can use like a quarry, but forms of an idea taken over from Aristotle and Plato. He also concedes that his material would be unconnected and contradictory without this 'basic idea'.[56]

So Bachofen combines the basic idea of natural philosophy with the theory of evolution and transfers natural history understood in this way to human history. This provides him with the equation: human history develops in accordance with the principles of natural history. What Bachofen does not note, but could have learned from philosophy, is the possibility given to human beings by self-determination in freedom to motivate themselves against their natural determination: 'Ontological reflection leads to human beings as entities with senses which emerge from evolution as part of nature. Transcendental reflection leads to human beings as subjects which are not part of this nature. Neither way can be rejected by philosophy. The two show human beings as "citizens of two worlds" (Kant). The contradictoriness of these two worlds and the tension between them form the human problem.'[57] The problem of ethics associated with this is not posed for human beings as nature, for here they are bound up with pre-existing regularities. Only the human being as subject is confronted with the question 'true or false?', the question of the good and the evil in his or her action. But Bachofen excludes this subject-side; human beings follow eternal laws.

This conception is matched by Bachofen's reconstruction of the development of human cultures in three or four periods. At the beginning of the history of humankind material motherhood dominated: 'Woman was not endowed by nature with all her charms to wilt in the arms of an individual: the law of matter rejects all limitations, hates all fetters and regards any exclusiveness as a sin against her divinity.'[58] According to Bachofen that is the period of hetaerism or the breeding-ground. The recollection of so 'unworthy a childhood' for the human race is painful to Bachofen,[59] but he believes that one must recognize as a realization of the law of nature that our history begins with the appearance of purely material, mortal form.

'By intensification to the extreme each principle leads to the victory of its opposite; misuse itself becomes the lever of progress, and the supreme triumph the beginning of defeat.'[60] Wearied to death by the lust of the male, women begin to rebel against humiliating hetaerism.[61] As universally as hetaerism, Amazonism now comes into being: armed combat of desperate women against men.[62] That is a 'degeneration', but a necessary one, which leads to the next stage, to gynaecocracy, to the rule of women.[63]

According to Bachofen monogamy is the decisive characteristic of maternal rule as a transition from hetaerism to the rule of the father as the spiritual principle. From the woman emerges the 'first civilizing of the nations'.[64] These women guard the divine mystery, the natural order, peace. The gynaecocracy is 'completely subject to the material and the phenomena of natural life, from which it derives the laws of its inward and outward existence'.[65] The nurture and beautification of material existence determine that motherhood; it knows nothing of inner, spiritual elements (= the Platonic idea).[66] The woman of the gynaecocratic period has recognized that she needs to be fertilized by the male, but she does not see the heavenly origin of the male principle. From her earthbound perspective the man must appear secondary, that which she brings forth must appear primary.[67] She believes that she is the divine bearer of the man, and presses the man into her service. Denying the natural law of the rule of the immaterial male spiritual principle, she herself provokes the struggle of the man for the lordship which is his due.[68] In a passing remark Bachofen refers to a disturbing phenomenon of his time. Women are beginning to depise men again, and he comments: 'Women are at their best in so-called barbaric times.'[69]

The woman is pure material form, the man the divine idea which gives form to the material. The next stage of development is therefore the age of 'paternity': 'The detachment of the spirit from natural phenomena...issues in the production of paternity.'[70] To achieve this goal, according to Bachofen there was a need for an intermediary stage beyond the rule of women. For the male is in danger of falling victim to purely material life and carrying on life as a sensual tyrant. So woman must rule as long as humanity is at the material stage.[71] Thus the male must serve so that the woman can educate him, by limiting his unbridled power.[72] Here in Bachofen there emerges his own version of the theory of evolution, namely that phylogenesis, the development of the individual, corresponds to ontogenesis, the development of the species: the son is born of a mother by whom he, the spiritual element, appears in his material form. Through her training he becomes capable of elevating himself above the material and arriving at himself, at the Spirit-idea that he represents. This development always takes place when a son is born; it corresponds to the development of the human race.

In this way, however, at the same time the man recognizes that it is not the mother, the wife, who is primary, but he, the man. For without him and his formative procreation the woman cannot give birth. In this way Bachofen distinguishes between a material and a spiritual beginning; the spiritual beginning, though invisible, is the primal beginning. Man progresses to this insight as soon as he has detached himself from the maternal primal material; 'He is not the material but the formative principle... but according to a view which often recurs in Aristotle and Plato, form is more divine than matter, because it is immaterial. God himself appears as the purest and finest form. In this view the male becomes the demiurge; he represents the woman over against the place of the creator.'[73] With Bachofen, we have thus reached by the most direct route that disastrous theocratic short cut which with more thorough systematic thought has proved simply to be false (see Chapter 1).

Bachofen's theory of development is not yet finished. The last stage is still to come: liberation 'from any connection with the woman'.[74] As long as the man begets children by the woman, the immortal spirit is bound to mortal matter and the battle rages to and fro between the two principles – always also a battle between the sexes. Granted, Bachofen praises the readiness of matriarchal cultures to make peace and misleads us into seeing them as forerunners of contemporary feminist interests. But for Bachofen this peace is identical with the rest of material mortal matter in the grave. The male battle over the liberation of the spirit from the grave is far more important for Bachofen; indeed it means everything to him. The feminine principle is in the way of our rise to immortality,[75] and so it must be removed: 'In the region of unchanging being, only the male God rules.'[76] And making himself sound Christian, Bachofen ends by writing: '...our relationship as sons can only be called forth by an action of a spiritual kind.'[77]

The negation of the human being as a subject of ethically responsible motives for action or actions emerges in Bachofen through a typical contradiction. If human beings in their cultural and individual development follow a law of nature, then their actions can never be good or evil, but only consistent. But in that case why, as Bachofen demonstrates, if women defend themselves against male rule, and men, though representatives of the immaterial principle of Spirit, act as cruel and lustful, is there talk of abuse? Bachofen gives another interpretation of what reasonably can only be understood as a motive for action: for him human action is the necessary consequence of a natural development which compels a person to act in a particular way and not in any other. In that case, however, he does not answer the question why some women have welcomed male rule and others have fought against it.

Arbitrary consequences

Those who suppose that they can take over Bachofen's historical material simply come up against Bachofen's basic idea. He did not write a history of the woman but a history of the man. Where feminists (and not only feminists, but also men) make use of Bachofen's 'results of scholarship' as an endorsement of their interest, they run the risk of more or less explicitly paying homage to that mother-cult which reduces women once again to nature, pleasure and childbearing, and which in the National Socialist period led to the award of the Mother's Cross. One strand of Bachofen's influence also leads to the adoption of his work by the 'Third Reich'. I do not mean to say that all those who accept Bachofen are 'Nazis'; what I want to say is that anyone who refers to Bachofen without reflection on his method will also, albeit imperceptibly, take over a dangerous ideology in the negative sense which is by no means well disposed to women.

Another strand in Bachofen's influence leads to the left. This use of him begins with Friedrich Engels,[78] and could only take place through the reversal of Bachofen's intentions. Here, too, the circular argument of interest and result plays a decisive role. Engels does not take up anything of what Bachofen says about the superior male spiritual principle, far less the natural philosophy that underlies it. Engels selects him only for the high social level of the woman in those days of grey prehistory. August Bebel takes the same line: 'Socialism belongs to the future, and that means primarily to the worker and the woman.'[79] Negatively he stresses that in no earlier period had so large a proportion of women been in such an unsatisfactory situation as at the end of the nineteenth and beginning of the twentieth centuries. To demonstrate that earlier societies had already been as socialist as later societies were to become, Bebel also refers, among others, to Bachofen: 'The sway of the rule of the mother meant communism, the equality of all; the rise of the law of the father meant the rule of private property, and at the same time it meant the oppression and servitude of the woman.'[80] Taking up Bachofen's naturalism, he even says: 'Our accounts show that the realization of socialism is not arbitrary tearing down and building up, but a natural development.'[81]

This model begins from the fact that the political intention represented is in a position as it were to introduce a healed society of a paradisal nature in the world. That is then justified with a legitimating reference to the idea of a once unspoiled, paradisal primal period which, it is claimed, was historical: what once was, can and must be again. In the meantime Socialists and Marxists have come to look on this model of their ancestors with a critical gaze.[82] On the popular level, however, the argument still takes this form, as is shown by Ernest Bornemann, who sees in the basic promiscuity postulated by Bachofen the future ideal picture of a free society.

Since the unspoiled, primal period is an idea, what it consisted of is a variable and therefore an arbitrary assumption, or rather one tied to particular interests. The Catholic ethnologist Wilhelm Schmidt argues that the rise of the woman in matriarchal law damaged the order of marriage and family. According to Schmidt, it is not in the nature of women to rule on the basis of the material possession of land.[83] Therefore the time of salvation was not that of matriarchal law but the one which preceded it, the 'bilateral, individual and extended family in which there was a natural division of work between man and woman.'[84] Jansen-Jurreit aptly mocks Schmidt for seeing the primal period as one of the realization of the form of marriage in Catholic natural law.[85]

Moltmann-Wendel thinks that feminist matriarchal scholarship is distinguished by its courage in using unconventional scientific methods.[86] I have looked for these in vain. The feminists from whom I parted and who play their special role in theology have taken over all their methodological conventions from men: the circular argument of interest and result, the idea of natural development which leads to the good or the identification of nature and goodness, and bound up with this the evolutionary approach which does not take any systematic account of ethics (which is reduced to moral interjections), the causal logic of the individual sciences and essential – unexamined – content, like the praise of divine motherhood and the periods of cultural history as listed by Bachofen – all mixed up in a tangle which is almost impossible to unravel. With Bachofen[87] his female successors feel themselves to be victims tried with suffering, when critical voices are raised.

Anyone who is looking for an attractive unspoiled beginning to the history of humanity can make use of Bachofen and indeed has done so. Bachofen's historical material is so closely connected with his theory that it is difficult to make a separation on the basis of his text. Anyone who wants to get through to historical material must take the laborious way to the primary sources and initially renounce any theory which formulates an interest. Beate Wagner speaks of the distinction between 'ideal models' and 'experienced social reality'.[88] Such a distinction is important not only for researchers but also for the sources, the literary genre of which must always be noted. Do the sources depict a praxis by observation, do they, like e.g. Aristotle, themselves offer a theory, or do they make demands like e.g. legal norms, from which one should argue to problems in praxis rather than to a corresponding praxis?

The first thing which shatters on this course of research is the 'inner necessity' presupposed by Bachofen. Ethnological research has sought to establish connections of causal logic in both past and present societies yet in the process has continually come up against deviations from such rules. Janssen-Jurreit rightly thinks: 'In our own civilization it is possible to demonstrate shifts of power and historical processes in the formation of relations between the sexes from century to century, from generation to generation and from state to state.'[89] Why should that not be true of other times and peoples?

Farewell to the matriarchy

On closer historical examination the evidence whether there ever was a matriarchy proves negative. What can be determined from a survey of the archaeological material and the scanty literary evidence, supplemented by a comparison with ethnic groups which exist at present, looks, briefly, like this. There were and are matrilinear social organizations. Where both characteristics appear at the same time, i.e. derivation of the kinship relationship from the mother and the dwelling of the women as the centre of life and work, the term matrifocality is used. These two terms do not yet say very much about the social position of women. It is only when matrifocality is associated with hoe-farming as the primary way of working the ground, with the work of women in collectives (producing and distributing products), and with the frequent absence of men that there is a greater equality in the social position of the sexes. The Iroquois, a group of Indian tribes in the north-east of the present USA and the south of Canada, are a prime example of this, but in the meantime they have lost their independence.[90]

The most important factor among the Iroquois 'was the separation of the world of women from the world of men, which was so effective because the men were always travelling. To put it more simply: the power of the women was the absence of the men.'[91] Ivan Illich calls that the gender structure: 'Under the reign of gender men and women collectively depend on each other; their mutual dependence sets limits to struggle, exploitation and defeat,'[92] whereas as a result of equality of opportunity for both sexes against a background of scarcity of resources the social structure of industrial states creates a situation of competition (= economic sex) in which the woman must always come off worse because she is hindered by pregnancy and the upbringing of children. This argument is illuminating. If a group can do or has something that another group needs without itself being able to do it or have it, the situation compels collaboration. Division of responsibilities is still an effective means against destructive rivalry in institutional conditions. But that also always means that one sex is separated from another, that each sex is given specific functions, whether these correspond to personal gifts or not. As at all events women must be involved in motherhood, their social status depends on whether production and control of the products which are necessary for a society can be made to fit in with the social conditions of pregnancy, birth and care of children.

It is not just the biological functions of the woman which therefore determine her social status: 'Only the manner of social involvement and the possibilities of independent direction of "reproductive relationships" make possible statements about the connection between motherhood and social status.'[93] That e.g. sedentariness favours women seems immediately obvious. In reality this element by itself is not enough. There are non-sedentary groups in which women do not have a bad position, and sedentary argrarian cultures in which women do not enjoy any great respect.

The status of women in agrarian cultures depends on a number of circumstances, e.g. whether priority is given to hoe-farming or grain farming, who draws the plough if grain is being grown, whether women as the producers of plant food also have control of its distribution, how high is the proportion of cattle-breeding and in what way the division of work takes place.[94] The organization of dwelling-places and the definition of kinship relationships are consequences of such social conditions, and not vice versa, since they represent a system of order which serves the consensus through which a society is kept functioning.[95]

The thesis that the patriarchy was introduced through popular movements into what were formerly matriarchal cultures also proves untenable on closer examination. The Spartans who migrated are one indication of this; in their social structure women had much more freedom than, say, Athenian women.[96] If we begin from the observation that collective organization of work determines the status of the sexes, it becomes plausible that the men in a society exercise more influence, the more continual occupation in waging war brings them together in independent co-operative units.[97] In all the attempts at reconstructing these early periods of human history, on which only a very little light can be shed by complicated processes of inference, there is an ultimate uncertainty which only allows verdicts with a small degree of probability.

For about two hundred years women have been trying to illuminate their history in order to discover connections which may be of help to their social status. According to Bachofen we are victims of an unstoppable development. Were we to follow the individual disciplines and their compelling causal logic, we would have to try to transfer to the present complexes of conditions for e.g. a social model favourable to women. Here Wilhelm Schmidt makes rather a touching suggestion. He begins from the fact that societies in which women practise hoe-farming and are tied to a place in and through possession of land display structures of matriarchal law. If we were nowadays to decorate the stone wildernesses of our cities with gardens in which women of all classes 'made their own contribution towards the provision of daily food by their own work, then alongside the money that the man earned in his profession the produce of this gardening could be the basis of a new, more moderate matriarchal law which would renew the old equal rights of man and woman in primal culture...'[98] Of course Illich refuses to offer strategies or recipes for the future. He thinks that we must take account of the irreplacable loss of the gender structure. Nevertheless at the end of his book there is the hint of a call to action: '... to renounce the comforts of economic sex',[99] which according to Illich can only mean that men and women cease to understand themselves equally as 'human beings' to whom all forms of action and life are possible and open, independent of gender. But, to be specific, if because of economic sex 'women were suddenly forced to join men in men's work in order to earn enough family income to buy what had formerly been grown in the garden plot',[100] would not the renunciation of economic sex mean here, too, a return to the allotment already recommended by Schmidt?

Ethics in the net of conditions

So there was never a rule of women like Bachofen's gynaecocracy or the feminist matriarchy. That must certainly be taken into account. To this degree our systematic-critical analysis of Bachofen has been confirmed by historical-critical analysis. But this finding is not so negative as might appear at first glance. Those who spoke of the rule of women, following Bachofen, at the same time condemned this morally: it was not on to enslave people: men, spouses, fathers of one's own children. With this argument they justified the 'patriarchal revolution'. But the same argument also justifies a 'feminist revolution', for is it on to enslave people, women, spouses, mothers of one's own children? Bachofen would answer this question in the affirmative, since he is not concerned with humanity: for him women, in contrast to men, are not human beings in the full sense, but 'material'. This is where the criticism of Bachofen ought to begin, and take up things much more vehemently than feminists do, since he detaches the Aristotelian metaphysics of form from an overall philosophical context which is well aware of freedom and the ethical responsibility of human beings who stand under the sign of humanity. Evidently it is difficult for some people to think in ethical categories. We can also learn a good deal from history in this respect: there was never rule by women, but there were periods and cultures in which there was a social equilibrium between women and men. That did not just happen in so-called primitive societies, but in high cultures like those of Crete and Egypt (in the latter down to the first millennium BC). Bachofen should not have all the credit for leading us on this journey. This had already been discovered by the French missionary J.E.Lafitau about 150 years earlier.

I am not an ethnologist, nor would I claim to have worked in this area sufficiently to have examined every single source. My examination is related to the methodological procedure and the soundness of the arguments. The findings of ethnologists, that there are many forms of human society and that the complexes of their conditions are not in the last resort to be derived from any principles, is confirmed by a basic systematic conception: if human beings are, and for millennia have been, subjects, because otherwise we would not be dealing with human beings who are distinct from behaviourally conditioned animals, then they cannot be reduced to rules, whether of causal logic or of natural philosophy. Thus in every age people have had to make decisions as to how best human society was to be regulated. The presuppositions were by no means always the same. The specific conditions of human beings have varied, depending on various factors, beginning with climate and terrain and going on to creative capacities. The reason why the forms of life did not have to be and do not have to be the same in comparable conditions follows from what makes human beings human beings: the capacity to decide for something on the basis of various motives. Otherwise one could not speak of actions, and certainly not of politics. That was true of past times, as it is true of today. And therein lies the opportunity for changes. Where it is a matter of actions and motives, there is always also at the same time a debate over ethics, a distiction between true and false, good and evil action, and thus the claim of humanity. Perhaps it is no longer possible to discover the field of conditions which e.g in Egypt evidently made possible a humane interaction betwen the sexes. But even if that were possible, what benefit would it be to us today, who are born into quite different circumstances? It is not all that easy to transfer what happened at that time down over the centuries. But it is already worthwhile to see that what happens today need not necessarily be so; it is already worthwhile to recognize that we cannot build on a progress in history which takes place as it were automatically; and it is vital to recognize that anyone who comes into the world is confronted with a responsibility which is his or her own.

Nevertheless it does make sense to be concerned with sociological analyses, since they help us to recognize that some social conditions make humane relationships difficult and others make them easier. Responsibility seeks to be transformed into specific, matter-of-fact steps which are appropriate to the social situation and remain ineffectual without considered strategies. At any rate the causal logic of the individual sciences can make us aware of the degree to which human beings, who in principle are capable of conscience, allow themselves to be trapped in what they do by mechanistic reactions, both in practice and in theory. In this sense it does us a service, so that both men and women can continually become human through insight into such danger. The thesis from which we began, namely that 'feminine oppression' cannot be justified in biological terms, can hardly be refuted by historical arguments, but it can be refuted by systematic arguments.

So it is no loss to the cause of women to bid farewell to the retrospective utopia of a matriarchal primal period. Where the relationship of the sexes has become inhumane, we do not need any comparison with a better past to prove that this is the case; and his orical evidence is varied enough to ensure that no change in present conditions is ruled out. The decisive factor is what women want and what they are prepared to do in order to accept a position of strength and equality. Do they want separation fom men in accordance with the gender stucture? A return to primal form of agriculture? The surrender of the individual in favour of mythical contexts? Or the trouble of conflict with the other sex? The burden of political and intellectual responsibility which so far has seldom been a matter for women? Many different ideas of how women want to live today and in the future are concealed behind the matriarchal utopias. The important thing is to put these things on the table and to discuss them. That would show how it is vain to look for an ideal state, for the 'whole' world of the woman or the man in the past or in the future; but it is worth a great deal of effort here and now to set aims and change conditions.

CHAPTER FOUR

Between Myth and Utopia

Copy, original, caricature

Johann Jakob Bachofen does not let us go so quickly. So far we have omitted a last decisive question of method. Can the myths of ancient peoples be regarded as a reliable historical source? Do the myths say anything about how things were then? Bachofen answers this question in the affirmative: 'The mythical tradition... seems to be the faithful expression of the laws of life of those times in which the historical development of the old world has its foundation... as direct historical revelation, and consequently as a true historical source notable for a high degree of reliability.'[1] Bachofen gives a closer definition of the relationship between mythological and historical truth as follows: they are twin sisters, different sides of the same 'civilizing'. Here the religious form of expression is the basis for the civil form of expression.[2] In the light of Bachofen's philosophy which I have already described in critical terms, such an association betwen myth and historical reality is understandable. In nature as in history, and thus also in the human spirit, the same laws of development prevail. And precisely this impossibility of distinguishing between nature and history, the linear transference of a law of nature which already transcends the natural by its formal metaphysical definition to the history of human beings who act and motivate themselves, discredits Bachofen's large-scale work, and makes it a ready prey to other semi-philosophical ideologies from the left to the right.

The association between myth and socio-historical reality which Bachofen seeks to communicate philosophically, at least in intention, is presented in the feminist matriarchal scholarship which has become so popular either with a reference to the Marxist theory of the correlation of the basis (economy/social relations) and superstructure (religious-ideal sphere)[3] or by a reference to the theory in the sociology of knowledge according to which the spiritual activity of human beings is the product of their social relationships.[4] This leads to the opposite conclusion to that of Bachofen: on this model, any human spiritual activity is secondary to the reality of contemporary experience as a linear copy of social conditions in the economy, social forms of communal life (here that of the sexes is particulary interesting) and religious and ritual practice.

The first critical objection is now made to the simplification of both Marxist theories and theories relating to the sociology of knowledge which are inherent in this thought-pattern. However different the two may be from each other, they begin from a link between reality and thought which is not linear and a copy, but dialectic. Thus Marxism criticizes the 'superstructure' as a negative ideology precisely because it conceals the real socio-economic conditions. True, Marx's starting point is that man makes religion and not vice versa, but with religion he is said to produce an 'inverted world-consciousness'. As the 'general theory of this world' religion is a 'ceremonial adornment', 'the universal basis of consolation and justification', the 'fantastic realization of the human being' and thus an expression of the fact that human nature has no true reality.[5] Marx argues from the fantasies of religious forms of expression to a contrary reality.

According to this theory the myths of the great goddesses should make one sceptical because they would be matched not by a high social position for real women but by precisely the opposite. We need not go back to the dim past to recognize the truth in the Marxist theory of superstructure: suppose we imagine historians of future centuries who in their researches encounter the present-day revival of Roman-Catholic Mariolatry. The feminist copy-theory would conclude from this that women had a particularly strong position in this church. By contrast, we do not feel drawn to such a process of argument and know how wrong those who used it would be, or how much everything depends on what is to be understood by 'strong position' or 'high position'. A new appreciation of motherhood and, associated with this, a division of work legitimated by biological factors go very well with this kind of Mariolatry. A similar complex would therefore also be conceivable for the periods of the other goddesses, and some ethnological material seems to confirm this suspicion.[6] At all events a critical examination is appropriate, so that we do not look on history in a detached and alien way or incur the Marxist verdict on the makers of superstructures.

The sociology of knowledge also fails to see the connection between spiritual activity and social conditions in terms of a linear copy. It begins from the primacy of praxis (in a good philosophical sense), i.e. from the primacy of living conditions. To the degree that these become a problem to us – and only the illusory idea of the possibility of a complete paradise on earth could be the basis for a dispute that historical reality is problematical – they prompt reflection. In this sense any thought is dependent on reality; but it is not only active in reproducing reality, it can also be productively active in developing utopias which are contrary to existence. 'When everything has been subsumed under the categories of the sociology of knowledge..., once we know that all human affirmations are subject to scientifically graspable socio-historical processes, which affirmations are true and which are false?'[7] Sociology is not blind to the human freedom to motivate oneself against the conditions of a particular context and thus to work to change circumstances. But this freedom does not exist *per se* as a 'hole in the fabric of causality',[8] but – to keep the metaphor – we are woven into the mesh of the fabric and nevertheless capable of parting it and knitting it together again.

Insufficient justice is done to the perspective of the sociology of knowledge if while we gain from its arguments the insight that in all our thinking we are always guided by an interest we always keep this interest immune from the insights of the sociology of knowledge. For example, Göttner-Abendroth does that again when she describes interest as conceptuality introduced 'intuitively', which must be gained from reflection on one's own biography and elevated to a scientific theory with the help of 'going through' historical material.[9] Anxiety that the interest which guides the author may thus be relativized can be detected in such quasi-methodological remarks. Since the sociology of knowledge discloses the connection any interest has with social reality, it in fact relativizes and does not allow interests to assume the garb of science and play the role of axioms. In this way scientific knowledge is freed from the 'tyranny of the present',[10] but also at the same time interest is freed from the tyranny of facts: our declared purpose to improve the situation of women is helped very little by the historical demonstration of matriarchies, just as the impossibility of demonstrating them does not harm it.

'The perspective of sociology, particularly of the sociology of knowledge, contributes a definitely liberating effect,'[11] so that we can really discover something new beyond our socially conditioned interest, which precisely because it is socially conditioned may well go wrong and become a false consciousnesss.

How little Marxism and the sociology of knowledge, to compare them both again on this one point, see speculation as being a copy of reality already emerges from their own critical relationship to reality: only a recognition of social connections of thought makes it possible to think new thoughts which leave aside these connections. So if a 'feminist method' argues for a 'copy' model of thought, it is following a different logic, namely that of the rationality based on causal logic which I have already criticized in the previous chapter and which cannot be identified with the theories of Marxism or of the sociology of knowledge. Here it is irrelevant to the result whether reality is regarded à la Bachofen as a copy of thought, i.e. of ideas, or whether thought, e.g. myths, is regarded as a copy of reality. The conception of the copy is itself the problem, since it simulates a false, impossible identity.

The subject, the thinking person whose actions are motivated, can never be or become identical with the 'objective reality' of his or her historical conditions: that would do away with the significance of history and the significance of the subject. Nor can objective social reality, which has a hard, independent objectivity over against the subject, however much it also owes this to the action of the subject. It cannot be fused with the subject. If that could happen, time could stand still. The subject always also represents objective reality, yet nevertheless can transcend it; correspondingly, objective reality always also represents the

subject and nevertheless proves elusive by developing a certain
life of its own, to which the subject can fall victim. The extreme
example of the martyr shows this dialectic in all its sharpness: out
of personal conviction the martyr refuses to recognize socio-
political reality and thus at the same time becomes its victim. So
are those right who raise a warning finger and say that we get
nowhere without sacrifice? They would be right if they thought
that to be the dialectic which has been shown, as a result of which
conviction always envisages resistance and must be prepared to
take the consequences (which need not always be physical death).
But they are wrong if they need the sacrifice of others to implement
their own interests. All those who make people suffer and are
motivated by the word 'sacrifice' rely on this confusion. Women,
too, do not simply face the question whether sacrifices should be
offered or avoided. That is indeed the wisdom of the cross over
against the ideological folly of the world; anyone who has become
capable of convictions can no longer be used as a toy, as an object,
and therefore as a victim of the interest of others, but is capable
of making a sacrifice for them. It may be painful that there is not
a third way, but that can only be taken by cynics to legitimate a
strategy of making victims.

In feminist theology – unless I am mistaken – the influence of
that short-cut of thinking in terms of copies which has made the
theories of matriarchy popular still prevails. Linear models of
thought are easy to produce and at first glance give the impression
of greater flexibility. However, anyone who looks at them more
closely will already discovers perspectives of a 'feminist critique
of reason',[12] which are capable of differentiation and are orientated on the future; but it seems that these have not yet been
discussed in theological circles. For example the art historian
Sigrid Schade criticizes thinking in terms of copies in connection
with her own specialist area: 'There is no original that might be
more authentic than the copies. The copies have no origin in
reality, but reality can be perceived through the copies.'[13] Anyone
who makes pictures is not reflecting reality but producing reality.
The relationship is not between reality and its representation but
between the realities produced, between the various 'representations', as Schade puts it.

Sigrid Schade's theory of images is not limited to the specific world of pictorial art. Just as there is no original that can simply be copied, so there is no human subject independent of any representation, e.g. an 'authentic' womanhood 'which is simply distorted or expropriated, say, by advertising posters'.[14] The feminine 'quest for a mirror image with which to identify', woman's 'presentation of herself as the remedy for the deficiencies in the other'[15] ends in a twofold contradiction to that self-orientated interest and can have very specific consequences. There is such a thing as a feministically motivated disguise of corporeality which inadvertently ends up with a reintroduction of Victorian morality. For by withdrawing from the gaze of the other, the man, so that they gain themselves, their corporeality, their own desires and do not become a copy of male desires, women produce what they abhor: without relation to another representation the avid gaze of the man is no more than self-centred and exhibitionist. Schade rightly used this argument to criticize the long-practised feminine tactic of concealment, which even today finds a remarkable following among feminists, and especially in church circles can take the wind out of the sails of anti-feminist preachers of morality. Nevertheless what we have here, far beyond being a fashion, is an impossible attempt to escape from the polarity of the sexes. The conceptions of matriarchy, too, are representations of a reduction to the feminine self, apparently independent of the other sex, a copy of femininity unsullied by the difference between the sexes, far removed from reality and art for art's sake. Schade contrasts the simulation of a false identity in the idea of a copy with the 'delight in dissimulating identity'.[16] In other words the relationship between the sexes, their forms, their possibilities and impossibilites, must become a theme if woman and man are to know who they are.

We began from the question whether the myths of the past can be reliable historical sources. First systematic considerations already compel us to a reply in the negative, at least to the idea of a linear-copy relationship. Now if the early myths of the great goddesses do not necessarily point to a real power of women in society, then hopes must be dashed that the revival of the goddesses would lead to a real restoration of the power of women.[17] But that is not to say that myth and reality represent separate spheres and have nothing to do with one another: the nature of their relationship must be defined in each instance. In that case we should attempt at least an approximate answer to the question what a myth in fact is.

In the labyrinth of interpretations

'...and everywhere people are immediately agreed that all readers throughout the world feel a myth to be a myth.'[18] All readers..., i.e. none of us can be directly involved in a myth if we recognize it as such: we do not tell one another myths in narrative innocence, as evidently people did in the dim past, before they became aware of the Logos, which since Plato has become the great counterpart of myth. Nevertheless the myths seem to have fascinated us, not just since some feminists discovered the great goddess, but for at least two hundred years. Bachofen is not least of those who have felt the spell of myths.

Interest in the reception of myth does not, however, lead to a direct relationship to it, but to its interpretation in a great many even contradictory forms. Those who interpret do not live in the world of sagas and myths but have to ask themselves: what did those who told myths mean when they said this or that? Are myths parables of the real, are the gods personifications of power experienced in nature and history, in the stars and fate? If so, they would be the metaphorical expression of the truth of what is real for people at a particular time, which the rationality of a later Logos cannot harm. In that case myth would remain bound to its time and would merely afford a nostalgic but attractively stimulating retrospect, perhaps tinged with a degree of nostalgia: when the gods were still alive...

But even those who are aware of the death of the gods must not consider their history closed. Reason is fond of recognizing poesy as an additional decoration. Those who reason can nevertheless foster the arts actively and receptively, take delight, for example, in the aesthetic form of mythical poetry; they can do this precisely because the gods are dead and no longer terrify them. In this way romanticism has found access to myth, in which it thinks it can see the free play of the imagination: absolute, unconscious poesy.

The term 'unconscious' should be understood here in the philosophical sense as a state of complete immediacy to the 'fall of reflection' (Hegel). So was there a period of the wholeness of the human spirit when the subject did not yet have to see itself as being detached from the object, was not yet called to become distanced from itself and the world in order to control itself and the world? Myth was and is also understood as the form of expression of such a total spirit which still thinks in preconceptual terms and communicates knowledge in, with and under metaphorical images. In this understanding myth is neither the terror of the powers nor an aesthetic game, but truth in a form that can be perceived by the senses.

Psychology had been said to have attempted to rescue the idea of human wholeness, if not for the spirit, at least for the life of the soul. In the postulate of the individual and the collective unconscious the myth is given a new sphere of life, as it were an underground one, where it develops its subversive power, making good the divided consciousness, and doing so all the more, the less one reckons with it: this is the archaic element in us.

But cannot precisely the opposite also be the case? Do not myths in particular bear the sign of lost human innocence? Driven out of nature and oppressed by society, human beings confront a breach which cannot be healed, which subsequently makes it difficult for them to understand what they perceive. This breach is the message of myths and their structure, which emerges from an appropriate analysis despite the apparent multiplicity of what is narrated.

Alongside these attempts at appropriating myths and relating oneself to them there are attempts at critical detachment. That myths are unworthy of both gods and men in that they narrate horrific, absurd and obscene things, was already noted by the ancient Sophists and Socratics: their argument continued down to the scientific history of religion and nineteenth-century ethnology. The charge that the myths and the cults that go with them are the result of a priestly deception aimed at keeping the people in tutelage and on theocratic leading reins can claim a comparable durability. Another method of explanation which since antiquity has permeated the enlightened part of history is that really the gods were nothing but historical figures who were elevated to supernatural status because of their special significance.

Evil intentions are not always deliberately imputed: superstition, defined as a lack of rationality, combined with magical practices, is said also to be the breeding ground of myth, all together being barbaric forms of expression of a primitive primal human history. Thus the old contrast between myth and Logos manifests itself for the umpteenth time in the garb of modern, empirically-orientated science. Once again let me refer to the opening thesis of this chapter. The fact that myth is an expression of real living conditions is also evident in the light of the manifold forms of the interpretation of myth as an inadequate perspective.[19]

All these attempts to trace myth either by seeking to follow it and understand it or by a detached explanation show, as through a negative screen, that myth belongs to the past. We do not live in a faith which is communicated through mythical narrative. But in that case, why are there these many attempts to use it, why is there the present stubbornness to want to understand and adopt something which has so many offensive and irrational elements?

Disillusioned by the Enlightenment

The capacity of the human spirit for reasoning began to seem radiantly hopeful as the cloud of superstitious attachment to the irrational slowly cleared away. Christian dogma, too, was accused of a deliberate compulsion towards a *sacrificium intellectus* (surrender of reason), as much a servitude of the conscience as of the physical body, even if Christianity had long beforehand itself set conviction against superstition. But now that demonic madness and wars of faith had devastated the European landscape, the message was of the human worth of humankind in its reason: God and all his powers were projections of true human nature. The God of humankind was its nature (Feuerbach), the light of reason was identical with the divine light (Spinoza). To arrive at reason therefore necessarily meant taking the way of perfection: becoming subject and becoming God coincide.

Being a subject is being whole, at ease with oneself and the world: 'No! It will come! it will assuredly come! the time of perfecting, when man, the more convinced his understanding feels about an ever better future, will nevertheless need to borrow motives for his actions from this future; for he will do right because it *is* right.' This is Lessing's prediction in his work on the education of the human race.[20] Do not some feminist arguments recall this certainty of the rationalists, which inevitably proved to be an illusion, when to being a subject and being whole is added being a woman, who is to free the world from all divisions?

If human beings as subjects had been lost, their rediscovery provided a breathing space, but only for a short space of time in which a false conclusion was to emerge. The rule of God and the demons was replaced by the rule of one human being over another – the 'self-destruction of the enlightenment'.[21] The fear of the gods was replaced by fear for human masters. On that logic would not a rationalism based on the feminism necessary lead to fear of human mistresses? Do we not already see similarly along the lines of this kind of logic the trivial products of science-fiction which takes its violence out on the fencing post?

Progress in knowledge aimed at the liberation of rational human subjects from a domination which keeps them immature is unmasked as an arrogant belief in progress, hybrid self-assertion and a diguised change in rule. That also applies to another variant of the Enlightenment, empiricism: the gaze of the subject leads to the terror of what is perceived. What can be observed in nature, in history, in human beings becomes an object at their disposal and precisely by becoming an object in this way gains an independence, the truth of the factual, which denies any possible truth of the subject because, rushing on ahead of the denial, it has long degraded itself into being a mere instrument. So finally the rule of facts would inevitably rob the rule of human beings of its power.

The terror of empiricism also sometimes haunts the feminist scene and its sympathizers with a powerful presence, when enquiries are made about the specifically feminine contribution to society or church or about the hoped-for 'feminization of society'.[22] Where else than from empirical observation of present conditions can attributes of the feminine be derived such as feeling, a-rationality or readiness for peace? Would we escape the thought-model of empiricism if we derived such attributes from other cultural and political conditions, say those of five thousand years ago? Moreover, the scientific beliefs of our cultures show how quickly empirical attributions turn into definitions with ontological, i.e. essential character. One should not pay homage to their readiness for adoration through new cult figures, in this case feminine.

As long as the Enlightenment had to fight against a real enemy it could develop liberating potential, to the point when it itself became the enemy. The comprehensive hope of salvation which was associated with reason come of age gave way to disillusionment. And as so often, this disillusionment tipped over into regression: if salvation did not lie in the time of the Enlightenment, it had to be before that; if it was not in reason, then it was in the irrational, e.g. in myth. One of the possible reactions to the experience that the golden age does not flourish beyond the modest beginnings of a dawn is in that case not critical reflection on the nature of perfection and its relationship to the real, but strictly speaking the refusal to allow oneself to be disappointed: what does not exist must at least have existed in an unspoilt virginal primal period which is thought of as having been historical.

The revival of this origin is always associated with a sweeping disparagement of the spirit and with it of the subject, with a protest against the 'servitude of life under the yoke of concepts'.[23] 'Our ego is passive, suffering, vulnerable, and it falls victim to the victorious power of life.'[24] Every ego, all thinking, willing and doing is finally extinguished. The drunken Dionysus, God of ecstasy, comes into his own, which is healthy for humanity, but Bachofen's goddesses and mother cults also celebrate their renaissance in the circle of the philosopher Ludwig Klages at the beginning of our century. The cult that went with this adopted the fine-sounding name 'Bloodlight' and was celebrated as a Dionysian rebellion against hypocritical bourgeois values. No less a figure than C.G.Jung gave his approval to this incarnation of the archetypes. He saw something of Wotan in such an urge and later called on the Führer, in all seriousness, to plant Wotan oaks throughout the land because in that way the German soul would be elevated. After the National-Socialist Götterdämmerung it was the same C.G.Jung who in 1950 welcomed the Roman Catholic dogma of the physical assumption of Mary into heaven because in it he thought he could see an incarnation and a revival of the anima.[25] In the light of this thought-pattern of 'the revival of primal time' (here the primal time in us), a call to set up Mary-pillars for women's emancipation would only have been consistent. We can immediately see the degree to which the content is interchangable in this thought-pattern. Let's leave the Führer and the German people out of it. We do not need them for our argument. The basic structure of this thought is not to allow oneself at any cost to be disillusioned in the face of the hybrid usurpation of perfection but rather, in the same way as the discredited Enlightenment, to delude oneself as to what is humanly possible. This also makes one extremely sceptical about a feminist revival of goddesses which follows the same pattern.

Another attempt to come to terms with the crisis of the Enlightenment which has now been going on for a long time can be termed synthesis or a concern for reconciliation. As the opening rhetorical question asks: are myth and science really the result of completely different activities of the human spirit? Do not myth and science begin formally from presuppositions which lay a basis for experience, and which themselves are no longer open to empirical examination? And can such presuppositions gain validity other than through an inter-subjective recognition which has come into being in history?[26] Granted, even in physics one must have the idea of the laws of gravity to be able to verify them empirically; granted, it is true of all inductive arguments and thus of empirical theories that they can claim no more than a hypothetical character, so that what at first sight seems exact at a secondary level is at best probable. But does that not mean that there is already a glimmering of myth on this horizon of the possible? Is not the self-decision of understanding enough?

Before myth comes, a further series of problems would have to be solved which are completely accessible to human reason. At all events, it is to the credit of Immanuel Kant here that he conceived of overcoming the Enlightenment split between subject and object. Any observation is blind without concepts which cannot be gained from experience, but without perception all concepts remain empty. Unless this dialectic is accepted, and accepted on the basis of Enlightenment logic, insight into its limitations again leads to regression to the merely subjective or the merely objective. In that case subjective and objective become interchangeable. Otherwise it is impossible to understand why e.g. Göttner-Abendroth stubbornly maintains a subjective starting-point (personal experience, biography, partiality) while at the same time speaking of an irrevocable fact of a matriarchy empirically demonstrated by myth.[27] Here myth is rationalized objectivistically and reason is mythicized in a subjective way. This is no reconciliation but the dusk before the night in which all cows must look black.

There is no doubt that today we have no uniform picture of the world and so we are plagued with the pluralism of arbitrary possibilities. We often move from one world to another completely different one in a conversation.[28] Withdrawal into subjective certainty or into small manageable groups is humanly understandable, but does not solve the problem. If myth once seemed to be capable of authenticating 'the existence and the composition of a society on the basis of a supreme value',[29] capable of justifying living conditions and social institutions, such a historical insight raises more questions than it answers. What kind of social order did myth justify? Was it worth justifying? What kind of a myth would we need to authenticate our present-day society (which society?)? If myth legitimates, can it not legitimate anything, and did it not do so earlier? Have we not long since had other quasi-mythical legitimations, and could not a myth of unity be created just as easily?

Myth is not just myth. Without doubt there were also varied changes in social forms, as in myths, in Greek history and prehistory. The chthonic myths with their earth- and mother-goddesses, with the symbols of night and moon, are distinct from the myths of the Olympian gods. Myths can be found in many places: in popular tradition, in Greek tragedy and epic, in philosophy. Their achievements in communication are not always and everywhere the same. It is doubtful whether all transformations can be reduced to the simple model of antagonism between matriarchy and patriarchy. One would only get nearer to the transformation of myth if it were possible to see the relationship between history and thought forms more accurately, to resolve their fusion in a more sophisticated way, and primarily to bid farewell to that simple one-track question of how they offer a representation or a legitimation.

That cannot be done within the limitations of this book, but we must be allowed to raise some questions. On what material is the investigation based? The Greek myths which e.g. Robert Graves takes as the basis for his hypothesis about the relationship between the goddess cult and the matriarchy certainly go back to older material, but they appear so markedly in literary-poetic form (Homer, Hesiod, the tragedies) that it is difficult to separate the interpretation from what is interpreted. If we start from the assumption that the mythical narratives were matched by a ritual praxis, though that does not always seem certain, then at best it could be noted that the Greek myths, like those of the ancient Near East, were not handed down in any kind of ritual context.

Mythical scholarship has therefore moved within the framework of ethnological research in quest of the living relationship betwen myth and ritual. The results are as astonishing as they are varied. Sometimes there is a feminine deity from which everything springs and sometimes a male deity; gods can 'give birth' to goddesses but also the other way round; the world arises either from the union of a divine couple or from a fight between them. The polarity between heaven and earth, i.e. between the 'higher' and the 'lower' powers, which is a constitutive element of myths, can lead to various assessments of these powers. If also as a rule heaven is identified with the male and the light side and earth with the female and the dark side, some tribes assign wisdom to the female and others assign it to the male.

Myths which are characteristic of the religion of a people in a particular cultural context are to be distinguished from those which seem secondary to it. To take both as being of equal weight would be to produce a false picture. Basic themes of myths can vary considerably by popular groups, geographical locations and periods. Myths, too, have a history, and as one generation succeeds another some themes are forgotten and others inserted. The differentiation between the sexes, an important theme in myth, also undergoes manifold changes. Given the difference between myth and praxis the question arises whether praxis is social reality, e.g. the form of work, or cultic praxis, what I have called poesis. The polarization of the sexes can go with dual orders of society, e.g. with the division of the clan into two spheres, or the separation of the working worlds of men and women, each of which then gets its own myths. However, that need not be the case. The same is true of dual religious ordinances. Often, but not always, the polarization of the sexes in myth is matched by specifically female and male rites of initiation and the practices of secret societies.[30]

In the case of social orders which are capable of maintaining an equilibrium between the sexes (these exist and have existed), we should then ask precisely what such orders look like, under what conditions and at what price this equilibrium is achieved. And finally the question arises how far one can argue from so-called primitive cultures to higher cultures; from ethnic groups which exist at present to peoples in history. There still remains the problem of the immense wealth of material for ethnology and the lack of source material for the period before the first millennium BC and earlier.[31]

Theology of myth

The activity of the human spirit is prompted by problems which arise from the experienced world of reality. If we begin from this basic insight of the sociology of knowledge, then we have yet to define the way in which people tackle their problems, and even what they regard as being their essential problem. Finally it remains open whether ideas for solution are successful or whether they do not create yet other, unforeseen problems. Again we should ask whether there are not basic human problems which show themselves in constantly new historical variants. It is also a basic thesis of the sociology of knowledge that worlds of meaning serve to support and legitimate, and thus oppose their power to the relativism which threatens all that is historical. Myths, too, can fulfil such a function, take on aetiological character as worlds of meaning,[32] and thus justify virtually anything. One could ask whether that feminist understanding of myths has not itself become an aetiological myth, in that only those myths are regarded as authentic which seem to confirm interest in the matriarchy; everything else is said to be a patriarchal falsification.

But not all myths are aetiologies in a limited sense.[33] Superficially the word myth means a story of the gods. But who are the people who tell themselves stories about gods? What 'attitude of mind'[34] is concealed in an awareness which seeks to communicate through myths? And could there not be something that connects us with the old myth-tellers, rather like common problems?

'Being born and dying, being shaken, being torn into conflicting parts, having no bounds, being directed towards ends the fulfilment or non-fulfilment of which would equally be the finish, these are the characteristics of the threat.'[35] That is the way in which the Berlin historian of religion Klaus Heinrich puts the concern of human beings at all times and in different specific historical forms. The Protestant systematic theologian Paul Tillich speaks of the 'conditions of finitude'; the Vienna philosopher Erich Heintel of the different forms of that which cannot be controlled. What individual ever sees the consequence of his or her decisions, can ever understand the course of his or her personal history, far less the history of his or her time? Who could evaluate or influence encounters with other people or an avoidance of them? Death, which cannot be calculated but which is nevertheless certain, casts its shadow forward in our awareness of having to die, and teaches us the transitoriness of all action and striving.

These are the basic problems which concern all religions, through which the human being is constituted as *homo religiosus.* One could agree with this concept. We can only survive this 'tottering'[36] life if we live in the certainty that there is order and not chaos, that our action also produces meaningful forms, that there is continuity and fulfilment, that the monstrous and ultimately inexplicable evil which culminates in death does not have the last word.[37] Measured by reality as we find it and the course of history, any such certainty must seem irrational. Nevertheless hope that threatening tensions will be overcome keeps us going.

Anyone who looks at the history of the destructive war between the sexes will find abundant cause for scepticism as to whether things could ever be otherwise. Despite scepticism, every love, every marriage, every child leads to the burgeoning of new hope in the midst of the multiplicity of disappointments. Here precisely that which remains outside our control seems to kindle hope. The religions in their concrete form give a name to that which we cannot control.

But for an answer to the question what a mythical attitude is, a reference to the *homo religiosus* remains too general. In this view the myths of the Greeks and the Christian confession of faith would be interchangeable, two possible answers to the basic view of humanity to which yet further answers must be added. My starting point is that the answer of myth to the basic problems of humanity is different from that of the Christ, and further that this distinction is significant for dealing with problems.

It would be a misunderstanding of the mythical outlook if one were to describe the stories of the gods as naive or even primitive. This outlook bears witness to the awareness of a truth, namely that of the separation of humanity from its origin, the loss of a growing unity. However, as unity is nothing which can be perceived or demonstrated empirically, the myth as it is already transcends reality in the direction of something which seeks to give a foundation and therefore significance to this: the presupposed unity of nature and history, of order and freedom, of good and evil, of beginning and end (birth and death) and – of male and female. So myth demonstrates simultaneously both the truth of the real in unity, in totality, and the real in multiplicity as being separated from the truth. Unity, totality accordingly belong to the origin, and the gods of myth are powers or origin.[38] Therefore the question arises for human beings: 'How does that which is remote from origins in terms of space, time and essence nevertheless have a share in these origins? How does that which arises fom the origins nevertheless have a share in the unconditioned power of the origin?'[39]

Existentially, what underlies this is the 'threat of being identical with nothing',[40] a threat which is posed to everyone from the cradle and which makes them anxious. Recourse to myth is supposed to allay this anxiety by seeking to derive humankind and the world 'from divine primal figures, forms and events'[41] and thus seeking to create a connection with the original wholeness. All the copy-models of the relationship between myth and reality, to return to that once again, overlook the fact that that original totality always already transcends reality, whereas immanence stands out by its lack of wholeness. Therefore the myths tell of gods and one can speak of a theology of myths.

The person who thinks and experiences mythically is thus aware of being on the one hand separated from an origin in totality and 'acquires independence from the origin – to the extent of anxiety and helplessness at being left alone by the origin which provides support. And on the other hand loss of independence is conversely the price to be paid for persisting in being in that origin – to the point of sacrificing the self to the origin that swallows it up'.[42] This polarity is also expressed in the myths themselves or in the ritual which goes with them; myths can narrate both the separation and the overcoming of the separation, by deriving both from a common origin.

To this degree myth derives its 'material' or, more accurately, its 'conflict material' from human reality, but transcends this in the direction of a presupposed unity. Ritual seeks to bring about this unity partly through orgiastic cults, whereas myth produces unity beyond fullness, the whole through the sum of all conceivably possible variations. Myth leads to conflicts, 'the alternatives of thought and action in which, and the attempts at the resolution of which, are quasi-experimental',[43] comparable to experiments aimed at an increase of knowledge, thought-experiments as the 'weighing up of possibilities'.[44] Conflicts understood as the impossibility of reconciling opposites are given solutions which in turn lead to new conflicts. This gives rise to a chain of permanent reinterpretations which never ends; neither conflict nor solution are ultimates. That is where the superiority of the gods emerges, but also the fact that human beings are given over to unlimited possibility,[45] which while being the only hope again gives rise new conflicts. The conflicts remain an insoluble riddle. 'It is the inner brokenness that constitutes its enigmatic character. Myth is not in fact just play (or poesy), and not only because it is also compulsion (or terror).[46] The truth of myth can be reduced to the statement that the solution of the riddle cannot be the riddle's solution.

Variations on androgyny

'If mythology had no kind of relationship to a reality which is not exhausted in relationships to time and space, it would not in fact be a living, ongoing material which continually takes changing form; it would not attract, it would provoke neither scandal nor fascination.'[47] As a mere historical source, mythology would be interesting only for historians and for answering the question how things once were. The attraction of myth, however, lies in two different elements, namely that the conflicts from which it takes its starting point are basic human conflicts which can be repeated at any time and that thinking through their unlimited possibilites (or also enacting them in ritual) makes possible in myth that which is really obscene, the breaking of bounds. I have already demonstrated that in Chapter 2 by means of eros.

So for myth conflict means antagonism, the impossibility of reconciling opposites, which are nevertheless understood as poles of a totality which belongs together. The differentiation between the sexes accords with this definition of conflict and therefore plays a similar dominant role in myth. So in terms of the logic of myth both the polarity and the transcending of antagonism are presented in very varied forms. Thus underlying the battle between goddesses and gods is not the succession of two different cultural periods (matriarchy and patriarchy), for which, moreover, as I have shown, there is no historical evidence, but the polarity of the sexes as opposites. In any case Robert Graves shows that it is impossible to reconcile myth with chronology;[48] however, he regards the dubious ways of bending myth against better insights to chronology as the particular achievement of 'science'.

If we begin from the antagonism between the sexes, it is clear that in the goddesses and gods there is a battle between the 'principles' of the feminine and the masculine, earth and air, night (moon) and light (sun), matter to be formed and formative power – metaphors for giving birth and begetting. The antagonism includes controversy over the answer to the question which comes first, begetting or giving birth, just as there can be controversy over the answer to the question which came first, the chicken or the egg. The basis of the unity of those elements which are referred to each other lies in the fact that this controversy can never be resolved in favour of the one or the other.

Gods and goddesses are in turn accused of sheer lust, but they are also praised as bringers of culture. The antagonism extends to forms of raw violence: castration, rape, murder and assassination, but through forms of transformation in terms of unlimited possibility they never represent an end. Disgrace, deposition, deceit and betrayal are the lesser forms of the war between the sexes in the pantheon of the immortals.

The wealth of variations also opens up the possibility of escaping the increasing tension and thus the war between the sexes by endorsing both of them through the *via negationis*. This sexual solipsism (each person as woman or man believes herself or himself to be self-sufficient in his gender) is either shown to be impossible by the revenge of the one who is rejected or is transcended by the union of the opposites in one person. This gives rise to the ideas of the androgynous figure as a 'relation of two complementary elements... which were one, are one or may be one'.[49] The forms of anrodgyny are manifold and are not just limited to the figure of the hermaphrodite, who bears the characteristics of both sexes. Sexual union, twins, marriage between brother and sister, virgin birth, birth from a man, can all represent androgynous unity.[50]

Finally, it is part of the pluriformity of myth that on each occasion one person, whether male or female, can unite all aspects of both antagonism and of androgyny. Thus the goddess can simultaneously appear to be both maternal and caring, life-giving, creating peace and all-consuming in destruction, fatal and belligerent; she can be mother and virgin, daughter or embodiment of delight. Therefore no deity can be reduced to a simple character. Myth also varies by selecting only one aspect and putting it elsewhere. In some contexts a goddess thus proves to be either only maternal or only fatal.

Heroes also take part in this summation of aspects, as can be seen, for example, from Heracles: as a 'superman' he performs in bed as well as in battle and impregnates fifty virgins in a night; as slave to Omphale he subjects himself to women and is subjected by them; he wears women's clothes and also does female house-work.[51] As elsewhere, all this can be understood as mythological, as an attempt to depict all the aspects of the antagonism of the sexes in opposition and unity, without opposition or unity having the last word. The antagonism which the feminist use of myths following Bachofen shifts to the level of historical chronology is the material of myth itself.[52]

It would be attractive to illustrate from the material this understanding of myth, which has been gained from the form of expression in myth itself and which follows its independent logic. However, that would take us beyond the framework and the scope of the systematic criticism that I am aiming at here. I would therefore recommend the reader to examine with the aid of this systematic criticism e.g. the rich material collected by Robert Graves. In so doing one should notice how often the author foists Bachofen's eloquence on to the silence of literary sources which are very late compared with the allegedly chthonic period. It is clear that because of its antagonistic structure any myth must also contain those chthonic aspects, but it is hard to see why anything that does not have chthonic character may no longer be called 'authentic myth'.[53] This selective procedure, which goes against the intention of myth, destroys the circle of myth and casts doubt on all non-chthonic material as being the result of deliberate 'manipulation'.

The concept of humankind

Since myth is a wealth of variations of unlimited possibility, no reality can match it completely and vice versa. Any reality is only a selection of the possible variants. At the same time, however, all that is real must appear as a variant in myth. That explains why myths can be claimed to have such varied forms; they can legitimate what exists but also present what does not yet exist as utopian hope. Here utopian futures do not always have only a hopeful side, but also express anxieties.

In this way myth confirms everything: the 'sexual revolution' through its obscene elements, the power of women, the power of men, motherhood or the demonic in the woman.[54] It confirms both antagonism and struggle and also the transcending of them in forms of wholeness; those with social privileges can identify with the heroic resistance, those without privileges with the victims of fate. Thus all of reality has its origin in myth, and no matter what social forms emerge anywhere in the course of historical change, a corresponding origin is already there for them in myth. Social forms with relative equilibrium between the sexes or with dominance of males, regions, places, virgins, mothers, warriors, poetesses, sculptors, peasants, merchants or market women, city-dwellers or seafarers, respectable people or thieves

– they all possess their own gods and divine histories. The message of these is ambivalent: they say that things could also be otherwise (which is the utopian element in myth) and they say that things must be as they are – and that is the yielding to destiny which myth teaches. The fact that there are two sexes the contrasts between which form the basis for their mutual attraction remains a 'scandal'.[55] No matter which of the manifold aspects of the relationship between the sexes one selects, one can never be sure which others are making an uninvited appearance. However inadequately myth solves this problem, it does put it clearly: man and woman do not exist for themselves as 'humankind', as a totality resting in itself, nor as a being with particular irrevocable attributes, but only in a relationship of polarity to each other.

Nevertheless, throughout all the previous chapters I have continually spoken of human beings, of basic human problems or of the human capacity for ethically motivated action. It could therefore be argued against me that there is no such thing as the abstract human being. If one began from individuals and left aside their differences, like size, hair-colouring, age, education, sex and so on, what would be left would be a monster without properties which eluded any attempt to envisage it: there is no human being who is neither small nor large, neither young nor old, neither man nor woman. Such an argument is based on empirical perception. The statement that one can speak of man and woman but not of human beings demonstrates the way in which we are fixated to this empirical thought-model. To think empirically is to observe, to sort out what is observed in terms of particular recurrent characteristics and to arrange it in 'classes': reality as a colourful collection of butterflies.

It can be observed that there are two different sexes, not only among human beings but also among the animals. What does that tell us about the distinction between man and woman? Nothing at all. Therefore it is necessary to look further. Women give birth to children, breast-feed them, bring them up and are housebound. Men do not and are not. That, too, can be established empirically, though we are now no longer dealing just with a natural given but with modes of behaviour. Giving birth is the natural and necessary outcome of pregnancy; pregnancy or being tied to the house cannot be thought of as being equally necessary, since in principle any woman can decide against both. Now if an empirical characteristic, e.g. the capacity to give birth, is taken as the criterion for the definition of the woman over against the man, then a biological characteristic turns into a definition of action. In that case action would no longer be a reasoned decision but a compulsive consequence.

Nevertheless we learn day by day how the results of the most recent empirical investigations are cited as a criterion for action, in that what is, is also uncritically regarded as useful, right and good. How much more deeply is this misunderstanding embedded in 'old' characteristics rooted in the centuries-long experience of our society, all the more so as there are always those who exploit the definition of existing circumstances! It can be useful for men who pursue higher goals outside their homes that women bring up children and look after the home. Therefore they will simply endorse the feminist argument that giving birth is a unique capacity and that a concern for human life is a specifically feminine virtue. This is also the context in which we find the popular statement that while men and women are of equal worth, they are not of the same nature. That they are not of the same nature can be confirmed empirically. The $64,000,000 question nevertheless remains the question of evaluation. If one considers this question empirically, it soon emerges that a housewife and mother does not have anywhere like the social prestige of a scientist. Thus talk of equal value becomes a husk, if not a downright lie.

If we leave aside the divergent attributions to the sexes and e.g. with Ivan Illich[56] begin from the point that the varied cultural worlds in the present and the past show considerable variations in the modes of behaviour and social functions of men and women, then it is still possible for us to keep to empiricism. That is what Illich does when he starts from the undeniable fact of the tension between the sexes rather than from specific sexual determination. This empirical characteristic now becomes the basis of his social utopia. The sexes have to be separated for the sake of peace. Men and women both need living space of their own. Whereas the distinguishing of biological characteristics leads to hierarchical 'solutions' to the difference between the sexes, Illich's model results in a reserved right.

Hierarchy or reserved right: that is the result of the refusal to talk of 'human beings' because there are no such things in empirical reality – a result of nevertheless extremely far-reaching significance. Only the content changes. Nowadays no one would speak openly of the superiority of blue eyes and blonde hair; the privilege of a white skin is not a respectable argument, but it is still an effective one. Instead, nowadays, for example according to Hoimar von Dithfurt, age plays an essential role. Youth will redeem the world. The slogan that women must redeem society takes its somewhat inglorious place in what are in fact the dangerous consequences of such an empirical thought-pattern.[57]

We get out of such dead ends only when we speak of human beings in terms of a concept which has at its correlate neither an observable reality not a concept derived from it. Conception and concept are two different things. The formation of the concept is marked out by the way in which it transcends all that is empirical. What is meant by that has been shown e.g. by Hegel in his distinction between human being and animal: 'The human being is an animal, but even in his animal functions he does not remain in himself, like the animal, but becomes aware of them, recognizes them and investigates them, as for example the process of digestion, so as to gain knowledge of himself. In so doing the human being breaks through the limitation of his restricted immediacy so that precisely because he knows that he is an animal he ceases to be an animal and gives himself the knowledge of himself as spirit.'[58] It also emerges from this that the human being with his nature can never be directly and totally bound to that nature, but stands over it and therefore against him or herself.

Whereas animals are as they are, human action escapes observation when we come to its motivation. Seen from outside, what we do remains ambivalent; we do not know whether individuals have good or evil intentions, whether they are shamming or whether they are merely inept. Moreover human motivation cannot be influenced to the same degree as action itself. We learn that from experience; parents, those in authority, state power can compel us to do something, but because this does not happen of our own free will, the motivation behind the compulsory action remains unaffected; without the compulsion we would act differently. Conflict can also ensue if external compulsion and our own motivation diverge to such an extent that we do not accept the compulsion, even if by doing so we suffer personal disadvantage. In this sense, Aristotle, for example, states as an extreme possibility that 'there may also be actions of such a kind that one cannot be compelled to it and to which one must prefer death in the most extreme torment'.[59] All forms of resistance are possible through this freedom which is bound up with the concept of the human. That is true for all human beings, and therefore also for both men and women.

In speaking of motivated action I mean deliberate motives, so that the individuals concerned can say why they regard this and not that as good and right. Knowledge is one decisive means of providing a basis for such judgments. In the light of the concept of the human, therefore, it is wrong to attribute the possibility of free-determination exclusively to males, or to males to a higher degree than to females. Thus anyone who denies freedom to women, logically also denies it to men. But anyone who robs human beings of their freedom, associating it with their empirical characteristics like colour of hair, colour of skin, sex and so on, by making arbitrary assessments of these characteristics and deriving socio-political criteria from them, offends against humanity. That amounts to racism or sexism.

But we could make further objections and say with Ivan Illich that a policy which starts from 'the' human being and which offers everyone the same chances in the same way must necessarily discriminate against particular social groups. One cannot begin from something, namely universal equality, which does not exist in empirical terms. Such an approach leads to inhuman competition, including competition between the sexes, which Illich describes as sexism. Illich is right; many people could not survive such competition because they are subject to social conditions which narrow down the room for movement. Children who grow up in a home with books can develop a relationship to the world of culture earlier than those whose youth is dominated by daily involvement in getting the wherewithal on which to live (conditions do not determine but offer opportunities). Women who decide to have a family and children must necessarily apply the greater part of their physical and psychological energy to these and fall behind in the field of professional competition if they do not fall behind by their own choice. The same is also true of men who devote themselves to their families instead of making use of them as a relief from burdens. But even given the same starting points, equality of opportunity is questionable. Not everyone can achieve everything, since there are few places at the upper end of the social pyramid, and there are many obstacles on the way up.

From this perspective the biological determination of human beings remains the fate of the individual and has far-reaching social consequences. If what makes the human being a human being cannot be distilled from empirical reality, then the concept cannot so easily contribute to that reality. The freedom which is possible in principle is never really complete freedom, nor is reality ever a complete tie. All social forms are also our work, that we shape and must justify in accordance with the claims of humanity. The concept and reality of being human are in a dialectical relationship; our action is in tension between theory and praxis.

Therefore we must always begin from reality, from how things are, without excusing anything, without closing our eyes to suffering. Much suffering arises from sexual determination, and from an empirical or statistical perspective there is more suffering among women than among men. If we keep to statistics and what the empirical sciences have to say about them, then we end up in that vicious circle which Elisabeth Moltmann presents in a solemn expression of her disillusionment: women, she reports, suffer as a result of their lofty, internalized moral conceptions, always wanting to be 'unselfish, loving their neighbours, patient and ready for sacrifice'. The findings of the humane and natural sciences should at last secure these women votes and rights, she demands, so that a new value system can come into being; an 'ethics of concern', a 'non-hierarchical relational thought', a 'method of empathy', 'sensitivity, reciprocity'.[60] Is not this new approach just the same old thing? Did not the ethics of care not always have its feminine privileges? Or are women today merely concerned to secure the official endorsement of science, because we think that we can no longer live without its blessing? Now, we can see, the provision of empirical definitions is free.

Thus for the sake of the humanity of human beings diagnosis should not be followed by confirmation but by criticism. Only in the light of the freedom possible to human beings can we come to say that things must not be as they are. This is where utopia abides and produces its promising blossoms first in theory, since utopia means that what is conceived, what is possible, what overcomes suffering as yet has no place. Anyone who is convinced by utopia sets his or her mind to bringing it about, to putting into practice that which does not yet exist and to changing that which does. Human beings cannot therefore define once for all the social consequences of their specific sexual determination, but they look for a worthwhile form in every context that is presupposed. Precisely because the ethics of concern has been part of the feminine tradition for centuries, while the world of the intellect has been part of the male tradition, it is time to shift the balance, so that men and women become freer to choose their own ways.

If from this perspective we take a look at the history of the Greeks, then two women of spirit emerge, each of whom in her own way has something to teach even the superior philosopher Socrates: Diotima and Aspasia.[61] The opposition between the sexes turns into a dialogue which creates knowledge. This tradition is worth noting!

The sobering effect of the covenant

Goddess feminism finds it easy to exchange the God of the Old Testament for revived myths and thinks that to do so is to advance the interest of women. Although the Old Testament contains mythological elements, it in fact rejects thinking in myth. In the theological statement of the narrative of the fall in Genesis 3 the *concept* of the human being comes into view: the fruit of knowledge is awareness of the difference between good and evil. Here no patriarchal principle of keeping under tutelage is at work; on the contrary, this is the basis for human freedom and thus for the necessity and possibility of acting responsibly, i.e. in a mature way. Only on this presupposition can the human being, can women and men, become God's covenant partner. This God does not control humankind in an omnipotent, arbitrary way but concludes a covenant in connection with ethical instruction. The utopia of a humane reality is formulated in terms of 'you shall'.

This is an opportunity, even for women, and it should not be exchanged lightly for a mess of pottage (Gen.25.29-33).

The idea of the covenant in the Old Testament is directed against the myths, the structure of which, with their unlimited possibility, also ultimately bars the way to the inherent utopian beginnings of a realization. To serve Baal or Astarte or whomever is to break the covenant, to betray that instruction which brings wholeness to human beings to the wild figures of unlimited possibility. That would also be the end of human freedom, self-determination, responsibility, and men and women would again fall victim to the manifold forms of sexual antagonism as the consequences of the striking 'small difference'.[62] The God of the Old Testament is not filled with hatred against human beings but is angry[63] at their lack of insight and their refusal to become free individuals. As long as they remain stubbornly as servants of the gods in their sexuality, they will never see in what way man and woman are bound together. The prophetic tradition is at the service of this good anger of God.

Now what I have said so far has not yet tackled the problem of freedom and humanity in its complexity. It already becomes clear in Genesis 3 that the recognition of the difference between good and evil does not make human beings good in themselves. They are under an obligation to discern and to choose, each at his or her point of time, what is right for themselves and the world entrusted to him. This is where all the possible abysses of which the myths sing their songs open up (as I said, myths show problems but do not produce a solution). There is no linear way from freedom to direct action in history. It is not just that the facts of reality and the motivation of other people which conflicts with one's own can get in the way; it is not just that people cannot perceive the best intentions or perceive them only in a distorted way. First of all we have to find and clarify our motives and become aware of them, and in this way there are already a variety of stumbling blocks. Anxiety about isolation, the confusing multiplicity of conceivable possibilities or the impossibility of seeing the consequences of my decision, for instance, can hamper me or simply make me revert to the usual demands. In that case others have decided for me. Or I might follow my innermost subjective feelings about what is attractive to me here and now.

In that case I would be following my nature and not my conscious will, which must reflect on whether what does me good is also right for others. I can also withdraw into the dreamy innocence of the great freedom apart from all ties which has no reality outside heady slogans. Freedom is always freedom only in, with and under the historical forms of life; what is lacking in any particular present in a fulfilment of the covenant awaits completion. Without this active element of utopia dreamy innocence is transformed into the sin of omission.

But the battle for utopia does not exclude errors in decisions, false estimations of the situations and guilt towards other people and includes tactical considerations and many compromises. We can learn a great deal about that from liberation theology, in terms of both hope and will, and in terms of strategies and coping with reverses and failures; more in fact than a European idealization along the lines of worlds of salvation within history (which we have already discussed) is prepared to perceive.[64] Thus no matter what the social context is, the realization of a relationship between the sexes in terms of a covenant can only take this weary way which never leads to a final goal, to a world in which one could say that nothing more is to be done because everything has been done. No utopia, whether in the past or the future, can ever attain the status of perfection, but the sobering clarity of the covenant allows people to set out for it freed from the omnipresence of mythical entanglements.

In a mythical outlook good and evil as original powers are just one opposing pair among others, which include male and female. Here good and evil, personified as figures, are fighting against each other and side by side, against human beings and for human beings, by providing explanations of why things are so and not otherwise. The powers can be conjured up *or* compel us to revolt against fate – there is no third possibility. In the spirit of the God of the covenant, on the other hand, human beings have powers of control over good and evil: they recognize their liberation from the spell of gods and demons; they need no longer conjure up anything but decide responsibly. Deuteronomy forbids trials by fire, consulting diviners or soothsayers, or resorting to sorcerers and magicians (Deut.18.9ff.). That the Jewish-Christian tradition is also full of evidence that people lapsed into these demonistic conceptions is not to be held against the God of the Old and New Testaments, but against those who do not want to have responsibility.

The near God

What Elisabeth Moltmann writes with reference to the American psychologist Nancy Friday is very true: women often (but not always) make giant demands on their goodness, fall short of their lofty aims, feel inferior and stew in the juice of self-accusation. Is the slogan 'I am good, whole and beautiful' an endorsement of their high claims, the falling short of which once again hastens the onset of feelings of inferiority? At any rate this misunderstanding is never far away.[65] Or does the slogan express God's promise to human beings who have succumbed to sin? That is how Elisabeth Moltmann wants to understand it. In that case we would have arrived at the decisive theme.

Responsibility does not remove evil from the world, but nevertheless there is no way of returning to origins. A new dimension opens up to those who cannot be completely good in that they have become aware of the fact: they recognize that they are directed towards Another, towards that which they are not and that promises them that which they themselves cannot achieve. This promise establishes community with the other person, the other sex, with the wholly Other: God.

There is hardly anything against which we are more on our guard than imputation of personal guilt, and talk about the unattainability of what we hope for seems to seek to compel resignation: Sisyphus comes into view. Without doubt there is a kind of Christian talk of sin which takes the form of contempt: there is nothing good in you, you can only do wrong, and all your efforts end in nothing. And in this 'pastoral' model there is a final condemnation of those who protest against being treated as a disposable article and with good reason appeal to their human capabilities: the more you insist on your human contribution, the further you are from God and from salvation; the more you humble yourself, the nearer you come to redemption. This way of talking about sin takes an ominous short-cut. Here sin is reduced to an empirical level and results in a basic mistrust which necessarily imputes evil intentions to any action that can be perceived or unconscious evil which disguises itself with good intentions. As the meaningful answer to the question whether there is such a thing as 'the' human being lay in the concept of 'the' human sphere, the meaningful answer to the question whether there is such a thing as 'sin' must be answered with the concept of sin, which is part of the concept of the human. Let me recall once again the difference between animals and human beings. It emerges from this that: 'One can mark the aspects given with the peculiar position of human beings in the world with the following concepts: reason, the capacity for language, freedom, sinfulness, historicity. They all denote the "leap" of human beings from nature, their primal leap. Therefore all these concepts do not denote anything that is specific and historical. They underlie all human reality. They have been called "existentialia".'[66]

Accordingly sinfulness or incurring guilt is not a matter of human beings failing to live up to the claims put upon them or being unable to realize them. It means not being able to rule out in principle the possibility of making mistakes. Sinfulness is the opposite of the perfection which is only the property of God (Mark 10.18). Therefore our human concern is not completely in vain, even if perfection is not achievable by any effort. Once again Martin Luther significantly expressed the final conclusion for action like this: to work with all one's might as if one could achieve the perfect; to trust with all our might in God as if all our action were in vain.[67] Without this dialectic the not exclusive, but inevitable, failure of our concerns would necessarily lead us to despair. The pressure for wholeness grows from the same root as resignation or destruction. A community life among human beings, and therefore also between women and men, is only human if we do not deny our sinfulness.

Wherever there is talk in theology of our inability to come to God as we have fallen victim to sin, there is something that has to be understood; we cannot be or become perfect, and in the language of faith that means that God remains alien and far from us. The answer to this knowledge, which also affects all areas of experience, can therefore be given only by God himself, and he gives it by overcoming his distance and becoming a human being among human beings. Nowhere is it written that God becomes male; as he comes into history, however, he must become either man or woman. If a theology reinterprets the incarnation of God as a matter of becoming male and argues from that that men are nearer to heaven, it shows itself to be rooted in the short-cut of empiricist thinking which has not understood anything either about God or about human beings.

The incarnation of God is an act of love which explicitly defines itself by promising perfection to all that is imperfect. Where faith looks at human beings in the light of this promise, the gloomy clouds of hatred move away. Anything can be abused, even the incarnation of God. In that case the love of sinful human beings becomes the love of active sin. However, if, for example, Paul says that faith in the incarnation of God makes us a new creation (II Cor.5.17) which replaces sinfulness with the certainty of forgiveness, which can help us to bear all the imperfections in ourselves and others, indeed in the whole world, then he is presupposing the knowlege of sinfulness. In the incarnation God is creating *his* utopia for us, which has its existence through guilt and death.

In such statements we are not on the level of the empirical, the observable or the demonstrable. That can never be the basis of faith. The question is a different one. Can sense be made of my existential problems in terms of the Christian tradition, so that I can live from certainty? Faith is not empirical, nor can reality be reduced to the empirical. Faith becomes real by being sustained in praxis. Only in this way are love and reconciliation prevented from being great and empty words. In, with and under its secular institutional form and its errors, indeed its sinfulness, the church is the community of those who believe in the incarnation, a claim which rebounds on it if it does not take it seriously. There can also be a community of those who believe in this way without its coinciding with the external form of the church. How to discern the spirits is always a living issue.

My starting point is that the message of the incarnation of God as the perfect human 'utopia' is really credible in the literal sense. The degree to which we are rooted in sinfulness is also evident from the difficulties in finding forms of linguistic expression. On the other hand, as I have shown, it is part of our existentialia that we have to communicate in language. A change in the level of language must accompany a change of subject. The empirical is matched by a different linguistic expression from that used in connection with existentialia or with faith. Therefore to develop the incarnation of God in relation to its significance for the relationship of the sexes, in the next chapter I have adopted the literary form of the sermon.

CHAPTER FIVE

Jesa Christa, or a Critique of the Ideal

A sermon

Jesus Christ: a man again.

God's Son: a man with divine authority.

Again a hierarchy of men in which women do not appear, or only at the very bottom of a long ladder, where they are hardly mentioned. The Swiss pastor Kurt Marti hopes for a female Messiah: 'Ah, if only a God, if only a God were made flesh in the flesh of a rather fat girl!'[1] Jesa Christa, says Ernst Eggimann, Joan of Arc, Angela Davis? 'Father, send us a daughter?'[2]

Son of God – daughter of God?

Physical procreation by God is a conception as alien to Judaism as it is to Christianity. In the Old Testament the term Son of God is applied to those who have allowed themselves to be seized by the spirit of God, the righteous who do the will of God. If one day, as the prophets hope, the whole of Israel turns to its God, then sons and daughters will prophesy (Joel 2.28), be prophetic, and that means speaking in accordance with the will of God. Thus human degrees of affinity can be an analogy for the relationship between God and humankind: those who do the will of God are also brothers, sisters and mothers (Mark 3.35). Biology and theology, nature and spirit are not to be confused: each has its place. It is not nature that binds God and man but the spirit of God. Jesus is begotten of the Spirit. Faith is not about natural, visible things, but about the things which are invisible (Heb.11.1), about justice, peace, love which are not obvious but which nevertheless seek to be realized by those who believe in them. God and faith go together, says Luther.[3]

Incarnation means that God comes into the world, into the flesh. Incarnation, God made flesh. No one has ever seen God (John 1.18); if we are to recognize him, he must show himself in such a way that we can perceive him. Thus God the unlimited must limit himself, take on flesh, enter into our confused finite world characterized by error, violence, lovelessness, the slaughterhouse of history. God does that without restraint, without reserve, without privileges – he lets himself be taken into the slaughter-house and slaughtered. The lamb of God is not a sweet Easter lamb.

Now everything gets turned round. What was above is below; what was below is raised up: 'He has shown strength with his arm; he has scattered the proud in the imagination of their hearts; he has put down the mighty from their seat and exalted the humble and meek. He has filled the hungry with good things and the rich he has sent empty away' (Luke 1.51f.) sings Mary in the Magnificat. Incarnation means the reversal of values: what people find respectable is not respectable; what is great becomes small; honour, praise and power burst like bubbles. And what are the disciples told when they want to get the first places? 'You know that those who are supposed to rule over the Gentiles lord it over them, and their great men exercise authority over them. But it shall not be so among you' (Mark 10.42f.). God does not become human in a prince, a king, a priest, a general.

Incarnation is the way to humility, to the invisible, to the helplessness of the many. This is not a masochistic way which goes happily into the attraction of pain. It is a way of conversion – the lowest becomes the uppermost.

Incarnation, the way to humility, is the way to representation: Jesus as the scapegoat.

He was executed as a rebel by those who provoked the uproar. Guilt is shifted on to the one who cannot defend himself, a mechanism which calls for its victim day in and day out.

The rebellious people is guilty, they break the laws – but are not the laws themselves often a rebellion against humanity, then as now?

The Jews are guilty because they separate themselves – but who is concerned to discover the alien in them to his own enrichment?

Women are guilty because they incite men to violence – but why do men respond to the charms of eros with despicable force?

No one has ever succeeded in ending this evil game once and for all. The game of evil representation recurs unceasingly and evokes another representation: the companion. Another, second, person takes the place of the one who cannot defend himself or herself. One who is not affected voluntarily becomes involved for the sake of the other. That is incarnation. Involvement stands over against desperation, togetherness against loneliness, compassion against grief, sympathy, solidarity, hope against the evil, fatal game.

Among the sufferers and victims of all times are both men and women, but more women than men. It is not long since women died giving birth, much too early. Even now, while still children, they are exposed to the violent inability of men to love. The development of personal gifts has remained the privilege of few, despite all kinds of progress. And whatever people do to one another to subject one another and assure themselves the first places where possible they claim to be an irreversible, natural and divinely willed determination.

Jesus goes the way of humility to the victims, to the lost, and that also means to the women.

Jesus, a man, goes the way of lowliness to the victims, to the lost, to women.

Jesus, God, goes the way of lowliness to the victims, the lost and to women. They may appeal to him, but the powers of this world may not. Those who appeal to him because they have first places blaspheme God. All powers, beginning with nature, to which we are exposed in our sexual determination, and extending to the many different forms of the power of human beings over human beings, stand under the criticism of the way of lowliness. God became man, not just nature, not king or priest.

So Jesus Christ and not Jesa Christa.

It is not insignificant that a man opposed the seductions of power. Power and the tempter are identical (Matt.4). Turn stones into bread! No, I do not want to live at any cost.

Hurl yourself down from the pinnacle of the temple into the bosom of the power of God! No, God's power cannot be hired out, as kings and priests may believe.

Rule over the whole world! No, ruling is not God's business, but serving.

That is the answer of a man, and that a man says that and that Jesus Christ says that is part of the transvaluation of all values. Let us work out this notion.

Jesa Christa says:

No, I do not want to live at any price. You are right, you too should not live at any price but perish in the fulfilment of your motherhood.

Jesa Christa says:

No, God's power cannot be hired out, as kings and princes may believe. You are right, you should not become either king nor priest; that is reserved for males.

Jesa Christa says:

No, ruling is not God's business, but serving. You are right, it is for you to serve and not to rule.

The devil would soon agree with these answers from the mouth of a woman. The rejection of such temptations would be impossible for a woman because what she could choose instead of the devil's offer would be always what is attributed to her: serving, renouncing, perishing.

So Jesus Christus and not Jesa Christa. A woman could not represent the humiliated because she herself is already where these people are. Representation involves the voluntary renunciation of power and privileges. It makes a difference whether we are already with others in the same boat or whether we voluntarily get into the boat out of love. Therefore God, who does not sit with us in the boat, comes to us in the boat. The one who could have kept away, journeys with us and becomes our companion. So God loved the world, we read in John (3.16).

The man Jesus also takes the place of women, as they are: the sick, the well-to-do, the highly placed, prostitutes, housewives, girls, children. His representation does not seek conditions but – as Luther says – the broken heart.[4] One wants to be healed – that is Mary of Magdala; another feels unfulfilled by the money and prestige of her husband – Johanna; one wants to be able to live without contempt – the great sinner; another begins to understand that housework cannot be everything – Martha.

Jesus the man turns things upside down.

Jesa the woman would always have been at the bottom.

Another woman plays the woman's role in the incarnation: Mary. What is made of her? Who does not also think of motherhood, the motherhood of God, of purity, sinlessness and virginity, in connection with incarnation?

Mary, the pure one, the ideal of femininity.

If Jesus is not son of God in a short-circuited biological sense, but is born of the spirit, then the virginity of Mary cannot be understood in hasty biological terms either. So in *De servo arbitrio* Luther thunders: 'What can be called more fleshly, indeed more blasphemous and contrary to religion, than that word which occurs in Jerome: "Virginity fills heaven and marriage the earth." That would mean that the married forfeited heaven while the pagan Vestals would be the best Christians simply by virtue of their virginity.'[5] Thus virginity turns from being a spiritual symbol into a human ideal, from being the unpredictable gift of the birth of God into a model to imitate.

That is also what has been made of Mary: Mary, the pure one, the ideal of femininity. Refrain from sexual impurity or compensate for the stain by motherhood! Thus motherhood is devalued so that it becomes a substitute for lack of continence, and the relationship between individuals, between wife and husband, between mother and child, which is both beautiful and difficult at the same time, is alienated to become an expiation.

No matter what the ideal may look like, whether of virginity or motherhood, the idealization itself contradicts faith. Ideal, *eidos*, the 'form conceived', is a picture of perfection: this is what you are to be, this is what you are to strive for, from bad to good, from good to better, to perfection. Ideals transcend reality, are derived from an idea which cannot be gained by perception. 'An idea is simply the concept of a perfection which does not yet appear in experience,'[6] says Kant. Not yet. That presupposes that this perfection is possible, can be fulfilled, attained. By anyone who makes the effort!

Mary, the ideal of femininity: women are to be like her – shy and subservient, virgin or mother, mother in a virginal attitude, passion-free motherhood.

That as a virgin Mary became mother of God was not a result of her constant effort but by a divine gift of the Spirit. Behind this theological statement stands the rejection of the ideal. Heaven strikes its blow against the tower of Babel and shatters the forms that human beings invent. It would be truly blasphemous to say that Mary achieved being the mother of God through applied effort. So Mary cannot be an ideal, but she is a woman who is seized by the Spirit because of the love of God for the world.

Ideals are all blasphemous and dangerous because they reach for heaven. Heaven could probably bear that, but it does not befit us. Anyone who strives for ideals becomes blind to the limitations which are now part of our reality. Under the aspect of the ideal everything in the world looks reprehensible: not only the inhuman, the evil, but also the human and fortuitous. Ideal and contempt for the world go hand in hand; reality is divided and declared to be half-reality, burdensome and useless.

Anyone who makes Mary the ideal overlooks the humanity of women: their desire to love, which remains incomplete, as does that of men; their desire and despair, which men have as much as women. Instead of embracing one another, sharing longing and despair, commending aims and failures together to the grace of God, men and women destroy each other by measuring themselves and others by ideals. The ideals change and are interchangeable; they prove pious and less pious, but they are all equally hostile to humankind:

Women should be beautiful and good.

Men should be superior, yet loving.

Women are capable housewives and mothers, ready to work their fingers to the bone.

At the same time erotic and always attractive to men.

Men are strong, a support for women.

Or men are weak and not aggressive.

Women are strong and unerotic.
Ideals change. The ideal is fatal.

Is it a coincidence that those who seek to improve the world often look at it in so bitter a way? Those who strive for heaven destroy the earth; those who follow illusions must find reality demonic, black; however, it is neither black nor white but at best grey. Yet that grey colour is a blow in the face of the white ideal. The feminist statement about God, 'She is black', is meant to be such a blow. God is not an ideal, for the consorts of the ideal are bitterness, disappointment, hate.

Those who divinize women and stylize them into an ideal are as guilty in respect of them as those who brand them as demons. Anyone who reveres Mary as an ideal must despise the real women of history, for how could they ever attain what comes from God's grace?

Jakob Sprenger, Prior of the Dominican monastery in Cologne, and Heinrich Institoris, founder of a Dominican reform movement with strongly ascetic tendencies, were both ardent worshippers of Mary. Sprenger experienced an appearance of the Madonna and in 1475 founded the Brotherhood of the Rosary. The same men who followed the ideal of Mary were the authors of the *Malleus Maleficarum*, the hammer of the witches. In the shadow of Mary as an ideal the real woman can only be a whore and a witch. 'Praised be the Most High,' wrote the two Mariologists, 'who has so well preserved the male sex from such shamefulness (of witchcraft) down to the present day: as he wanted to be born for us and suffer for us in the same sex, he therefore so preferred it.'[7]

That is the fearful consequence of a theology which is incapable of distinguishing the divine from the human, which blasphemes the divine by the ideal of the feminine and excludes the feminine side of humanity from the incarnation of God. If it is also not unimportant for women that Jesus was a man, it is nowhere said that God became male. He became human, a human being for women and men with broken hearts.

Thus idealization is followed hot-foot by demonization; they are a blasphemous pair. 'The claim of something finite to infinity or to divine greatness is the characteristic of the demonic,'[8] writes the theologian Paul Tillich. Anyone who denies the finitude and limitations of our reality is already in the grasp of the self-made witchmaster.

This sharp comment also applies to a feminism which counters the demonization of the feminine with a new idealization. Since women have no aggression, if women were in power, they would love peace and the world would look different. Can power ever look different from the rule of one human being over another? Power, too, is one of the conditions of finitude; it cannot be 'got rid of'. There is no plausible reason for excluding women from power, quite the contrary; but power has its own temptation which both women and men have to be able to withstand. Both sexes are required to deal with power by walking on the knife-edge between responsibility and guilt. That is unavoidable. Here, too, lack of illusions in an unidealistic attitude proves an advantage. If women develop their own ideal, they themselves produce the demonic and do themselves a disservice.

Is it really so difficult to recognize that both women and men in our finite history undeviatingly come to the limit, to the limit of what is at their disposal, to the limit of their own capacity? Is not the death to which they are both subject an undeniable symbol of this? Women and men are brought together by their laws, by their dependence on grace and forgiveness. Those who, whether woman or man, cease to form ideals and run after them so as to provoke hatred and demonism; those who, whether woman or man, cease to attribute and to shift guilt, show themselves to be freed for a love which can bear many things, among themselves and others.

Only: this love, too, cannot be demanded and compelled; if that is the case we have again made it an ideal, the ideal of love, the non-fulfilment of which embitters us.

Let us beware of ideals, those of women as well as those of men.

Let us beware of demoting God to the ideal of the good. Then there will be incarnation.

Incarnation, God made flesh. God made flesh becomes our friend. The incarnation of God in the human Jesus of Nazareth. And since then that has meant that anyone who looks for God finds God in the other person who is encountered. We can see God as in a mirror in the eyes of a woman, in the eyes of a man, in the eyes of the father, the mother, the children, friends and strangers. None of them are themselves God; they reflect God's turning towards us in the moment of saving encounter, in the *kairos*. That is when, not permanently and not with our being able to count on it, the gates of paradise open to us through the other person.

This other person is not sexless; the other person is always either male or female. When God moves in the human world, he moves in the reality of the difference between the sexes, since he has become like to us in all things (Heb.2.17). And we can be certain that that is what he has willed.

The divinized idea of the feminine did damage to women. What would Jesa Christa be? Not a redemption for women and a temptation for men to subject God. Incarnation means neither removing the human nor bringing near what is always near to us.

Incarnation. The alien becomes near. God comes near to the feminine in the masculine thou.

Therefore, once again, Jesus Christ and not Jesa Christa.

Jesus Christ, the man, and for men too an alien: the man who comes near, the man who serves.

Feminine Science

1. Finally, let us once again take the sociology of knowledge seriously and enquire into the basis of those forms of feminism and feminist theology which we have subjected to systematic criticism in this volume. This criticism could be understood as moral reproach and a personal attribution of guilt, but to do that would be a misunderstanding. My starting point is that those feminist positions which have become most popular are the ones which cannot be approved; they articulate problems characteristic of our day but without showing a way of overcoming them. Even worse, they show the spirit of the 'dialectic of the Enlightenment', as Horkheimer and Adorno have called it, and once again drive a wedge into the existing division between rationalist and empiricist views of reality without being aware of doing so. It was and is my interest to demonstrate this and to communicate it by means of argument.

In his novel *The Man without Qualities*, Robert Musil says something which still makes us think:

So there are in reality two outlooks, which not only conflict with each other but – what is worse – usually exist side by side, without exchanging a word except to assure each other that they are both desirable, each in its place. The one contents itself with being precise, and sticks to facts; the other does not content itself with that, but always looks at the Whole and draws its knowledge from what are called great and eternal verities. Thereby the one gains in success, and the other in scope and dignity. It is clear that a pessimist might also say the results of the one are worthless and those of the other not true. For where will it get one, on the Day of Judgment, when mankind's works are weighed in the balance, to come forward with three treatises on formic acid – or thirty, for that matter? On the other hand, what can one know about the Day of Judgment if one does not even know what may have come of formic acid by then?[1]

Now one does not need to reflect long on the question to which of the two outlooks the feminist positions that I have been considering belong: they look at the Whole and prophesy the downfall of the world of facts. Eternal truths like the Last Judgment or other Christian things do not seem very promising to goddess-feminism, so the contents are exchanged: the place of the God of the Christians is taken by the goddesses of myth as eternal truth. But that does not destroy the scepticism of the pessimists, for why should the goddesses be true and the Last Judgment not? The world of facts does not know a world beyond its calculations and the world of the goddesses is beyond all reasoning. For those who believed in myths the myths were as much reality as weather conditions are for us, and that is what separates us.

Goddess feminism has, however, a feeling for this difference and therefore makes use of authentication by facts without noting this trick. Feminists, too, are children of our time and have difficulties with all that is eternal; they too suffer from the terrible feeling that they cannot put a stop to the independent course of facts which, accelerated by constantly new facts, has taken an immediately threatening and destructive form. And yet all that remains for them with which to confirm the truth of the goddesses is the fact of a matriarchy that can be demonstrated in primal history. But in that case once the opposite of this is demonstrated, or even if there is doubt as to whether the sparse sources allow such clear conclusions, the truth of the goddesses falls. By clinging on to the fact of the matriarchy at any price they demonstrate something different, namely our difficulty in believing that there is that which is valid and certain yet cannot be proved. The 'fact' of psychological archetypes can take the place of the historical fact of the matriarchy, in which case, for example, dreams bear the burden of proof, or the 'fact' that it is the nature of a woman to be yielding and faithful which empirical investigations cheerfully confirm. It is always a matter of proofs, because like Ulrich, the man without qualities, we cannot believe anything. The two outlooks of which Musil speaks still stand side by side or over against each other. Even feminism cannot heal this split. In contrast to Musil, however, who is aware of the problem and addresses it as such, goddess feminism makes use of the concealments of the dialectic of the Enlightenment, of which it is to be seen as an expression.

2. Anyone who, following empiricism, becomes open to the world of facts, is shown reality as a kaleidoscope of varied forms which, infinitely variable, offer constantly new combinations. Think of all the things that are and have been! Think of all the things that people have believed, thought and done! Between the natural phenomena and the artefacts of human productivity opens up the field of unlimited possibility which does not allow us to rule out anything for the future. Think of all that can still be done! In this sense, for Ulrich, Musil's man without qualities, a real thing is no more than an idea in accordance with which God has made and conceived of the world: 'it could just as easily be some other way'.[2]

So Ulrich is a person of possibilities. Whenever he imagines something, he thinks of the opposite. When he faces the task of completely rebuilding his castle, the styles of all the centuries including contemporary theories of art pass before his mind's eye, and as soon as he decides to get down to things he begins to dream. Finally he in fact leaves it to the 'genius of his tradespeople'.[3] Here we see the affinity between empiricist and mythical outlooks. Over against reality, which gains its forms from the figures of unlimited possibility as a never-ending chain of contrasts and transitory agreements, the human being is condemned to hand himself or herself over to the fate of the gods or the tradespeople. The reassurance is only apparently provided: empiricism and myth alike explain that it is so but could also be different, So Ulrich and his ancestors who think in myths waver between dreams and a powerful unrest that cannot be banished.

In its recourse to myth, goddess feminism does not make a clear enough distinction between mythological figures and that mythical outlook which is so close to belief in the facts. In this sense goddess feminism even corresponds to the Enlightenment consciousness. The women who revive their goddesses do not believe in them. However, if it is not a matter of the content – here facts, there gods – but of the way in which people relate to their reality and at the same time constitute it, then, as Musil can show, mythical and empiricist attitudes cannot be separated. In that case the great feminist criticisms of the modern world smash like soap bubbles against male belief in facts. Goddess feminism disguises the dilemma by one-sided attributions of guilt, whereas it would be better to come to an understanding with one another. In that case it would be discovered that we are all in the same boat, regardless of our sex. Whether the waves which toss the boat to and fro are moved by sea gods and goddesses or follow the laws of nature is irrelevant to the question how we can live together in the dangers.

3. Walter represents the other side of the coin of the 'dialectic of the Enlightenment' in Musil's novel. In his youth he had been a friend of Ulrich's, but this friendship had changed into mutual antipathy. Walter despises Ulrich, the man of possibilities, who cannot commit himself to anything because commitment is something he does not know. Walter's comment that 'in the old days, instead of death and logical mechanization, it was blood and wisdom that prevailed'[4] could have been spoken by a goddess feminist. He tells his wife Clarisse that 'there is nothing that everybody needs so urgently today as simplicity, nearness to the earth, health'.[5] 'Real people feel the warmth of the earth, no more analysing it than one analyses one's own mother.'[6] Over against that, 'Everything is crumbling nowadays.'[7] Walter is as incapable of acting as Ulrich:

> But while his condition had become steadily worse in the course of the last year, he had also found wonderful help in a thought that he had never before valued highly enough. This thought was none other than that Europe, in which he was forced to live, was irreparably decadent... the tangle of clever, stupid, vulgar, and beautiful is... so dense and involved that to many people it evidently seems easier to believe in a mystery, for which reason they proclaim the irresistible decline of something or other that defies exact definition and is of a solemn haziness.

It is fundamentally all the same whether this is thought of as the race, or vegetarianism, or the soil, for all that matters, as in the case of every healthy pessimism, is that one should have something or other that defies exact definition and is of a solemn haziness... Had it up to then been he who was unfit for work and felt out of sorts, now it was the time that was out of sorts, and he the healthy one. His life, which had come to nothing, was all at once given a tremendous explanation...[8]

Whereas Ulrich is open to the glittering world of facts, Walter takes shelter in the firm fortress of a subjective well-being which is only apparently self-sufficient ('good, beautiful and whole') and as long as the buck does not stop with him. The fact that before Europe became degenerate, everything was different and indeed was whole in comparison to the present day, even lends a certain necessity to the regression and bestows on the one who has regressed the halo of a missionary of those former worlds who cannot fail, as the hopelessly degenerate present hinders his actions. Robert Musil's Walter cultivates 'matriarchal spirituality'. We cannot enter into a detailed comparison; it is enough to substitute the degenerate male world for this degenerate Europe.

At a purely superficial level the attitudes which Ulrich and Walter represent are opposites. They can be taken as the two faces of the Enlightenment which I have described with the terms empiricism and rationalism. Responsibility is shifted on the one hand from people to circumstances, 'a world of qualities without man' (and, one could add, 'without woman');[9] so on the other hand it only seems logical that human beings, robbed of their responsibilities and their qualities at the same time, find themselves thrown back on the element of spontaneous feeling, and are only concerned, whether as individuals or along with some sympathizers, to give substance to this fine feeling by conjuring up whole worlds following the motto: 'The one who is with himself is with God' (Anne Wilson-Schaef).

Such feminism is therefore an authentic expression of that permanent crisis of the Enlightenment, since neither the logic of facts freed from the subject nor that of the godlike subject, the human being, released from all facts, can supply what they have been counted on to produce. The feminist solutions which are called for, however, once again show the crisis of the Enlightenment. Therefore the most appropriate reading would be to regard as a symptom and take seriously what emerges as a solution.

4. The talk is of feminine science, of feminist method, of unconventional thinking, and finally of healing the world by feminine nature. That 'the ideas and ideal demands which have grown out of the male and for the male have become absolutes transcending the sexes has ominous consequences for assessing the role of women', namely the 'mysticizing overestimation' of the woman, and also the loss of the independence of the feminine, in that it is merely taken as a supplement to the masculine. Whereas the male is a divided being, either given over to mere impulse or, if this is satisfied, devoting himself to material things and the world of ideas, the woman, as she is not by nature dualistic, is the 'authentic human being'. The woman 'rests in being... through an immediate, more instinctive, to some degree more naive contact, indeed identity'. Therefore standing beyond morality, 'she is not at all affected by the ethical problem'; she is good in herself. Therefore only she can heal the division of the male world.[10]

These characteristics of a whole matriarchal world as we have come to know it from feminist literature, and which represent the result of female science and the feminist method, do not stem from a woman but from a nineteenth-century philosopher who died in 1918: Georg Simmel. What is offered us today as the result of feminist scholarship was invented by men a century earlier. At first sight it may seem hypocritical and strengthen personal narcissism to be given redemptive quality as an attribute; on closer examination it is simply a matter of passing the buck. Feuerbach's God-man has failed; now let us see what goddess humanity can do. As the world has not yet been healed by anyone, either German or male, it cannot be healed by females either, and on the basis of such an insight it is easy to make a clear attribution of guilt. At some time in the future it will again be said that women failed, and this statement could not be refuted on existing presuppositions.

The main aspect of this kind of feminism that I would criticize is its blindness to method, its arbitrariness, in confusing and exchanging levels of thought to suit itself. Method is not self-sacrifice to the God science but literally the way of distinguishing the actual from the conceivable, the empirical from the conceptual, and at the same time recognizing how they are related to one another. What feminists claim to be feminine science is a false kind of thinking which takes short cuts, and if one were to judge these women by the criterion of their own thinking only one conclusion would be possible: once again it emerges that women have no logic, as is also confirmed by Georg Simmel.

However, one can make a virtue of feminine illogicality by declaring logic itself to be a vice and disqualifying all those who concern themselves with it, both men and women.

This kind of feminism is therefore dependent upon men in two ways and thus supports all conservative and reactionary tendencies:

(a) A blind and sweeping opposition which cannot distinguish between e.g. the virtues and vices of its opponent strengthens the power of the opponent, gives it a sacrosanct character and precisely by refusing to worship it confirms the conviction of this opponent (which may not be so certain) of being worthy of worship.

(b) The shift of perfect virtue into the opposition camp either represents a powerful challenge to the opponent or the opponent is happy to let it happen, whether because it relieves him of responsibility or because in this way he gets rid of something which in any case seems to him inferior and unworthy of him. 'Feminine science', which bases its claim on what is alleged to be specifically feminine, confirms all patriarchal arguments.

5. From where does Georg Simmel get the knowledge that the nature of woman is in a relationship of identity to being, forms the basic foundation of nature and therefore is to be described as 'supernaturally magic', metaphysics in the pure sense? Simmel gets it from the 'phenomena', from what he observes; and yet again the empirical, that which is subject to the changes of history, as we already saw in the case of Bachofen, is elevated to ontology, the essential foundation of the world.[11]

But that which is not true in the ontological sense nevertheless has some decisive elements of truth in the empirical sense. In arguing that woman is the 'whole sex' and that by contrast the male is sex only in relation to the woman, whereas outside this relationship, in the world of the spirit, man is free from the sexual, Simmel is giving an accurate description of a social condition. That is usually the case; whereas women squander their energies between bed, kitchen and nursery, men can regularly escape this world of the house, and indeed have to, because otherwise the world of business, politics and science would lie fallow. Business can only be carried on effectively if it is free from feminine elements and keeps the man who is so easily divided from being distracted by desire, by the woman.

Once again it is Barbara Sichtermann who provides an acute analysis of this problem.[12] What is being brought about is not a feminizing of science but the solution of a social problem which bars access for women to a 'zone' unburdened by any sexual element, because they alone are concerned with clearing away the consequences of sexuality. Sichtermann writes about 'feminine aesthetic'. If we replace the term aesthetic by science, then everything fits: 'All the misunderstandings which have burdened debates about "feminine aesthetics" (science) derive from the fact that people renounce the useful supposition of a "free zone" and instead of this toil in the polarity of male and female, with the result that such frivolous constructions as those of a male or female art (= science) emerge, or a new version of the prejudice that women are no good at art (science).'[13]

Neither art nor science has a sex. They are expressions of the human spirit, made possible by freedom from the sexual dimension. The relationship between the sexes does not have the character of a universal ontology, the nature of which permeates all things, but has a social context. Science has another location. The problem of women is that they are assigned to a particular place which is then defined as the feminine place. If women through 'feminine science' transplant the only place assigned to them to libraries and lecture rooms, then they will never be free of that under which they suffer, that which limits the development of their individual capacities.

I can easily imagine the anxiety that seizes men when femininity, which they usually encounter in bed and at the table, invades the sphere that had previously been a zone free from sexual tension. Now new attitudes and patterns of behaviour have to be learned, since it has not been agreed that female colleagues at the conference table shall show tenderness, discover that a button has come off or have aspirins ready. The experience that things are not the same when working with a woman as they are with a wife or lover can also have liberating and enriching aspects. A realistic way must and indeed can be found between the sweat of anxiety and officiousness.

Those who do not want to have a place assigned to them must themselves be able to discern when and where something particular is in place. It would be too easy if only men had to learn new modes of behaviour. Thus the first commandment in Friedrich Schleiermacher's *Rational Catechism for Noble Women* (1798) might be altered to read: '...you shall be a friend (colleague) without sexual overtones, without flirting or making eyes at men.'[14] When the question of the ordination of women was debated in the 1960s, a reciprocal relationship was forecast between the woman in the pulpit and the lascivious male onlooker. In the meantime it has proved that the female pastor can be as effective as the male. Such a 'sex-free zone' is not free of tension, any more than is the domestic hearth. Each of the tensions is distinctive and each requires to be dealt with separately. But the woman cannot avoid the demands of performance and competition in the public market place simply by withdrawing into her need for protection. If she does so, she will be told that she should not expose herself to the battle; after all, she alone has the privilege of warming herself by the fire, with knitting needles and purring cat. That would once again bring us back to Simmel, even without ontology.

The world of the home as a place of retreat and idyll is, however, only one perspective and life-style and not even the decisive one. The realities of a classical feminine life involve dealing with living people and their everyday pains and delights. As a rule women are much less able to escape the daily tasks of loving care than men, nor do they want to. Women more than men are confronted with the mistakes and confusions of children and old people and have to deal with what they encounter, which continually surprises them, because it evades scientific systematization. That in this way women vicariously take on tasks for their husbands to leave them free for other, allegedly 'specifically male' tasks does not further the humanity of men and at the same time bars them from socially rooted thought, which can give an account of its social relevance.

Here again the sociology of knowledge should be taken seriously, according to which all questions and problems which provoke reflection come or must come from the reality of living, since reflection which forms theories otherwise becomes a pointless game or turns into knowledge as power. The hostility of many students to theory, for example, is not a coincidence, since the packets of knowledge which are pressed into their hands are not opened; the students are not told why, in what circumstances, on the basis of what existential questions, and so on, people follow particular courses and abandon others. If the students were told, then one could speak in a positive sense of 'feminine science' as a criticism of current science detached from any biographical or social location. The opportunity for women in science is thus a chance for science, not because women shift their household activity to the university, but because even in their new location they do not forget to further life in all their thinking and theorizing. Granted, this scientific-critical perspective is not new, and the sociologists of knowledge around the turn of the century who formulated it were men. But by virtue of their tradition of a closer connection with life here and now women could further a socially rooted thought and thus at the same time counter the exile of men from the world of the home, also to the benefit of the human spirit, in this case the male spirit. Anyone who is not just playing a game in his or her thinking or in so doing is seeking to steal a march on the rest of humanity must also presuppose a relationship with the reality of human life if he or she is to work out real solutions to problems. In this connection classical philosophy already speaks rightly of the primacy of praxis.

A 'feminine science' understood in this way can thus appeal to the best traditions of science. Just as feminist theology would be superfluous where a responsible theology – in both sense of the word – transcended it, so too science will do justice to its tasks only if it does not go on ruling out that reality which our civilization has foisted above all on to women. Anyone who looks more closely therefore discovers that the fronts between 'feminine' and 'masculine' science do not run between women and men but between a science with an interest in communication and one which gains social prestige from its detachment. Women can contribute ways of stimulating the first kind of science, and in so doing they will rediscover themselves in the society of men who like themselves have become alienated because they connect knowledge with life and hand it on, and therefore betray the unwritten rules of educated society.

6. The subtitle of this book is 'Systematic criticism of a feminist theology'. The article is indefinite, not definite. It is easy to overlook this distinction, especially as in the text it was impossible to keep on stressing that I am concerned with a particular kind of feminism. I am not concerned to make sweeping judgments on all the thoughts and writings of women for their own cause; otherwise I would probably have had to forbid myself my typewriter. So the concept of feminism is located in a context not only of criticism but also of assent. The argument is the reason for drawing on both the one and the other.

The positions which I have criticized have one thing in common. They are particularly popular, and at the moment are particularly in vogue in all the educational institutions at a middle level: high schools, institutes of higher education and schools. As a secondary effect this has now produced a distinctive genre of literature which I have called 'popular'. The best example of it is the book by Else Sorge, *Religion und Frau*,[15] which has also appeared specifically in a series for instruction, study and adult education produced in collaboration with the educational specialist Siegfried Vierzig. Thus the literature with the widest influence includes what is read by those at a middle stage of education or produced for it. Perhaps this observation may also help us towards some understanding.

In terms of social context, then, this kind of feminism or feminist theology (and when I go on to speak of feminism I shall always mean only this kind) can be defined as 'midcult' (= culture of the social middle class) as distinct from masscult and avant garde.[16] The cultural forms of expression (which include literature) of masscult and midcult have in common 'the sale of prefabricated effects, the preparation of conditions for use along with the product, and with the message a prescription of the reaction that it is to produce',[17] whereas the avant-garde seeks the cause of a possible effect and represents the course of this search in order to stimulate thought-processes.[18]

However, the midcult also feels superior to the masscult in that among the avant-garde it attributes to itself those motives which meet the desires of its particular public not to feel that they have to belong to the mass. It exposes the consumers of its products 'apparently to a privileged and difficult experience';[19] 'it satisfies the consumers by convincing them that they have heard the heart of culture beating (in this context one would have to add: and that of science)'.[20] Both elements, the prefabricated effects and the privileged experience, to a large degree shape this feminist literature. The readers cannot but be angry at the crime of the patriarchy, which has now lasted for millennia. Such feminist literature evidently makes it possible finally to see through one's own life; in the light of the patriarchy all possible personal mistakes are given a comprehensive explanation.

How much more honest it would be, however, to have personal reports of experience in which the author told of her hard life, her bad experience with men and how she was able to free herself from them (or not: there is this kind of literature too). It would also be honest just to write literary works, like Gerhard Hauptmann with his *Island of the Great Mother* or Christa Wolff with her *Cassandra*. The literary products of midcult feminism are different, for here the reader is given the privilege of participating in high science. All statements are 'is' statements; everything is garnished all the way through with a salad of every possible genre of text and content; quotations, pictures, the suffering of woman in the form of evidence create a collage which leave no room for doubt: no matter what, the patriarchate is guilty.

7. What is suspicious is not mass production and consumption, nor even that writers fulfil the needs of their readers, seek to create an effect with their product, or popularize knowledge. That very good midcult literature is devoured by many people, and is indeed written for this purpose, does not disqualify it. But there is a suspicious variant of the midcult, marked out by definite characteristics, those associated with deception. Even if there is no deliberate intent behind them, they nevertheless express a particular relationship to reality. Away from the heat of the argument and the call for unconditional solidarity with the interest expressed, it is important to summon up courage to

submit this kind of literature to an analysis which explains its effect. It has two features. It 'does away with reality',[21] for this seems on the whole to be simply dismaying, and its tensions and pluriformity are intolerable. On this ground a second element flourishes – the search for synthesis at any price. Those who write like this 'synthesize the presuppositions of their intelligence away by ignoring boundaries which are open to criticism. Where analysis is needed they offer synthesis.'[22]

The false, deceptive syntheses are capable in principle of lumping together all the elements at their disposal without making any distinctions at all. Isolated motives from history, art, myths, and indeed methods are picked out without any note of the context from which they come; time and again a totality is broken up with its wealth of tensions. But this synthesis no longer arrives at a totality; it forms a sum, a conglomerate, in which the wealth of individual elements simulates the totality. Such syntheses are produced by a single theory which does not arise from the material but holds the material together. The feminist literature that I am describing here knits its material together from the centuries with the help of the theory of matriarchy or the victory of the patriarchy over the matriarchy.

The secret of this trick is as follows: the individual elements which do not really fit into the new conglomerate context derive from another, recognized context. Each individual theme, whether it be the dancing goddess, the sacred marriage, a particular social structure like matrifocality, the Jesus whom feminine disciples follow, the Marxist theory of superstructure and so on, appears in academic literature, which in this way is able to lend corresponding authority to the conglomerate. It is thus claimed that the syntheses are demonstrably scientific, indeed that they are the better, true science, because they no longer contain open questions, unresolved contradictions: in short, they no longer have any tensions. No wonder that the readers come to see salvation (or disaster). The solution necessary here and now for the specific problem here and now is left once again to the 'genius of the suppliers'.

It is not altogether clear why such literature comes into being and how it can emerge posing as the bringer of redemption. Since increasing numbers of women nowadays are conquering the sphere of the 'sex-free zone' which was formerly reserved for men, they are finding themselves faced with new experiences, tensions and problems. How difficult it is to leave an accustomed social place, even if one protests against being firmly assigned to it, is shown not least by the way in which women attempt to take this place with them everywhere: 'feminine science', 'feminine art' are the result, and of course they do not work. To emerge from the commonplace causes anxiety; the dream, in this case that of the matriarchy and its spirituality, provides comfort.

Assurance is sought: but its popularity still does not have any political success to show for itself. I regard the popular variants of feminist theology, in which I include more than just the Christian positions, as being politically dangerous. The false syntheses arouse false hopes in that they falsify reality. Deceptions, illusions and schematizations are always more popular consumer goods than the stubborn fight on the field of confusing reality. Wherever the roles of the wholly evil and the wholly good are assigned, where dogmatic schematizations reach around themselves, regress disguises itself as progress. 'The democrat is the one who rejects schemes and recognizes nuances, makes distinctions and justifies contradictions.'[23] The logic of the reactionary also contains the step from reason to magic.[24] And experience confirms that argument, cross-checking, self-critical questioning are virtually impossible in this kind of feminist circle. In that circle it is said that criticism strengthens the forces of reaction. But the opposite is the case: reactionaries have always been characterized by the way in whch they brand criticism as 'destructive'. If women have given themselves up, they are now in danger of seeking themselves somewhere outside the real world and thus losing themselves to their solipsistic selves. But if there is to be change, if there is a concern for human criteria and realistic steps, then over-hasty syntheses are a temptation on the way. Anything that 'escapes exact judgment and is of solemn obscurity'[25] merely creates the illusion of a new start and ultimately always supports those who regard the traditional as desirable. Those who dream of the matriarchy and feminine spirituality produce opium for women.

8. Thus systematic and political considerations, including literary and political ones, show the degree to which even that

feminist literature has been infected by the sickness of our scientific age. It looks for proofs because it thinks that only what can actually be proved can claim validity. But who could ever 'prove' conclusively and once for all that discrimination against women is false and is therefore to be shunned? The truth of the *humanum* or of faith does not stick to the facts: on the contrary, the patterns of life as it is lived are an expression of what people regard as true and right, and that can be very different. The fact itself is dumb; only the significance that we attach to it makes it speak, and again in the sense of what we regard as true. So the battle has to be waged on the level of truth-claims, and what is called a fact is no help to us here.

One cannot exempt the churches from the charge that their preachers seldom succeed in detaching the truth-claims of faith from rigid formulae of doctrine and morality and in making them understandable. This is because they speak of sin as though it were like greenflies and of the incarnation of God in the same way as of the 'mysterious' powers of micro-chips. This facts-and-data talk of faith is also a fact in the Christian tradition. Similarly, even now doctrinal statements and praxis show that the weight is decisively on the side of discrimination against women. To this degree the feminist theology which throws out the whole of Christianity on the rubbish heap of history is at least consistent: if one took the dominant fact of Christian misogyny as the criterion, we would have to do away with Christianity. Those forms of feminism which keep within the framework of reducing Christianity to an idealized beginning and on that basis promise women the time of salvation here and now are not so consistent. But these beginnings lie a long way back in the past, and the centuries between carry more weight and put the facts of the contempt for women on the line. Thus historical facts neither rescue Christianity nor help women. Nor is it any more use to abandon oneself to deceptions and illusions, whether with reference to the Christian tradition or to other religious traditions like that of the goddess myths. What helps is the removal of deception.

Here I mean the removal of deception in a particular sense, namely that facts do not offer the support that they promise, that precisely that which seems to be certain and unshakeably established proves to be a deception. Ingeborg Bachmann calls the last of her five Frankfurt lectures 'Literature as Utopia'; in them the poetess formulates very clearly the struggle which is carried on between constantly new sketches of the future and their association with the facts of the past. She bases her discussion on the critical interchange between literature and literary criticism. If one thinks how much literature is always a 'confession of faith' directed towards the future, how much its critical power, whether it chooses the present or the past as the scene, consists in not accepting what is (and that means developing utopias), then it is not surprising that Bachmann's analysis is also relevant to our question. 'We all want to prove literature or prove something with it,' writes Bachmann, and here she means that literature which has in it the power of a utopian faith: '...moreover all possible disciplines come up against it and it is compelled towards regularities and conditions or revelations, to which it does justice today – pleasing everyone and no one – and then contradicts tomorrow.'[26] The irreplaceable character of faith is shown by the fact that it escapes all regularities and conditions and has always already left the history of its realizations (always deficient, and often also unsuccessful) behind it, in so far as it is alive. What follows from this is none other than the demanding conclusion that each generation and each individual must pose the question of theological truth afresh in order to do justice to faith as utopia and eschatology.

There is no evidence that human beings have an independent value, that men and women in their freedom for creative action are images of God, but in the impossibility of ever being able to become perfect remain creatures; that God became human, not male, in order to redeem both man and woman equally from their imperfection; that God has no respect of persons and thus also no respect of gender, and that this claim of faith is meant to be realized here and now in this world. There is only the testimony in faith of those, whether in the present or the past, who believe this claim to be true. And there have been and always will be those who avoid this claim, and by virtue of this refusal are also in a position to mobilize their whole power of thought. Therefore history as the praxis of that of which human beings are convinced can provide confirmation for all possible convictions, and everyone is thrown back with empty hands on the credibility of his or her thought and action. Here and there at all times people have succeeded in shedding light on this confused history of deceptions and illusions through credible practice, as utopia become reality or, as it is called in theology, a present eschatology. Therefore Christians can only be utopian existents, and they must reckon with contradiction, with struggle.

Faith as utopia sheds its own light 'when we turn off the searchlights'.[27] What we know as the perfect, the whole and the healed in it 'sets the incomplete going again'.[28] So if women are really concerned with confirmation from the past for the sake of their future, are they really concerned with legitimation at all? 'For what we are left with,' says Ingeborg Bachmann, is 'having to struggle with the unsound language that we find towards this one language which has never yet prevailed.'[29] The utopian destiny spoken of here, that of being homeless in this world or only a transitory guest, affects everything that cannot be communicated by means of facts but only through hope and certainty, including Christian faith. 'We have to go on writing,' says Ingeborg Bachmann,[30] and I would adapt her remark to our problem: we have to go on believing, because we are concerned with the future of faith and not the past of error. Utopia means giving language and real form to unwritten history, as a history which has never yet been.

It is to that end that I have written my two books, concerned to remove deceptions and to make room for utopia. But, it might be objected, do not many women live by what I call deceptions? Is it permissible to want to take away from people something that gives them power and self-awareness? In reply I would ask: Would not the energy with which so many feminists invent a pseudo-reality which appeals to them not be better put to another cause? Does not the constant search for firm support in the facticity of history or in the ontology of the feminine promise nothing but continual disillusionment? I understand very well the wish to 'derive models from an origin' and thus 'set up a forward projection', but that is 'a misapprehension rather than a criterion, which will never be attained however near one gets'.[31] To say that it will never be attained is not an expression of resignation; it is not meant to make people despondent, but to protect them from ideals of perfection which have so often had disastrous consequences. For in human hands all that is perfect trickles away into illusion or runs away into the fanaticism of the totalitarian. Talk of a criterion, a human criterion, means that there cannot be a fixed and permanent support in history or in human nature. Therefore what theology calls futuristic eschatology points to a hope according to which the whole, the total, the perfect will only appear at the end of earthly days.

One of the classical misinterpretations of the Christian hope of the 'last things' was to derive the flight from earthly realization from such hope. The one who hopes is necessarily already determined by that hope all his or her life, and the one who cannot hope is already dead during his or her lifetime. And those 'patriarchs' who give themselves such airs, deny their sinfulness, derive theocratic claims for themselves from God and the masculinity of Jesus, who avoid contradictions and corrections by human standards, substitute domination over women for a relationship to them, thus truly ruin themselves and in the good biblical sense bring down judgment upon themselves.

And over all this there is God's cause, and the matter of doing, in trust, the utmost justice to it that we can. 'To the collapse of all proofs the believer answers with a *Salve* to the future.'[32]

Notes

Introduction

1. The spectacular church wedding of the well-known feminist Edit Schlaffer is not an isolated instance or an exception, but represents a typical variant of the 'modification' of feminist interest; cf. my *Women and Early Christianity*, SCM Press 1987 and Augsburg Publishing House 1988, 48f., 163 nn.170-2. As far as the hopes of the authorities mentioned further above are concerned, such arguments were used in Austria at the time of the first ordinations of women.

2. In September 1986 there was a conference of women art historians in Vienna at which Sigrid Schade of the Technical University of West Berlin gave a notable paper on the problems of representing the mutilated (female) body. She associated the 'myth of the sound body' with the Fascist totality 'ideal' of the Third Reich, and in so doing criticized the ideological approach in the concept of Gestalt therapy.

3. Barbara Sichtermann, *Weiblichkeit. Zur Politik des Privaten*, 1983, 10.

4. This quotation comes from a lecture given by Alexandra Petzold at the conference of women art historians (see n.2 above).

5. I have come to this conclusion above all from my experience in discussions with feminist women theologians.

6. H.Lübbe, *Religion nach der Aufklärung*, 1986, 324 n.68.

7. Sichtermann, *Weiblichkeit* (n.3).

8. See n.2.

9. For this concept drawn from Erich Heintel see *Women and Early Christianity*, 37.

10. See Peter Heintel, *Modelbildung in der Fachdidaktik*, 1978, 77ff.

11. The concept of the distinction between levels of meaning comes from Erich Heintel. Cf. the careful account in H.Gehrke, *Theologie im Gesamtraum des Wirklichen. Zur Systematik Erich Heintels*, 1981, 49ff.

12. Here are some technical details. For both biblical and extra-biblical texts I have tried to refer to translations which are not just available to expert scholars. Where I have been able to translate the original text myself I have sometimes provided my own translations which I indicate as such in the notes, or have checked the translations. Where I have not had access to the original text, as for example in cuneiform documents, because the translations often differ so considerably I have had to limit myself to warnings against basing too crucial an argument on one of the variants. The notes in no way offer a complete bibliography, even of all that I have read. Above all I have listed the most popular literature so that the reader can follow my argument for himself or herself. I have

also felt it important to substantiate my judgments from sources and so show 'where I got it from'. In so doing I am offering anyone the opportunity to check what I say. (Where possible, English translations have been consulted or used; however, it has not been possible to gain access to some rare books, so in these cases, while bibliographical details are given of the English versions, the page references are to the German edition.)

1. God the Father, God the Mother

1. The quotation is an excerpt from the Eighteen Benedictions, the main prayer of the Jewish synagogue after the Shema, 'Hear, O Israel'. The main part of the text goes back to the end of the first and the beginning of the second century of the Christian era. Quoted from *The Authorized Daily Prayer Book*, ed.S.Singer, London ⁹1932, 44, 54.

2. Translations of Old Testament texts are largely taken from the Revised Standard Version. All the examples quoted below are only a selection from a far great number of instances.

3. RSV.

4. G. Schrenk, 'Father', *Theological Dictionary of the New Testament*, 5, 975; further instances are given here.

5. Flavius Josephus, *Jewish Antiquities* I,13,4.

6. The apt term 'theocratic short-cut' comes from the Viennese philosopher Erich Heintel: cf. e.g. 'Gott ohne Eigenschaften', in *Gott ohne Eigenschaften?*, ed. S.Heine and E.Heintel, 1983, 9ff. (41).

7. K.Knohl-Hoberg, 'Sexismus in den Gesangbuchliedern', in *Nennt uns nicht Brüder*, ed. N.Sommer, 1985, (310ff.) 311.

8. Cf. Elga Sorge, 'Thesen zur Kritik am männlichen Bild von Gott', *Religion und Frau* 1985, 44-6. Cf. also the literature cited in n.31. This criticism is a constant theme in feminist theology.

9. B.Kavemann and I.Lohstoter, *Väter als Täter*, 1984; Florence Rich, *The Best-Kept Secret: Sexual Abuse of Children*, Prentice-Hall 1980; Valeska von Roques, 'Das geheimste Verbrechen', *Der Spiegel* 29, 1984, 30ff. Cf. also Susan Brownmiller, *Against our Will*, Simon and Schuster 1975; S.Plogstedt and K.Bode, *Übergriffe. Sexuelle Belästigungen in Büros und Betrieben*, 1984; C.Bernard and E.Schlaffer, *Die ganz gewöhnliche Gewalt in der Ehe*, 1978. In all the books I have cited there is a wealth of further literature on this theme.

10. van Roques, *Der Spiegel* (see n.9 above), 33; cf. Kavemann/Lohstöter, *Väter* (n. 9), 28.

11. Kavemann/Lohstöter, *Väter*, 100.

12. Ibid., 25.

13. van Roques, *Der Spiegel* (see n.9 above), 34; cf. M.C.Baurmann, *Sexualität, Gewalt und psychische Folgen*, 1983. For the problem in 'literary form' see B.Frischmuth, *Haschen nach Wind. Erzählungen*, ²1974, 74ff.

14. Kavemann/Lohstöter, *Väter*, 36f.

15. *Der Spiegel*, 40.

16. Cf. C.Bernard and E.Schlaffer, *Gewalt in der Ehe* (n.9).

17. Plogstedt and Bode, *Sexuelle Belästigungen* (n.9). Male clergy, too, are not above all suspicion, cf. e.g. H.Mynarek, *Eros und Klerus*, 1980; cf. the bibliography in n.38. That perpetrators and 'victims' of sexual abuse are also to be found among the psychologically sick where a degree of 'complicity' can be attributed to the victims does not justify including all offences under this model

and vice versa. It is important to make a careful distinction. The same goes for ethical assessments.

18. 'Sexism – to be thought of as parallel to racism – means oppression, exploitation and discrimination not on the grounds of belonging to a race but of belonging to a sex, in our historical tradition and in the present the female sex' (Rosemary R.Ruether, 'Die neue Frau und die neue Erde: Frauen, Ökologie und soziale Revolution', *epd Dokumentation* 44, Frankfurt 1976, 24).

19. Cf my comments in *Women and Early Christianity*, 37ff.

20. The relationship between the father God and the king as his son can imply different conceptions: the divinity of the king, the adoption of the king as son of God, the elevation of the king to be son of God through the enthronement ceremony, or simply the close relationship between God and king which can also be expressed by individual faithful. It may be taken for granted that the king as son of God has something to do with the one 'by the grace of God'; why should the monarchy in Israel not also have modelled itself on other oriental images on this point, too?

21. See n.35.

22. The new foundation of the state of Israel in 1948 is irrelevant to our purposes.

23. W.H.Schmidt, *Introduction to the Old Testament*, SCM Press and Crossroad Publishing Company 1984, 129.

24. Gerda Weiler, *Ich verwerfe im Lande die Kriege. Das verborgene Matriarchat im Alten Testament*, 1983, 143, 343, etc.

25. It is striking that many feminists use psychological and psychoanalytical terms to condemn authors who are no longer alive. On the one hand the question arises here whether and how psychology and psychoanalysis can be applied outside living (therapeutic) dialogue; but on the other hand these terms are not used analytically but in the form of moral verdicts. This fundamentally goes against the intention of psychology and psychoanalysis, the specific nature of which consists in abstaining from value judgments. A psychological judgment may not be made an accusation! Cf. also the verdict of M.Janssen-Jurreit (*Sexismus*, 1976) on J.J.Bachofen (97), or that of K.Deschner (*Das Kreuz mit der Kirche*, 1974), on Paul, that he was 'brimful of sexual complexes' (67). For a criticism of this 'method' cf. J.Scharfenberg, 'Martin Luther in psychohistorischer Sicht', in *Europa in der Krise der Neuzeit*, ed. S.Heine, 1986, 113ff.

26. Though I do not want to suggest that it does this deliberately, feminist literature, which sweepingly makes 'the Jews' and their allegedly martial God responsible for all women's suffering down the centuries, affords a powerful stimulus to antisemitism. As Christianity and Islam also derive from the sphere of Jewish religion, possibly the Jews still have to bear the blame for all the evil in the history of these two other religions.

It can be argued against this that for example neither Buddhism nor Hinduism show themselves to be particularly well disposed towards women. The conclusion to be drawn is that inhumanity of all kinds has at all times and in all cultures sought legitimation from a particular religion by means of the theocratic shortcut. Therefore the legitimizing process must be criticized, but not the authority which is utilized. To talk of 'the Jews', 'the Moslems', 'men', is a sign of the tiresome strategy of finding scapegoats, to which the other side answers 'women'. The one is no better than the other. Something else needs to be stressed. A dominant feature when Jews reflect on their own history is self-criticism: Jews (not all, but a great many of them) from Old Testament times down to the present day seek the guilt for their disasters not among others but among themselves.

27. Cf. W.Eichrodt, *Theology of the Old Testament* I, SCM Press and Westminster Press 1961, 392f.

28. Chancellor Kreisky of Austria has rightly seen this. He constantly stresses that it is better not to have a referendum on certain problems like the death penalty and the emancipation of women. For example, according to an opinion poll in September 1986 (under the impact of a wave of terrorism) 77% of the French called for the death penalty, which was abolished in 1982 (*Salzburger Nachrichten*, 20 September 1986, p.2). The same would be true of Britain.

29. *Women in Early Christianity*, 55ff.

30. I developed this notion further in an article 'Zeitgeist und Gottesgeist – Glaubensvermittlung im Zeitalter der Religionskritik', *Amt und Gemeinde* (published by the Bishop of the Protestant Church in Austria), 5 May 1986, 45. Here Paul's argument against the Jews in Rom.11 is transferred to the church.

31. Some literature on this theme is: J.E.Bruns, *God as Woman, Woman as God*, Paulist Press 1973; P.D.Hanson, 'Männliche Metaphern für Gott und die unterschiedliche Behandlung der Geschlechter im Alten Testament', in *Frauenbefreiuung* (ed. E.Moltmann-Wendel), ³1978; A.Greeley, *The Mary Myth. On the Feminine Dimension of God*, Seabury Press 1977; A.Vergote and A.Tamayo, *The Parental Figures and the Representation of God*, Paris and New York 1981; Virginia R.Mollenkott, *The Divine Feminine. The Biblical Imagery of God as Female*, Crossroad Publishing Company 1984; R.Laut, *Weibliche Züge im Gottesbild israelitisch-jüdischer Religiosität*, 1983; Christa Mulack, *Die Weiblichkeit Gottes*, ²1983; E.Moltmann-Wendel, *A Land Flowing with Milk and Honey*, SCM Press and Crossroad Publishing Company 1982, 91ff.; R.R.Ruether, *Sexism and God Talk*, Beacon Press and SCM Press 1985. When I go on talk about 'feminism' or 'feminists' I am essentially referring to this literature.

32. Cf. e.g. E.Moltmann-Wendel, *A Land Flowing with Milk and Honey*, 98ff.

33. Rachel Wahlberg, 'The Woman's Creed', in *Growing together in Unity. Discussion Documents for the Faith and Order Commission, Bangalore, 16-30 August 1978*.

34. That emerges clearly in V.R.Mollenkott, *The Divine Feminine* (n.31); the feminine aspects that she stresses are: midwife, mother bear, female pelican (who sacrifices herself for her young), the presence, housewife, beloved, help, baker, mother eagle, hen.

35. I do not have space here to outline the history of Israel in any detail. Nevertheless the following section can only be understood in connection with this history. So here is a brief chronology as a guideline. The time of the so-called patriarchs (Abraham, etc.) is generally dated to the nineteenth century BC; the Moses traditions to the thirteenth century; Kings Saul and David reigned around 1000 BC. The first fixed date is the death of David's successor Solomon in 926 BC, which was followed by a division of the state into a northern and a southern kingdom, each with its own king. In 722 the northern kingdom was finally destroyed by the Assyrians, and in 587 BC the southern kingdom was destroyed by the Babylonians (first destruction of the temple). The sixth century BC is the exilic period (deportation of the Jewish upper class to Babylon; life in independent communities); some of the exiles returned to Palestine under Cyrus, king of the Persians, in 537, and rebuilt the temple with Persian support. From then on the Jews were always under the rule of the great powers of the time.

168   Notes to pages 30–36

36. E.Schilling, *Manchmal hasse ich meine Mutter. Gespräche mit Frauen*, 1984, 193. For conflict between sisters see e.g. L.Siebenschön, 'Schwestern', in *Psychologie heute*, 2, 1983, 38ff.

37. Schilling, op.cit., 12, 173, etc.

38. The literature of psychoanalysis provides numerous instances of the problem of parent-child relationships in all their varieties, cf. e.g. S.B.Kopp, *If you meet the Buddha on the Way...*, Sheldon Press 1974, 43ff.; S.R.Dunde (ed.), *Vater im Himmel – seine Söhne auf Erden*, 1986 (concerned with 'males and religion'). H.Hemminger, *Kindheit als Schicksal?*, 1982, is helpful here: his starting point is that all childhood experiences represent need and injury which need to be overcome in the process of growing up.

39. A.Miller, *The Drama of the Gifted Child and the Search for the True Self*, Faber 1983, 96f.

40. Ps.2.7 is the only passage in the Old Testament which speaks directly of God begetting.

41. E.g. Matt.1.20; Gal.4.29; and especially in the Johannine literature: I John 2.29; 4.7; 5.4, etc.

42. G.Weiler, *Kriege* (n.24), 112.

43. Ibid., 112f.

44. For the sake of clarity on the following philosophical problems I have kept to literature which is fairly widely available: A.Anzenbacher, *Einführung in die Philosophie*, 1981: H.Gehrke, *Theologie im Gesamtraum des Wirklichen*, 1981.

For Aristotelian forms of activity cf. A.Anzenbacher, 215f. Aristotle discusses this problem above all in the Nicomachean Ethics (distinction between action and production) VI, 4-5, see *Nichomachean Ethics*, Loeb Classical Library 1926, translated by H.Rackham.

45. H.Gehrke, *Theologie* (n.44), 272.

46. For the significance of the form as a sense-image cf. Yorick Spiegel, *Glaube wie er leibt und lebt*, three vols, 1984.

47. The term *deus ex machina* comes from the Greek theatre. When conflicts had resulted in an inextricable tangle, with the help of theatre machinery a god was made to descend, to resolve everything for the best. See this theme in Bert Brecht, *The Good Man of Szechuan*.

48. In very general terms 'projection' is understood to mean that an inner perception which is not consciously realized as such is claimed to be of something external. Thus for example an individual can project repressed (to use the Freudian term) hatred on to other people or even on to God (there is no moral judgment here!).

49. Cf. E.Heintel, *Die beiden Labyrinthe der Philosophie*, 1, 1968, 91, etc.; Heintel describes ontological reductionism as 'bad metaphysics' or 'ghost metaphysics'.

50. For reasons of space I have dispensed with giving a history of 'analogy' or 'analogous speech' an account of the many layers of its meaning. I am limiting myself to the aspect which is relevant to our theme and thus to Kant's remarks.

51. Gehrke, *Theologie* (n.44), 237.

52. I.Kant, *Prolegomena to any Future Metaphysics that will be able to present itself as a Science*, ed. Peter G.Lucas, Manchester University Press 1953, 124.

53. Op.cit., 124.

54. *Kant's Critique of Aesthetic Judgment*, ed. J.C.Meredith, Clarendon Press 1911, 222f.

55. Ibid., 222.

56. Kant, *Prolegomena* (n.52), 125.

57. Kant (see n.54), 223

58. One could take the objective understanding of the word 'is' even further, *ad absurdum*: in that case God is not just father and/or mother, but also animal (hen, eagle, bear). No one would take such an analogy seriously, but why does that happen with 'father' and 'mother'?

59. Kant, *Prolegomena* (n.52), 125.

60. Gehrke (n.44), 239.

61. The book by H.Halbfas, *Das dritte Auge*, 1982, is an example of how quickly communication can get involved in that polarity in which theory either appears as mere factual knowledge or seems devalued as a formal structure.

62. Cf. e.g. K.Rahner, 'Observations on the Doctrine of God in Catholic Dogmatics', *Theological Investigations* 9, 1972, 127-44; id., 'Reflections on Methodology in Theology', *Theological Investigations* 11, 1979, 68-114.

2. Eros of the Goddesses

1. The 'initiates' are members of the cultic personnel of a particular temple. It is no longer to determine their rank and function, and these probably varied. The Old Testament texts suggest that we should see the initiates as hierodules, as cultic prostitutes. Whether this view is right or is the result of Old Testament polemic against 'heretics' is also difficult to determine. There are arguments for both positions. Cf. e.g. the conflicting standpoints of Hans-Walter Wolff, *Hosea*, Hermeneia 1974, and Hans M.Barstad, *The Religious Polemics of Amos*, Leiden 1984. We shall be returning to this question below.

2. It certainly does not emerge with any certainty from the passage quoted that the queen mother had an influential and indeed official position in Israel. However, no more is said in the texts, which are coloured by later polemic. It remains questionable whether the far-reaching conclusions drawn by Gerda Weiler, *Ich verwerfe im Lande die Kriege*, 1984, 310ff., are legitimate.

3. A reconstruction of the early history of Israel with a more marked sociological orientation challenges the classical theory of nomadic origin. There are supposed to have been oppressed groups on the periphery of Canaanite society who detached themselves in order to develop social forms in opposition. This theory does not date the polemic from the time of the exile but sees it as a characteristic of the history of Israel generally. The Canaanite feudal rulers would have fought against 'mono-Yahwism' and a concern for equal social rights. But however one dates or explains the polemic, that is not an answer to the question of its theological significance. Precisely for that reason there must also be a systematic criticism. For the sociological theories see e.g. N.K.Gottwald, *The Tribes of Yahweh. A Sociology of the Religion of Israel*, Orbis Books and SCM Press 1979, and the critical discussion of it by W.R.Wilfall, 'The Tribes of Yahweh. A Synchronic Study with a Diachronic Title', *ZAW* 95, 1983, 197ff.

4. Else Sorge, *Religion und Frau*, 1985, 84,

5. A.K.Rush, *Moon, Moon*, Random House 1976, 297.

6. For this topic see above all: J.Schreier, *Göttinnen*, 1978; H.Göttner-Abendroth, *Die Göttin und ihr Heros*, 1980; Elizabeth Gould Davis, *The First Sex*, Dent 1973; Robert Graves, *Greek Myths*, Penguin Books ²1960; id., *The White Goddess*, Faber 1952; G. Weiler, *Ich verwerfe im Lande die Kriege* (n.2). The literature mentioned is specially related to a perspective with a feminist interest.

7. It is not even certain whether these female figures (like the Willendorf Venus) are goddesses. We might think more in terms of fertility amulets which also play a role in birth magic.

8. H.Göttner-Abendroth, *Die Göttin* (n.6), 119. For the following account see 79ff.

9. In particular periods and places names and functions of the goddesses can be confused or shifted in relation to those of other goddesses. In the Old Testament Baal is mentioned together with Asherat but not with Anat. It is no longer possible to determine whether the traditions are confusing the two goddesses, did not understand the names in this way, or whether the increasing significance of Baal over against El led to an adoption of Asherat by Baal.

10. Cf.John Gray, *The Canaanites*, Thames and Hudson 1964, (119ff.) 121.

11. For a description of the gods and goddesses of the Ugaritic pantheon cf. E.O.James, *The Cult of the Mother-Goddess*, Thames and Hudson 1959; C.F.A.Schaeffer, *The Cuneiform Texts of Ras Shamra-Ugarit* (1937), reprinted Munich 1980; O.Eissfeldt, *El in the Ugaritic Pantheon*, 1951; A.S.Kapelrud, *The Violent Goddess (Anat)*, Oslo 1969; id., *Baal in the Ras Schamra Texts*, Copenhagen 1953.

12. J.Aistleitner, *Die mythologischen und kultischen Texte aus Ras Schamra*, Budapest 1959, 39f.; cf. the sometimes very different and also freer translation by A.Jirku, *Kanaanäische Mythen und Epen aus Ras Schamra-Ugarit*, 1962. Goddess feminism tends to attribute to the transition to the patriarchy any motif that is not evidence of the dominance of feminine deities; however, it has to be said that there are no literary sources for the preceding period.

13. E.O.James, *Cult* (n.11), thinks that the two goddesses could be Asherat and Anat; possibly Anat was originally the spouse of El before she turned to the younger, ambitious Baal (74f.). Cf. Kapelrud, *Goddess* (n.11), 34f.

14. Thus e.g. Weiler, *Kriege* (n.2), 96f.; H.Göttner-Abendroth does not mention El once.

15. J.Aistleitner, *Texte* (n.12), 41.

16. However, it has to be said that the texts, too, are not free from contradictions. Anat, who normally fights with and for Baal, can also oppose Baal's interests (cf. Kapelrud, *Goddess*, 115).

17. Aistleitner, *Texte*, 25f.; cf. also Anat's battle against Aqhat, with which we shall be concerned later.

18. Cf. James, *Cult* (n.11), 74f.

19. Aistleitner, *Texte*, 27.

20. See G.Weiler, *Kriege*, 5.

21. Kapelrud, *Goddess*, 101.

22. Aistleitner, *Texte*, 19.

23. Ibid., 52ff.

24. Feminists and indeed a number of male scholars take offence at these terms; some because they seem too derogatory, others because they seem too limited. The gods and goddesses are said to be lords of nature, 'life', generally. That seems to me to be pedantic, since fertility, life and death are indissolubly connected. Cf. the discussion between U.Cassuto, S.E.Loewenstamm and A.S.Kapelrud, *Israel Exploration Journal* 12/13, 1962/63.

25. Cf. H.Gollwitzer, *Das hohe Lied der Liebe*, 1978, 29.

26. Aistleitner, *Texte*, 60, 53.

27. Ibid., 56f.

28. E.M.Yamauchi, 'Cultic Prostitution. A Case Study in Cultural Diffusion', *Orient and Occident, FS C.H.Gordon*, ed. H.A.Hoffner Jr, 1973, 213ff. (214).

29. Ibid.

30. Ibid., 215.

31. According to E.Sorge that would be a patriarchal perspective, *Religion und Frau* (n.4), 76.

32. Weiler, *Kriege*, 307.

33. R.Otto, for example, uses the term 'numen' or 'numinous' to denote the specific form of the experience of the holy 'in contrast to the ethical model in its ambivalent aspects of anger and grace', *Brockhaus Enzyklopädie*, ^{17}1971, XIII, 606.

34. See n.13 above.

35. Aistleitner, *Texte*, 27.

36. Ibid., 26.

37. Ibid., 67ff. Cf. D.R.Hillers, 'The Bow of Aqhat', in *Orient und Occident* (n.28), 71ff.

38. H.Donner and W.Röllig, *Kanaanäische und aramäische Inschriften* II, *Kommentar*, 1964, 31 (Kilamuwa Inscription from Zinjirli, ninth century).

39. Ibid., and 37 (from Karatepe, eighth century); J.Gray, *Canaanites*, 107ff.

40. Schaeffer, *Cuneiform Texts* (n.11), 42ff.; for the source text see 86f.

41. H.A.Hoffner Jr, 'Incest, Sodomy and Bestiality in the Ancient Near East', in *Orient and Occident* (n.28), 81ff.

42. Gray, *Canaanites*, 138; Schaeffer, *Cuneiform Texts*, 59; this is attested by many inscriptions, see n.38.

43. Plato, *Symposium*, 195-7 (speech of Diotima).

44. Thus e.g. in Minucius Felix, *Octavius*.

45. Cf. e.g. *Partnerschaft: Liebe mit Verantwortung*, published by the Bundesministerium für Familie und Bundesministerium für Unterricht, Kunst und Sport, Vienna 1986 (the empirical sections).

46. For criticism of this model cf. A.Elsigan, *Sittlichkeit und Liebe*, 1972, 34ff.

47. Plato, *Symposium*, 176-80 (speech of Phaedrus). It is explicitly stressed here that even women can give up their lives for love.

48. Ibid., 202ff. (speech of Diotima).

49. Plato, *Phaedrus*, 249 BC.

50. Plato, *Symposium*, 202ff. (Socrates and Diotima); *Phaedrus*, 249.

51. Cf. A.Elsigan, *Sittlichkeit* (n.46), 55f.; G.Krüger, *Eros und Mythos bei Plato*, Klostermann Texte Philosophie (ed. R.Schaeffler), 1978.

52. Cf. Georges Bataille, *Eroticism*, 1984; also id., *Literature and Evil*, 1973; id., *Les larmes d'éros*, Paris 1981; Lou Andreas Salome, *Die Erotik*, 1979; D.O.Schmalstieg, 'Aber-aber... zur kritischen Funktion erotischer Literatur', in A.Grabner-Haider/K.Lüthi, *Der befreite Eros*, 1972, 60ff.; M.Treut, *Die grausame Frau, zum Frauenbild bei de Sade und Sacher-Masoch*, 1984; B.Sichtermann, *Weiblichkeit. Zur Politik des Privaten*, 1983; id., 'Krieg und Liebe – apropos Lysistrata', in *Lysistrata*, new translation by E.Fried, 1985, 9ff.

53. Sichtermann, *Weiblichkeit*, 36.

54. Bataille, *Eroticism*, 252.

55. Weiler, *Kriege* (n.2), 270, 306,309.

56. Gollwitzer, *Das hohe Lied* (n.25), 33, 35, 42.

57. In what follows I shall refer especially to Bataille and Sichtermann, since both see this problem clearly, even if in other respects they are not comparable.

58. Sichtermann, *Weiblichkeit*, 35.

59. Ibid., 39-40.
60. Ibid.
61. That is especially the case with the literary works of de Sade, somewhat less so with those of Bataille and Sacher-Masoch; the writings and films of Pasolini are also vulnerable here. Sichtermann mentions in this connection Oshima's film *In the Kingdom of the Senses*, which depicts the relationship between eroticism, cruelty and death (*Weiblichkeit*, 39f.).
62. Bataille, *Eroticism*, 263.
63. Sichtermann, *Lysistrata*, 10.
64. Ibid., 23.
65. Ibid., 13.
66. Ibid.
67. Ibid., 14.
68. Ibid., 15.
69. Tuli Kupferberg, 'Bayonet Drill', in *Schmalsteig*, 'Aber-aber' (n.52), 61.
70. M.Enigl, 'Warum muss ein Kind derart elendiglich verrecken?', article in the Austrian weekly *Profil*, 7, February 1986, 49f.
71. Cf. Bataille, *Larmes*, 162f.
72. Bataille, *Eroticism*, 236f.
73. Cf. Bataille's reminiscences in *Literature and Evil* and the biographical note by M.Luckow.
74. Sichtermann, *Weiblichkeit*, 42.
75. Sichtermann, *Lysistrata*, 12.
76. Bataille, *Eroticism*, 115.
77. Ibid., 118.
78. This principle is among the demands of Kant's 'categorical imperative' (*Foundation for the Metaphysic of Morality*).
79. At this point I cannot go more deeply into the question why that is particularly the case with the Roman Catholic church.
80. The fallacy of this argument lies in the thought that as nature is a 'good creation of God', human action is also *eo ipso* good in so far as it is orientated on the natural. The absurdity of this conclusion becomes particularly clear in the Roman Catholic prohibition of 'artificial' means of birth control. Whatever the means, it is a means, i.e. something that human beings decide to use on the basis of their freedom. So even 'natural' means of contraception are 'contrary to nature', as the free development of nature, i.e. the origination of a child, is hindered. Structurally this thinking is no different from that of Ernest Bornemann, who has in mind a sexuality free from moral restrictions and, as he supposes, therefore natural and 'innocent', as a way to 'improve the human race'.
81. Cf.M. Treut, *Die grausame Frau* (n.52).
82. Bataille, *Literature and Evil* (n.52), 235.
83. See my *Women and Early Christianity*, 131.
84. -There is a wealth of literature on this, e.g. M.Greiffenhagen (ed.), *Pfarrerskinder*, 1982; J.Richter, *Himmel, Hölle, Fegefeuer*, 1982; D.Scherf, *Der liebe Gott sieht alles*, 1984; see R.Dunde (ed.), *Vater im Himmel – Seine Söhne auf Erden*, 1986.
85. Sichtermann, *Lysistrata* (n.52), 20.
86. Ibid., 17-18.
87. Ibid., 13.
88. Sichtermann, *Weiblichkeit* (n.52), 40.
89. Ibid., 42.

90. One example from the Christian sphere is Buttlar's trio, named after its founder Eva M.von Buttlar (1670-1721), who was active particularly in Hessen.
91. Cf. R.A.Knox, *Enthusiasm*, Oxford University Press 1950.
92. I have not given any sources in the following account of the positions of Erasmus and Luther, but would refer to my article 'Erziehung in der Reformationszeit: Luther und Erasmus als Pädagogen', in *Europa in der Krise der Neuzeit*, ed. S.Heine, 1986, 129ff., where there are similar examples.
93. Ibid., 150.
94. Cf. the basic notion of the relationship between eating and love in the work of Gerard Neumann, e.g. 'Hungerkünstler und Menschenfresser', *Archiv für Kulturgeschichte*, ed. E.Boshof, 2, 1984, 347ff.; cf. also the eucharistic symbol in Dante's *Vita Nuova*, Chapter 3.
95. Cf. E.Bornemann, *Das Patriarchat*, 1975.
96. E.Heintel, *Grundriss der Dialektik* I, 1984, 72.

3. Matriarchy: The Lost Paradise

1. M.Janssen-Jurreit, *Sexismus. Über die Abtreibung der Frauenfrage*, 1976, 113.
2. H.Göttner-Abendroth, *Die Göttin und ihr Heros*, 1980, 11.
3. E.G.Davis, *The First Sex*, Dent 1973.
4. J.Schreier, *Göttinnen. Ihr Einfluss von der Urzeit bis zur Gegenwart*, ed.G.Meussling (1968), 1978. There was an English edition: *Goddesses*, New York 1948.
5. R.R.Ruether, *Sexism and God-Talk*, Beacon Press and SCM Press 1983, 55ff.; K.Lüthi, *Feminismus und Romantik*, 1985, 125ff.; for popular summaries see e.g. E.Moltmann-Wendel, *A Land Flowing with Milk and Honey*, SCM Press and Crossroad Publishing Company, 1985; E.Sorge, *Religion und Frau*, 1985; school books include *Zeiten, Völker und Kulturen. Lehrbuch der Geschichte und Sozialkunde für die Oberstufe der AHS* (5 Klasse), ed. E.Fijala and J.Mentschl, Vienna ²1973, 38.
6. Göttner-Abendroth, *Göttin* (n.2), 17-22.
7. R.Fester, 'Medias in res...', in R.Fester, M.E.P.König et al., *Weib und Macht. Fünf Millionen Jahre Urgeschichte der Frau*, 1979, 7ff., 30.
8. Göttner-Abendroth, *Göttin* (n.2), 15.
9. Davis, *First Sex*, 133, 121.
10. Ibid., 96.
11. Schreier, *Göttinen*, 37f.; here she refers above all to two works by Freud: New Introductory Lectures on Psychoanalysis and Mass Psychology and Ego Analysis.
12. Ibid., 38.
13. Ibid., 61f.; this argument also appears in Davis, without reference to Freud, *First Sex*, 37ff.
14. Ibid., 5, 8.
15. Ibid., 120.
16. Davis was a trained librarian and Schreier a trained photographer.
17. Davis, *First Sex*, 18.
18. Ibid., 351f.
19. Göttner-Abendroth, *Göttin*, 9.
20. Ibid., 8f.
21. G.Weiler, *Ich verwerfe im Lande die Kriege*, 1984, 30.

22. Ibid., 33.
23. Ibid., 372.
24. Ibid., 394.
25. Göttner-Abendroth, *Göttin*, 14.
26. Davis, *First Sex*, 76, for example, makes explicit use of this doubtful argument with a quotation from Erich Fromm: 'The violence of the antagonism against the theory of matriarchy arouses the suspicion that it is... based on an emotional prejudice against an assumption which so foreign to the thinking and feeling of our patriarchal culture..' After that, who would dare to express doubts? However, the argument should not be illegitimately generalized as though there were no psychologists who would look critically on such a simplification.
27. P.Watzlawick et al., *Menschliche Kommunikation. Formen, Störungen, Paradoxien*, ²1971, 82.
28. Schreier, *Göttinnen*, 5.
29. Ibid., 8.
30. Ibid., 7f.
31. Sorge, *Religion und Frau* (n.5), 60.
32. Cf. G.Schwarz, *Was Jesus wirklich sagte*, 1971, 60ff.; A.Anzenbacher, *Einführung in die Philosophie*, 1981, 203f.; H.Gehrke, *Theologie im Gesamtraum des Wirklichen*, 1981, 106ff., etc.
33. Cf. e.g. Weiler, *Kriege* (n.21), 112 etc.; Sorge, *Religion und Frau*, 27ff.; E.Pagels, *The Gnostic Gospels*, Penguin Books 1982: however, in a different way Ruether wants to argue from the 'working paradigm of some main trends of our consciousness', *Sexism and God-Talk*, 45.
34. Davis, *The First Sex*, 94.
35. Ibid., referring to Karen Horney.
36. Ibid., 95, with reference to Edward Carpenter.
37. This phrase is a variation on the title of a work by G.E.Lessing, *The Education of the Human Race* (1780).
38. Schreier, *Göttinnen*,38.
39. Ibid., 104.
40. Davis, *First Sex*, 95f.
41. Weiler, *Ich Verwerfe*, 394f.
42. U.Wesel, *Der Mythos vom Matriarchat*, 1980, 31.
43. Robert Graves (see the books listed in Ch.2 n.6); L.H.Morgan, *Die Urgesellschaft* (1908), 1976; Wilhelm Schmidt, *Das Mutterrecht*, 1955; R.Briffault, *The Mothers*, three vols., London 1926.
44. Johann Jakob Bachofen, *Das Mutterrecht*, 1 and 2, Gesammelte Werke 2 and 3, ed. Karl Meuli, 1948, 55.
45. Davis, *First Sex*, 36f.
46. Ibid., 148.
47. Once again to ward off possible misunderstandings: I mean this kind of popular feminism. By contrast Janssen-Jurreit, herself a feminist, is very sceptical about the matriarchal theses. Moreover the popular literature encourages sweeping verdicts by identifying matriarchal research with feminism.
48. E.Moltmann-Wendel, *A Land Flowing with Milk and Honey* (n.5), 45.
49. Bachofen, *Mutterrecht* (n.44), 1, 22f.
50. Ibid., 23.
51. Ibid., 22.
52. Ibid., 2, 925.
53. Ibid., 1, 24.

54. Ibid., 431.
55. Ibid., 283.
56. Ibid., 23f.
57. Anzenbacher, *Einführung* (n.32), 209.
58. Bachofen, *Mutterrecht*, 1, 38.
59. Ibid., 36.
60. Ibid.
61. Ibid., 37.
62. Ibid., 49.
63. Ibid., 134.
64. Ibid., 124f.
65. Ibid., 34.
66. Ibid., 35.
67. Ibid., 157, 163.
68. Ibid., 49, 134.
69. Ibid., 249.
70. Ibid., 54.
71. Ibid., 123.
72. Ibid., 123f.
73. Ibid., 432.
74. Ibid., 59.
75. Ibid., 468.
76. Ibid., 469.
77. Ibid., 2, 641.
78. F.Engels, *The Origin of the Family, Private Property and the State*, 1968.
79. A.Bebel, *Die Frau und der Sozialismus*, reprinted 1977, 557.
80. Ibid., 58f.
81. Ibid., 550.
82. Janssen-Jurreit, *Sexismus* (n.1), 118f.
83. W.Schmidt, *Mutterrecht* (n.43), 185.
84. Ibid., 27.
85. Ibid., 126.
86. E.Moltmann-Wendel, *Milk and Honey*, 44.
87. Bachofen, *Mutterrecht*, 26.
88. B.Wagner, *Zwischen Mythos und Realität. Die Frau in der frühgriechischen Gesellschaft*, 1982, 19.
89. Janssen-Jurreit, *Sexismus*, 130.
90. Cf.U.Wesel, *Mythos der Matriarchat* (n.42), 107ff.
91. Ibid., 117.
92. I.Illich, *Gender*, Marion Boyars 1983, 178.
93. B.Wagner, *Mythos und Realität* (see n.88), 34.
94. See the numerous examples in Wagner, *Mythos und Realität*; Wesel, *Matriarchat* (n.42).
95. Wagner, *Mythos und Realität*, 201.
96. Ibid., 67ff.
97. Ibid., 279f.
98. W.Schmidt, *Mutterrecht*, 128.
99. Illich, *Gender*, 179.
100. Ibid., 174.

4. Between Myth and Utopia

1. J.J.Bachofen, *Das Mutterrecht*, Gesammelte Werke, ed. K.Meuli, 2.1, 1948, 13, 27, etc.

2. Ibid., 30.

3. H.Göttner-Abendroth, 'Zur Methodologie der Frauenforschung am Beispiel einer Theorie des Matriarchats', in the proceedings of the conference on *Frauenforschung in den Sozialwissenschaften*, Deutsches Jugendinstitut Munich 1978, 10, 16.

4. In feminist literature the reference to this position (following e.g. the sociological model of E.Durkheim and M.Mauss) is more implicit than explicit.

5. K.Marx, *Critique of Hegel's 'Philosophy of Right'*, ed. J.O'Halley, Cambridge University Press 1970, 131.

6. Cf. e.g. H.Baumann, *Das doppelte Geschlecht*, 1955; B.Wagner, *Zwischen Mythos und Realität*, 1982; or also M.-L.Janssen-Jurreit, *Sexismus*, 1976 (chapters 6-8).

7. Peter Berger, *A Rumour of Angels*, Allen Lane 1970, 57.

8. Ibid., 65.

9. H.Göttner-Abendroth, 'Methodologie' (n.3), 2,7, etc. Under the heading 'Notes for Readers who have escaped the Decline of the West' (A critique of Spengler), the Austrian poet Robert Musil has some apt 'Comments on Intuition' (1921) which apply to this variant of feminist thought: 'For today it is the case that anyone who wants to assert something that he cannot prove or has not thought through sufficiently refers to intuition... people cannot say the most important things; they are sceptical to extremes... but amazingly credulous about all that occurs to them; they shoot only with blanks instead of with bullets; that is the clinical picture of the spirit which is softened by excessive continued enjoyment of intuition, the aesthetics of our time' (*Gesammelte Werke*, ed. A.Frise, 8, 1978, 1053, 1055).

10. Berger, *Rumour* (n.7), 62.

11. Ibid.

12. *Weiblichkeit in der Moderne. Ansätze feministischer Vernunftkritik*, ed. J.Conrad and U.Konnertz, 1986.

13. S.Schade, 'Cindy Sherman oder die Kunst der Verkleidung', in *Weiblichkeit in der Moderne*, 229ff., 238.

14. Ibid., 232.

15. Ibid., 128, 133.

16. Ibid., 238.

17. H.Göttner-Abendroth takes this course only in the illuminating statement: 'But after that it (= feminist scholarship) goes over into praxis', 'Methodologie', 7.

18. M.Detienne, 'Die skandalöse Mythologie', in *Faszination des Mythos*, ed. R.Schlesier, 1985, (13ff.) 13.

19. A general survey of the main arguments of the most important positions in the reception of myths is given on 100, 101. Cf. e.g. M.Frank, *Der kommende Gott. Vorlesungen über die Neue Mythologie*, 1, 1982; K.Hübner, *Die Wahrheit des Mythos*, 1985 (Chapter III); Jan de Vries, *Forschungsgeschichte der Mythologie*, 1961.

20. G.E.Lessing, *The Education of the Human Race*, in *Lessing's Theological Writings*, ed. H.Chadwick, A.& C.Black 1956, 96.

21. M.Horkheimer and T.W.Adorno, *Dialektik der Aufklärung*, ⁸1981, 1 (Preface).

22. Cf. R.Garaudy, *Der letzte Ausweg. Feminisierung der Gesellschaft*, 1962.

23. L.Klages, *Der kosmogonische Eros*, Sämtliche Werke, ed. E.Frauchiger et al., III, 1974, (355ff.) 391.

24. Ibid., 392.

25. Cf. the account in M.Frank, *Der kommende Gott* (n.19), 33; cf. further C.G.Jung, *Answer to Job*, Collected Works II ²1969, 458f., 461f.

26. See the argument in K.Hübner, *Wahrheit des Mythos* (n.19), 269.

27. See n.3.

28. Berger, *Rumour*, 52.

29. Frank, *Der kommende Gott*, 11, etc. A clearer distinction should be made as to whether this term relates to empirical reality or to the categories of experience (e.g. good and evil).

30. M.Eliade, *Myths, Dreams and Mysteries*, Fontana Books 1968, 201f., 209ff.

31. For the whole catalogue of questions see M.Eliade, *The Quest: History and Meaning in Religion*, University of Chicago Press 1969; H.Baumann, *Das doppelte Geschlecht* (n.6).

32. I gave a detailed definition of aetiology in *Women in Early Christianity*, 20f.

33. Cf. e.g. the discussion 'Mythos und Dogma' on the contribution by H. Blumenberg in *Terror und Spiel. Problem der Mythenrezeption*, ed. M.Fuhrmann, 1971, 527ff., 535f.

34. For the term 'attitude of mind' or 'disposition' as the productive consciousness cf. K.Heinrich, 'Die Funktion der Genealogie im Mythos', in *Parmenides und Jona*, 1966, 9ff. 11ff., etc.; for the basic problem see also W.Schmithals, *Die Apokalyptik*, 1973, 22ff.; Schmithals speaks of Daseinsverständnis.

35. Heinrich, *Parmenides und Jona*, (61ff.) 87.

36. K.Heinrich uses this term 'totter' in connection with the difficulty 'of saying no to the threat of nothingness which is manifest in loss of identity, speechlessness and the pull of self-destruction', op.cit., 68, etc.

37. Cf.Berger, *Rumour*, who means his terms to have wider application than the specific subject-matter of sociology, which I shall later call existentialia.

38. Thus K.Heinrich with reference to P.Tillich, W.F.Otto, K.Kerenyi, M.Eliade.

39. K.Heinrich, 'Funktion der Genealogie' (n.34), 12.

40. Ibid., 13f. M.R.Svilar, *Denn das Dunkel ist heilig*, Europäische Hochschulschriften 24, 1976, has also noted the substantial degree of anxiety.

41. K.Heinrich, op.cit., 14.

42. Ibid., 15.

43. R.Schlesier, *Faszination* (n.18), 9 (Preface).

44. B.Gladigow, 'Mythische Experimente – experimentelle Mythen', in *Faszination* (n.18), 61ff., 68, 79 etc.

45. K.Heinrich, op.cit., 22.

46. R.Schlesier, *Faszination*, 10 (preface).

47. Ibid.

48. Robert Graves, *The Greek Myths*, Penguin Books ²1960, 18.

49. A.Aurnhammer, *Androgynie. Studien zu einem Motiv in der europäischen Literatur*, Vienna 1986, 2.

50. Cf. M.Eliade, *Longing* (n.31), 158f.

51. Nicole Loraux, 'Herakles: Der Über-Mann und das Weibliche', in *Faszination*, 267ff. As emerges from the study, no variant of love is alien to Heracles. H.Baumann, *Das Doppelte Geschlecht*, gives a wealth of examples for possible ritual enactments of the the androgyny theme.

52. J.Bollack/P.Judet de La Combe, 'Der Mythos zur Schau gestellt', in *Faszination*, 145ff., 152, 155ff.

53. Graves, *Greek Myths*, 18.

54. E.g. M.-A.Macciocchi points to the close connection between the feminine maternal and the feminine demonic in Fascism in her book *Jungfrauen, Mütter und ein Führer*, ²1978, 80ff.

55. N.Loraux, 'Herakles' (n.51), 168.

56. I.Illich, *Gender*.

57. Even the great Protestant theologian Karl Barth is not free from this: on the one hand he speaks very aptly of the relationship between the sexes as an exemplary sphere of cohumanity; on the other hand he stresses that the human being exists only as male and female and derives the pre-eminence of the male from that (*Church Dogmatics* III.4, § 54).

58. Hegel, cited with commentary in A.Anzenbacher, *Einführung in die Philosophie*, Linz 1981, 209.

59. Aristotle, cited with a commentary in E.Heintel, ' "Herr aller Dinge, Knecht aller Dinge." Zum Begriff der Freiheit in philosophischer und theologischer Hinsicht', in *Sprache und Begriff. Festschrift für B.Leibrucks*, 1974, 122ff.: Bert Brecht, too, has the dialectic of freedom and real conditions as one of his central themes, e.g. in the stories of Herr Keuner: measures against power.

60. E.Moltmann-Wendel, 'Wir sind bei Gott, weil wir bei uns selbst sind', *Deutsches Allgemeines Sonntagsblatt* 7, February 1987, 16.

61. Cf.the Platonic dialogues *Symposium* (Diotima) and *Menexenos* (Aspasia).

62. Cf. K.Heinrich, 'Der Floss der Medusa', in *Faszination*, 335ff.

63. K.Heinrich works out very well the difference between myth and the idea of the covenant or that between hatred and anger (see n.35).

64. Cf. especially C.Boff, *Theology and Praxis*, Orbis Books 1987, and the works of Paulo Freire.

65. E.Moltmann-Wendel, 'Wir sind bei Gott' (n.60).

66. H.Gehrke, *Theologie im Gesamtraum des Wirklichen*, Vienna 1981, 156.

67. The formulation of this dialectic, 'in the light of a context of "contradictory sentences"', is typical of Luther (see n.59, Heintel 130).

5. Jesus Christus, Jesa Christa

1. K. Marti, *Leichenreden*, 1969, 45f.

2. E.Eggimann, *Kontakt*, October 1972, 11f.

3. Luther, Greater Catechism, explanation of the first commandment.

4. M.Luther, *De servo arbitrio*, in *Luther and Erasmus*, ed. E.G.Rupp and A.N.Marlow, Library of Christian Classics 17, SCM Press and Westminster Press 1969 (also contains Erasmus, *De libero arbitrio*).

5. Ibid.

6. I.Kant, *On Pedagogy*.

7. J.Sprenger and H.Institoris, *Malleus Maleficarum* (Hammer of the Witches), 1486, ed. J.W.A.Schmidt, 1, 1920, 106f.

8. Paul Tillich, *Systematic Theology* 3, University of Chicago Press 1963, reissued SCM Press 1978, 102.

Conclusion

1. Robert Musil, *The Man without Qualities*, Volume 1, Secker and Warburg 1953, 295.

2. Ibid., 15.

3. Ibid., 17.

4. Ibid., 70.

5. Ibid,. 73.

6. Ibid., 72.

7. Ibid., 69.

8. Ibid., 67.

9. Ibid., 180.

10. Georg Simmel, *Philosophische Kultur, Gesammelte Essais*, (1923) 1926. All the quotations come from the article 'Zur Philosophie der Geschlechter', 64ff.

11. Cf. ibid., 16 (Preface by Jürgen Habermas).

12. Barbara Sichtermann, 'Schwule Musen', *Die Zeit* 45, 31 October 1986, 49f.

13. Ibid., 50.

14. *F.D.E.Schleiermacher in Selbstzeugnissen und Bilddokumenten*, dargestellt von F.W.Kantzenbach ²1974, 72.

15. Elga Sorge, *Religion und Frau*, 1983. I have been unable to take account of the second edition which appeared recently and is again sold out.

16. Umberto Eco, 'Die Struktur des schlechten Geschmacks', in *Apokalyptiker und Integrierte. Zur kritischen Kritik der Massenkultur*, 1984, 39ff., 67ff.

17. Ibid., 64.

18. Ibid., 65f.

19. Ibid., 68.

20. Ibid., 71.

21. Helga Pross, 'Kitsch oder nicht Kitsch?' in *Kitsch. Soziale und politische Aspekte einer Geschmacksfrage*, ed. H.Pross, 19ff., 25, with a reference to K.M.Michel.

22. Ibid.

23. Umberto Eco, 'Die erzählerischen Strukturen im Werk Ian Flemings', in *Apokalyptik und Integrierte*, 273ff., 297.

24. Pross, *Kitsch*, 26.

25. Musil, *Man without Qualities* (n.1), 67.

26. I.Bachmann, 'Literatur als Utopie', in *Frankfurter Vorlesungen*, 1980, 79ff., 89/90.

27. Ibid., 92.

28. Ibid.

29. Ibid., 94.

30. Ibid., 95.

31. Ibid., 89.

32. Ibid., 95: the passage quoted comes from René Char. However, I have changed the sentence and replaced the word 'poet' of whom Char is speaking with the word 'believer'. This seems to me to be possible because of the affinity between poetry and faith, even if Char does not explicitly include the future in the sense of Christian futurist eschatology.

Index

Sarah,
with an H

Also by Hadley Irwin

Jim-Dandy

The Original Freddie Ackerman

Can't Hear You Listening

So Long at the Fair

Kim/Kimi

Abby, My Love

Sarah, with an H

Hadley Irwin

MARGARET K. McELDERRY BOOKS

Margaret K. McElderry Books
An imprint of Simon & Schuster Children's Publishing Division
1230 Avenue of the Americas
New York, NY 10020

Book design by Michael Nelson
The text of this book was set in Berkeley Book
Printed and bound in the United States of America

First Edition
10 9 8 7 6 5 4 3 2 1

Library of Congress Cataloging-in-Publication Data
Irwin, Hadley.
Sarah with an H / Hadley Irwin.—1st ed.
p.   cm.
Summary: When a bright, talented Jewish girl moves to the small town
of LaMond, her presence brings significant changes and evokes subtle
prejudices in the local inhabitants.
ISBN 0-689-80949-2
[1. Anti-Semitism—Fiction. 2. Prejudices—Fiction.
3. Jews—United States—Fiction.] I. Title.
PZ7.I712Sar   1996
[Fic]—dc20
95-52559
CIP
AC

*In memory of Lee Hadley,
who loved words*

Contents

Instant Replay

I was caught in a dream, enough awake to know I was dreaming, enough asleep to want to know what happened next. I heard the crows that spent the night roosting in the trees outside my dormitory wake and begin their insistent cawing at the dawn. I heard the rustle of their wings and the shudder of tree limbs as the birds, hundreds of them, beat skyward from the college town to forage in fields a few miles away. The harshness of their calls and the flapping of their wings became the sound of my sneakers as I ran up Downer's Hill.

In my dream I was in high school again, taking my early morning run from our house at the edge of Lake Ulmer across Main Street and then up to Hill House. If I could have chosen my ideal home, it would have been that house—faded red brick overlooking the town, its

pillars glistening white in the morning sun, its silhouette the last to fade in the darkening twilight.

I was asleep enough to dream and awake enough to know I didn't want to live again what happened the year Sarah-with-an-H came to live in Hill House.

Tip Off

"That's my seat." She had velvet-black hair, eyes the color I'd always wanted, pierced ears, and clothes that didn't come from a discount store.

"Oh. I'm sorry."

She didn't sound very sorry.

Just then Mrs. Crawford, our homeroom teacher, appeared with her seating chart in hand and motioned the new girl to the desk behind me. "Your name is Sarah, isn't it?" Her smile switched on and off.

"Yes. Sarah. With an H. Irvine."

I hadn't known about the "H," but everyone in town knew about the Irvines. They'd moved from Chicago to open the new Handy Harry's Hardware and Appliance Store on Main Street. It was the only chain store ever located in LaMond.

The classroom was filling up, and just when the tardy

bell rang, Muffie Barnes walked through the door as if she were making a guest appearance on TV. I figured the shorts and top she was wearing must be new and she wanted to make sure everyone got a good look. Muffie was my friend. I liked her, but I didn't always like how she acted. And she acted a lot. We'd known each other from the first day of kindergarten when she borrowed my new poppy-red crayon and wouldn't give it back. Instead, she made me take her broken dusty-gray. I guess Muffie was just someone I'd gotten used to. Maybe that's what friends are.

As it was, we ran around with the same kids and were both out for basketball, and that made us special at LaMond High.

After roll call and announcements from the loud-speaker, Mrs. Crawford, as if she were conferring some kind of honor, asked, "Marti, why don't you take Sarah to her classes this morning and make sure she finds her way around? You two have almost the same schedule."

I looked across at Muffie. She crinkled her nose and rolled her eyes.

"Is that all right, Marti?"

"Okay." I slumped in my seat. I could feel the new girl's eyes on my neck as if she were trying to read the label inside my shirt. I reached around and tucked the label farther down. Mom had picked the shirt off the clearance rack at the Save-It-All store in Boyer. I glanced at Muffie again. She was grinning the way she always did when she pretended I'd fouled her in basketball practice when I hadn't even touched her, but the coach called me for it anyway.

4

"Why me?" I mouthed across to Muffie. "You come too."

"Can't."

"Why?"

"Because."

"Because why?"

"Just because."

I gave up. Muffie never had a straight answer. She always argued in dead ends.

Sarah-with-an-H followed me out into the hall.

"Where's the first class?" There was something different about the way she talked. It wasn't the words; it was the way she said them.

"Mr. Hawley's room. History," I answered, trying to ignore the kids staring at us as I hurried down the hall.

"American history?" She took an extra step and caught up with me.

"Iowa history."

"Isn't Iowa part of America?" She sounded as if she was laughing at me.

"I didn't mean that. I mean we're spending two weeks on what Hawley calls 'our heritage.' He said that by the same token we have to write a paper about something in LaMond's history that is memorable as well as influences who we are."

We'd reached Hawley's room when she asked, "Did you ever wonder what 'by the same token' means? It sounds like what you need to get on a bus."

"There aren't any buses in LaMond except school buses and they don't take tokens."

"But you just said it."

"Did I?"

"I think"—and her face screwed up as if she really was thinking—"people use words like that to make their sentences longer than they need to be."

I didn't answer because as we walked into the classroom the chatter quieted down. I led her up to Hawley's desk and said, "This is Sarah-with-an-H Irvine," and left her standing alone.

I slapped my notebook down on my desk and pulled out my pen. Hawley stuck Sarah at a desk in the back of the room. At least she couldn't read my clothes labels from there.

"What I'm looking for in this assignment," Hawley began, "as I explained in detail earlier this semester, is some careful research and creative treatment of the ethno-cultural environment of LaMond, past or present."

"I don't understand what 'ethno-cultural environment' means," Muffie said in that suck-up voice she always used with teachers.

It was enough to set Hawley off.

"'Ethno' or 'ethnic,' if you prefer, has to do with people of one cultural group. People classed according to a common religious, tribal, linguistic—that's language, Muffie—heritage. Or a common national or cultural background. So perhaps you will want to define the people of LaMond and how its culture has affected you—or some historical figure of the town. The possibilities are limitless."

Hawley's explanation went on for the rest of the

period. Once, I glanced over my shoulder at Sarah. She was looking at me and when our eyes met, she smiled just as if we'd known each other forever and were friends! I felt the corners of my own mouth start to grin back, but I turned away. It wasn't that I didn't like her. I didn't even know her, but I wasn't going to get suckered into instant pal-dom just because she was new in town.

Evidently my not smiling back didn't matter because Sarah was still talking to me as we made our way to the next class. Since it was only three doors away, we didn't have to hurry.

"Does he always use that many words?" she asked.

"Only when you ask him a question," I said.

"Have you got an idea for your paper?"

"Not yet. I'll probably work on it Sunday. English is next—Ms. Hansen's class— and it's a lot better. And a lot harder."

"Great!" Sarah sounded honestly excited. "I love English."

I thought of telling her that at LaMond High, it was definitely cheesy to like anything about school. Then I decided she could find that out for herself. I was going to suggest that she walk on into the room since she couldn't possibly get lost on her way through the door, when Jason came loping down the hall with Chaz two steps behind.

"Yo, Marti," Jason said, glancing at me but focusing on Sarah.

Jason was a genuine hunk—tall, blond, with a great

bod that drew girls to football games by the car loads. He'd lettered in every sport LaMond High offered, been voted Homecoming King twice, and was president of the Student Council. Muffie practically salivated every time she saw him. She wasn't alone.

Chaz, on the other hand, wasn't exactly ugly, but close enough to make him look like an undernourished raccoon. He was smarter than anyone else in school, but he had slick, no-color hair, ears that stuck out, and an Adam's apple that moved when he talked.

Automatically I assumed my role as appointed care-taker with, "This is Sarah-with-an-H."

"What a coincidence," Jason said, grinning down at her. "That happens to be my name too."

I groaned. Jason would do anything to impress a girl. Sarah looked puzzled. I shrugged. I didn't think she really got the joke, though.

"Don't listen to him," Chaz broke in. "He's really Jason—with an S, and I'm Chaz—with a Z."

"You three sound like alphabet soup," I said, attempting a funny, but no one heard me. Jason was standing as if posing to have his picture taken. Chaz looked as if he'd seen a dream come alive, and Sarah was smiling at both of them. Her teeth were as perfect as the rest of her.

"Tell you what . . ." Jason began, touching her arm, but whatever he was going to say was lost in the clang-ing of the warning bell.

"Come on," I ordered. "Nobody's late for Hansen's class. Ever!" I shoved her toward the teacher's desk and collapsed in my assigned seat. I was tired of explaining

how to spell Sarah, and I wondered how I could avoid herding her through the lunch line with me.

"Okay," I said when class was over, "now it's time for the pits. Biology with Frog-Face Phelps."

Sarah pulled out her schedule card and scanned it. "No. Look."

I did, but what I noticed were her fingernails. Perfection again—not chewed and ragged like mine. I concentrated on where she was pointing. "Chemistry! How come you're taking chemistry? That's for seniors. It must be a mistake."

"I don't think so, Marti." She glanced at me sideways like she was apologizing. "I took double science courses last year. Biology was one of them. But maybe you could tell me where to go."

I thought of at least one good answer, but I didn't use it. Instead, I pointed toward Jason and Chaz, who were standing at the end of the hall. "Just follow them," I said and turned in the other direction. I didn't look back.

Biology class ran late as it usually did because Phelps could almost always think of one more thing to say about frogs or worms or whatever disgusting thing we were slicing up. I thought he scheduled the class before lunch on purpose.

"I saved you a seat," Muffie called as I walked into the lunchroom. "What do you think?"

"About what?" Muffie always started conversations before her brain clicked in.

"Her! You know. Sarah-with-an-H."

"She's okay, I guess. We didn't talk much."

"I don't like her."

I took a swallow of orange juice and opened my bag of chips. "Why not?"

"She acts so stuck up. I was going to ask her to sit with us, but . . ." Muffie scanned the lunchroom. "And didn't you notice in Hansen's class? She not only knew all the answers, she knew the questions before Hansen asked them."

"I'll bet her clothes come from Marshall Field's." Cindy, our senior starter on the LaMond Tigerette basketball team, chimed in. Cindy told anyone who would listen that she was going to college to major in *haute couture*. I didn't think she was smart enough to spell it, let alone major in it.

"I heard they have piles of money. Do they, Muffie?" Angie played guard and it was a constant toss-up whether she'd beat out Muffie for a starting spot.

"Well, I don't know if they're rich." Muffie leaned forward and lowered her voice. "But they are definitely well off. They didn't borrow any money from Dad to remodel Hill House." It wasn't easy to forget that Muffie's father owned the town bank. She turned back to me. "What did she say? What did she talk about?"

I tried to remember. "She has kind of a Chicago accent. And she's had biology. She's in chemistry."

"Weird." Angie raised her eyebrow.

"She'll be sorry," Cindy said. "I almost didn't get through it last semester."

"Do you suppose she plays basketball?" Liz Fisher finally opened her mouth to do something besides put food in it. "I mean with Cindy graduating, we're getting short on depth."

We all nodded. Liz's coordination was not what you could call graceful, but she took up a lot of space under the basket. It took at least three good dribbles to get around her. "Did you ask her, Mart?"

Liz was the only person who called me that and I hated it. I'd never told her. Liz guarded me in practice and she could do a lot of physical damage when she was upset.

"Monday, Liz. I'll ask her Monday. I don't think she's into sports, though. She has perfect nails."

"Manicure!" Cindy was triumphant. "Anyone who buys her clothes at Marshall Field's would have manicures."

I joined Muffie in scanning the lunchroom. "I wonder why she didn't show up here. Maybe she went home for lunch."

We all laughed. The only kids who went home for lunch were losers or still in elementary school. Some of the seniors—if they had cars and money—drove down to the Sail-Inn Truck Stop.

Liz looked up from her empty plate. "Wherever she went, it was with Jason and Chaz. I saw them leave the building together."

I tried to swallow but the chip stuck in my throat. No one said anything. Then Liz looked across at Angie. Angie sneaked a sideways glance at Muffie. Muffie set her Pepsi can down with a bang. "Talk about nerve! If she thinks she can horn in—" Muffie looked around at all of us as if taking a vote—"that JAP has another think coming."

"JAP?" Liz almost shouted. "I thought she was a Jew!"

"It's an acumen."

"A what?" Liz stopped in mid-chew.

"It's where a letter stands for the real word. JAP stands for 'Jewish American Princess' . . ." Muffie emphasized each word as if she were translating from a foreign language.

"It's 'acronym'—" I tried to tell Muffie, but the others stood up and started walking out of the cafeteria.

I sat alone for a while. I didn't like how the word "Jew" was making me feel. Suspicious, somehow. The word made Sarah different . . . not one of us . . . one who, if given a chance, would try to take over and run everything. But then, nobody put me on a committee to change the world, so I wadded up my potato chip bag and slammed a one-hander into the trash.

After lunch we usually hung out around Muffie's locker—because it was on the way to the boys' room.

"After all," Muffie explained once, "you have to be where they are if you want them to notice you." Muffie had a way of staring at you through half-closed eyes and making you believe what she was saying.

That day we stood around waiting until the last minute to go to the next class. Halls were emptying and, as I was congratulating myself for being done with guide duty, striding down the hall between a grinning Jason and a nonchalant Chaz came Sarah-with-an-H.

The guys ducked around the corner without saying a word. Muffie and Liz disappeared down the hall in the opposite direction. Cindy and the rest floated off as if wafted by a sudden gust of wind.

"Where do we go next?" Her "we" stuck in my ears.

"It's free period. I'll show you the library."

I left her there alone and headed for the student lounge. I figured that next hour she could find the gym by herself.

After school was out, Muffie latched on to me and we hurried out of the building before Sarah showed up. It wasn't friendly, but she wasn't one of us so I didn't owe her anything.

When we reached the corner of Muffie's block she said, "Come home with me. We can shoot some baskets or play one-on-one."

"I've got that stupid paper to write for Hawley."

"Mine's done." Muffie fluffed her hair. "All I have to do is print it."

"What did you write about?"

"Girls' basketball at LaMond High in the 1920s. My great-grandmother played with the team. There wasn't much to say, so I had to fill in by listing the wins over the years. But to get to eight pages I had to list the losses too."

I should have gone home and started my paper, but after herding Sarah around all day, I wanted to forget my "ethno-cultural environment," my grades, homework, and school in general. "Why not?" I agreed.

We were walking up Muffie's drive when she grabbed my arm. "Here comes Sarah-with-an-H. Don't look. Pretend you don't see her." She jogged toward the house.

I started to follow, but something made me turn around. Maybe it was guilt. I waved and said the first

thing that wandered into my mind. "How was the rest of your day?"

I felt my neck getting red because I wasn't sure which was worse—ignoring her or pretending I cared about her day—so I kept talking. "We're going to shoot some baskets. Want to join us?"

"Sure. It sounds like fun."

Muffie came around the corner bouncing the basketball and stopped in mid-dribble. "Well, hi. Do you play ball? Catch!" Muffie threw a bullet pass at Sarah. That was one thing about Muffie. She was a good ball handler.

Talk about peripheral vision! Sarah caught the ball, dribbled around Muffie before she could move, and sank a one-handed bank shot.

"I guess you've played before," I said like an idiot.

"Some." She grinned and tossed the ball to Muffie, who still hadn't moved.

"Are you going to try out for the team next fall?" Muffie's voice sounded as if it belonged to someone else.

"Come on," I said. "Throw me the ball. We can play two-on-one and rotate."

Sarah moved between me and the basket. She'd played "some" all right! She never took her eyes off the ball and blocked the first two of my shots without fouling me.

She was almost as good a shooter as she was a guard, but both Muffie and I picked up on the moment of hesitation she sometimes took before a shot and were able to knock the ball away.

As for Muffie, she'd been okay with six-girl basket-

ball when all she had to do was guard, but next year, with a five-girl team when she'd have to play both ends of the court and make points as well as wave her arms around, she'd be in trouble.

It was an hour later before we stopped.

"I have to go," Sarah finally said as she sank a sure three-pointer from the farthest edge of the drive. "This has been fun."

She was in good shape, not even out of breath. "And you two are really good. You must have been playing all your lives."

"Since grade school," I said. "Mom got me started. She played when she went to school at LaMond High."

"Marti's one of the top scorers in the state. After next year she'll get a scholarship to any school she wants." Muffie tucked the ball under one arm. "Did you play six-girl basketball at your school?"

"Five," Sarah answered. "I played on the JV team. I was lucky. There was a lot of competition and I'm not a natural. I have to work hard at it. Grades are easier than basketball."

Muffie and I looked at each other. Muffie worked for the C's she got, which, she figured, would be high enough for her after-high-school ambition to be a television weatherperson. I scrabbled for the A's and B's I got that would help a lot at college if I could pull a scholarship.

"Are you going out for the team?" Muffie asked again.

"I may. The coach talked to me about it after gym class today."

"Have you heard about Basketball Camp?" I asked.

Muffie's look could have wilted a thistle.

"It's really important if you want to go out for the team," I babbled on. "It's right here in LaMond in August after Summer Karnival, and the girls come from all over the state."

Sarah started walking away, then half turned toward us. "Coach Carlson invited me today. I told her I'd think it over. You make it sound like such a good idea, I guess I'll sign up. Thanks for telling me, Marti."

Muffie watched until Sarah headed up the street to Hill House. "Sure hope she's not a guard. Why did you have to tell her about Camp? She's too good already."

I turned to leave. "I don't know," I said. "I was just making conversation."

But that wasn't it. Maybe I'd mentioned it because I'd thought it was too late for her to possibly get in. Was that why? Sometimes the hardest questions to answer are the ones you ask yourself.

I turned down the street toward home. Our town began with Sarah's Hill House on Downer's Hill and ended with our little house perched on the backwater bay of Lake Ulmer.

I always wondered why Cyrus LaMond, when he founded the town, built his house on the hill instead of down by the lake where he could watch canvasback ducks and Canadian geese and pelicans drop in every spring on their way north and again every fall on their way south.

That's when I got the idea for the paper. I'd write about Cyrus LaMond and how he founded the town and

how he ordered the bricks for his house brought clear over from Mortonville by wagons pulled by four-horse hitches. Sometimes you get the best ideas when you're not thinking. Maybe it's because the rest of your body is so busy walking and your head is just riding along, not worrying about anything.

Mom was home, but she wasn't cooking. She had kicked off her shoes and was sitting at the kitchen table wearing the little sailor hat and plastic name tag that were part of her uniform at the Sail-Inn Truck Stop. "Verda's sick and I'll have to work her shift. You'll have to help me out. We shouldn't be too busy and maybe Barney will close early."

I'd practically grown up at the Sail-Inn. From the time I was in junior high, I'd helped out by clearing the tables and the counter. "Do I have to?"

"No, but . . ." She looked like she should take a nap instead of head back to work.

"Okay, but do I have to wear that dumb sailor hat?"

"I guess not. Anything new at school today?"

I doubted that Sarah would like being called a "thing," but she *was* new. "The Irvine kid showed up. She's Sarah-with-an-H. She's in my grade."

"What's she like?" Mom wiggled her feet back into her shoes.

"She's . . . kind of different, but she's okay, I guess. She plays basketball. Where she came from they had five-girl teams."

"Good." Mom stood up and smoothed her skirt. "Coach Carlson should be happy to have her go out for

basketball. Come on. We'd better get moving."

Mom backed our car out of the drive and headed for Main Street. She called our old Chevy "Silas" because, she said, it was prone to falling into a catatonic fit and stopping right in the middle of traffic. Mom said she named it after a book called *Silas Marner* that she'd read in high school. In fact, she made me read it so I'd understand. I didn't like it, but Mom said it was a classic and that if kids didn't get a good background in literature like that, all books might disappear some day. I think, if given the chance, Mom would have revised the entire school system, reorganized the government, and restructured the whole world.

Barney tore off his apron as soon as we walked in the door. It was his bowling night down at Maple Grove, so Mom and I were left to run the Sail-Inn by ourselves.

Bud Newby and his carpentry crew lined the counter. Bud grew up in LaMond building corncribs with his dad, but when cribs went out of use, he shifted to building and remodeling houses. That's probably why his houses looked like corncribs. One thing about him, though—his work might not be pretty, but it was hammered together so solidly that it'd never fall apart. Mom called him LaMond's Frank Lloyd Wrong.

Mom grabbed the coffeepot and began filling all the guys' cups. It was "bottomless coffee cup" night at the Sail-Inn. I started clearing the counters of dirty dishes and wiping up spilled catsup and smeared mustard blobs.

"Take Hill House," Bud was saying as he spooned sugar into his coffee. "Would you believe them pillars were full of

termites? And the whole dern house had settled. Roll a marble across that floor and it wouldn't stop till it hit the south wall. And then that Irvine fella insisted on covering the roof with shakes! Real shakes, mind you! Any fool knows shakes don't last in LaMond. Something about the lake. They shrivel in summer, crack in winter. We put them on. Nothing harder on a man's knees than laying shakes."

"Cost him a pretty penny too—that roof." I hadn't noticed Muffie's dad sitting on the other side of Bud Newby. "Speaking of houses, Bud, have you heard any reaction against our development plan for the south shore?"

"Just Elva Beals." Bud stirred his coffee thoughtfully. "She sits up there in The Home and writes letters against it to everyone she knows. Newspapers too! Hear she's getting the State Conservation Board riled up about our taking over that shoreline and moving the road back."

"Elva was the town librarian so long, she thinks she's the mayor," Muffie's father said. "She's been sticking her nose into everything since I was born. She'll stir up a little fuss about how we're robbing fishermen of access to the lake, but it won't amount to much."

"Well." Bud sipped his coffee. "I'd sure hate to lose out on all the new houses that'll go up there. We got all the shares sold, haven't we?"

"Just two left and they'll go. That Irvine fellow might be interested." Barnes stared down into his coffee cup. "We're having a little trouble getting clear title, though. I've got a lawyer working on it. I figure it's practically a done deal."

"Fella ought to be able to get at least ten new houses out there." Bud gazed up at the ceiling as if he were actually plating the lots and filling them with hip-roofed houses that looked like corncribs. "Well, keep me posted, man." Bud stood, hitched up his Big Boy jeans, and gave one of his crew a slap on the back. "Flip you for the bill, kid."

The "kid" looked older than Bud. "Sure."

The kid lost. Bud walked over to the cash register and slapped the bill down in front of Mom. "Hi, beautiful. The kid's paying tonight."

"Thank you, Bud," Mom said without looking up.

"The only trouble with Bud Newby," she once told me, "is that he's obnoxious, but he doesn't know it. He can't even do something wrong, right."

Mom's hope that we might be able to close early slowly faded as Mr. Barnes continued to sit alone with his coffee cup, which Mom kept filling and he kept acknowledging with a "Thanks, Marge." Hope faded completely when a stranger walked in.

"Working late tonight, Mr. Irvine?" Mom asked as if he was one of the usual Sail-Inn customers.

"Oh, yes. A truckload of new merchandise came through. It took a lot of moving and rearranging."

Mr. Barnes looked up and motioned at the empty stool next to him. "Come on over and sit down, Bob. I was just thinking of a little opportunity you might be interested in."

"Our special is pie—apple, cherry, or lemon—and it's bottomless coffee cup night." Mom filled a glass of water

and grabbed a napkin roll of silverware.

"No coffee, Marge. Just a glass of milk with apple pie, please."

I busied myself cleaning up the booths. So this was Sarah H's dad. He was tall, blond, blue-eyed, and looked like he'd just stepped out of a J. Crew catalog. Mom hurried around dishing out a piece of pie and pouring a glass full of milk from the carton in the refrigerator.

After another cup of coffee Mr. Barnes finally stood up and I wondered if he'd been trying to sell Mr. Irvine a share in his Lake Ulmer Development Association. He slipped a dime under his empty coffee cup, walked over to the cash register, and paid his bill with a "Good night, Marge."

Mr. Irvine left a fifty-cent tip.

That night before I went to sleep I looked out of my bedroom window at Hill House. I saw a light on the second floor and wondered, just for a minute, what Sarah H thought of her first day at LaMond High.

After breakfast the next morning, I shot baskets for an hour as I usually did unless it was too dark to see or too cold to hold on to the ball. Then, when I couldn't put if off any longer, I headed to the town library. Hawley had said he wanted a bibliography with the paper and the library seemed a logical spot to begin.

I was lucky. For once the place was empty. Usually, on weekends during the school year and almost any day in the summer, Marvia had her library crammed with little kids for story hour or read-your-eyes-out projects.

The rest of the time it was full of discussion groups or writing clubs sitting around talking. I didn't see how she had time to put all the books back where they belonged.

In the entryway I stopped as I often did in front of the bisque doll display—a collection of antique dolls in a glass case. Dressed in clothes of satin or lace, they peered out with shiny eyes that had given me nightmares when I was little.

Of all the dolls, the one that had always frightened and fascinated me most stood alone on the top shelf— Bebe Jumeau. I must have been four or five when I first saw her at one of Elva Beals' Kiddy Hours. I was sitting on the floor with the other kids when the doll came walking toward me with an awful jerky motion that was almost, but not quite, human.

Her hair was real, and her eyes, unearthly blue, moved in time with her body. The doll's face was white and smooth and her mouth was open as if she were going to speak. I know now that Elva, who was the librarian back then, was behind her, manipulating the walking mechanism and the mama-papa pull cords that gave her a voice. All I knew then was that Bebe Jumeau stopped in front of me, lifted her arms, and said, in a rusty, unused voice, "Mama, mama, mama."

I was still screaming when Mom rescued me.

Even now I felt the doll's eyes following me as I walked toward Marvia. Before I could open my mouth, Marvia said, "Sorry, Marti, but no, every book even vaguely relating to the history of LaMond has been

checked out. Sarah Irvine took the only one I had left last night."

It wasn't fair! She'd just found out about the assignment yesterday and she hadn't even waited to begin. "What am I going to do? It's really important. . . ."

Marvia smiled and patted my arm. "I don't know what your topic is, but you have two choices—oral history from people who remember the past, someone like Elva Beals—or basics like the cemetery and street names and buildings. You'll have to use your imagination."

My imagination started with strangling Sarah H. Then I decided that a trip to the cemetery was a better idea. I could get at least a page out of describing Cyrus LaMond's grave, two pages maybe, if I went into detail. After that there'd be time to go to The Home and talk to Elva.

The gate to the cemetery was never closed. I always wondered why they bothered with a fence and a gate anyway. Who was going to leave? Muffie and I used to have an elaborate game when we were little kids that involved carrying on long conversations with some of the people who were buried there. Our favorite spot was the Smythe grave with its polished, white marble statue of a lady, her hands outstretched over all the other Smythes, only someone had broken off one hand so that her arm looked like a baseball bat.

"Hello, Elroy," I said, half whispering to the nearest grave. "It's a great day. Sorry you can't enjoy it. And Enid, how's it going?"

That none of the Smythes answered didn't bother

me. If they couldn't spell their name right, they wouldn't be much help with the paper.

"Did you know them when they were alive?"

I whirled around. Sarah was standing there watching me. She wasn't laughing at me, but she looked like she might.

"Of course not. But I figure if you're stuck in Hope Cemetery, you need all the extra hope you can get. I'm just doing my part." I tried to sound sarcastic.

She nodded as if she took me seriously and pointed at the statue. "Who is that supposed to be?"

"I don't know. I call her Hope, like the cemetery."

Sarah stepped across Elroy and Enid to look up at her. "Her eyes are blank."

"What's there to look at?" I said. "I think she's lonely. She's the only statue in town."

"Then maybe you should call her Hopeless."

It wasn't very polite, but I was curious, so I asked, "What are you doing here?"

"The history paper. I'm writing about Cyrus LaMond and he's buried here . . . somewhere."

My mouth dropped open. I tried to change my gasp into a cough, but it didn't sound much like one. It felt like someone had stolen the ball from me on my way to a winning basket. Sarah had taken *my* idea for *my* paper! The LaMonds were part of *my* history, not hers. Watching her, I remembered something Bud Newby had said about her folks—"pushy." It seemed to fit Sarah.

Sarah turned away from the statue. "It's funny to think all these people were alive once. There's so much

to know about them and if someone remembers, then they're not quite so dead. The assignment makes sense, doesn't it?"

I almost agreed because she made it sound so logical. Her words mixed with the breeze as it rippled the tops of the tall oaks throwing patterns of sun and shade down on us.

"Do you realize that you're standing on Arthur?" I sounded as if the cemetery belonged to me.

"Arthur who?"

"Arthur Smythe. He was killed in some war and you're stepping on him."

"Is that what the little flags are for?"

"He didn't have any, so one day I borrowed some from around and stuck them here."

She looked at me and smiled. "See? That's what I mean. At least you think about him. Are you writing your paper about him? It's a great idea. You could call it 'Lest We Forget.'"

"I don't think there's enough about Arthur to fill eight pages. The only time he got out of LaMond was to join the army, and he caught the measles and died three weeks later. Can you imagine anything dumber than dying from measles?"

"Maybe you could make up a history for him, Arthur, I mean, and let him die heroically. That could be a really creative paper and I'll bet Mr. Hawley would like it."

"Is that what you're doing with old man LaMond?" I asked.

She sat down on the grass and leafed through a note-

book. "I don't have to. He was really interesting. He built our house before there was even a town. And he invented a lightning rod before anyone else ever thought of it by running wires from stove pipes on the roof to the ground. It even worked. Somebody else got the patent, though."

I'd heard most of it all before, but Sarah made it sound like a story about someone who'd been a real person, not just a name.

"There was another man," Sarah went on, "named Fred Ulmer who wanted the town to have *his* name, but after Hill House was built, Cyrus LaMond took a team and a plow and made a big furrow right down the hill from his house to the lake and called it Main Street and since he made the first street, nobody could argue with him! Fred got to name the lake, though."

She'd probably taken that last book from the library and run home to read it clear through. Bud Newby was right. She *was* pushy.

"You've got your paper practically written." I tried to sound complimentary.

"Not quite, Marti. Perhaps you could help me find . . ." She looked as if she was seriously considering something, and then went on. "Marti, could you help me find where Mr. LaMond's buried? For a small town, this is a pretty big cemetery."

"The cemetery's big because most of these people were born here and this is as far away as they got." Since she'd taken my paper topic and already knew a whole lot more about Cyrus LaMond than I did, showing her

where he was located couldn't make things worse. "Come on," I said, "you couldn't miss it."

Next to Hill House and the angel statue, the LaMond mausoleum was the fanciest thing in town. It was in the oldest part of the cemetery in the middle of a bunch of scraggy pine trees that must have been growing there before there was a town.

"Ugly!" Sarah said when she saw it. "How could he have such a nice house and such an ugly place to be buried?"

I tried to see it with her eyes. I was so used to it, I'd never really thought about what it looked like. She was right. It was a square, squat marble lump with wrought iron bars across the door and what would have been windows if they hadn't been filled with cement.

"Maybe his wife built it," I said.

"Nope," Sarah answered. "She died when she was only forty-five. That was in 1879. He lived until 1900."

"Did you get all that stuff from the book?" If I'd been to the library first, my paper would have been as good as written too.

"Mostly the dates and facts. The really interesting parts, the stories, most of what I'm going to use in my paper, I learned just today. Marvia calls it 'oral history.' She sent me to see someone at the nursing home."

I knew the answer, but I asked anyway. "Who did you talk to?"

"A woman named Elva Beals. She used to be a librarian and she knows enough history for a dozen papers."

"Elva Beals," I repeated.

"She's really interesting, Marti."

She used my name as if we were lifelong friends.

"She told me all about the lake and how it had an ancient wall of rocks along the shoreline until early settlers carried them off to make foundations for their houses. Now, she said, there's a Development Association that's trying to get the county to move the paved road back so they can build a bunch of houses on the lakeshore and close off public access. She's trying to stop them."

"Yeah," I muttered. "I heard about it. The developers will probably win, though."

"I don't know." She sat on Sadie Parker's headstone. "Elva says she has a trump card she hasn't played yet. It's funny. Do people in little towns like LaMond always take sides and fight about things like that?"

"Most of the time all of us think the same way." She was criticizing LaMond and she'd only just moved here!

I left Sarah sitting on Sadie's headstone, jotting down dates of births, marriages, and deaths of every LaMond listed in marble on the mausoleum. She didn't even notice when I left. I walked toward Main Street marveling how she could have stolen my idea. She'd even stolen Elva Beals.

I stopped in front of the library trying to decide what to do next. Then, as if something had made me stop, the idea came. I'd write about the dolls!

I didn't have to waste Elva Beals after all. She'd told us all about the history of the dolls—all I had to do was remember. Besides, there was a pamphlet

about them—if Marvia could find it.

A couple of hours later and I had all the material I needed. I did have a little trouble at first tying the dolls to my "ethno-cultural environment," but I finally pointed out, in my conclusion, that my intense interest in French art and history had sprung from these dolls in our local library. It wasn't true, but it fit and provided a nice little personal touch that I was sure Hawley would love.

We got our papers back the next Friday.

"Can you believe it?" Muffie almost shouted as she caught up with me. "Hawley gave her an A."

We had fallen in the habit of saying "her" or "she" instead of using Sarah's name.

"Plus! An A plus!" I reminded her. "He's never given anyone an A plus in his life until now."

"What did you get?"

Muffie knew very well what I'd got. I'd seen her look when Hawley handed back my paper.

"B," I replied, trying to sound as if the grade meant nothing to me.

"No plus?"

"No plus!"

I didn't bother to ask what she got. I'd seen the C before she tore off the corner of her cover sheet.

"And he even read her whole paper out loud. I thought if it was history it had to be facts, not a bunch of stories put together. And did you see the gold chain she was wearing? I'll bet it was eighteen karat."

"I didn't notice." I'd been too busy looking at her amethyst ring that I could have died for.

It was just too much. Not many people moved to LaMond. Most people graduated from high school and just stayed around, so when someone like the Irvines came and opened up a fancy store on Main Street and bought the oldest house in town, it was upsetting. And then to have Sarah be a sure threat in basketball and pull the top grade in class for a paper that was my original idea . . . not that I was jealous.

At home, when I walked in the back door, the kitchen looked as if a gang of thieves had stopped in the act of carrying away everything we owned. I knew without asking. It was Mom's turn to entertain the Atheneums, the only club in LaMond that she belonged to, and that was only because her mother had been a charter member. No one knew for sure what the Atheneums did except meet and eat—desserts mostly.

"I made out a list," Mom said, climbing down from the kitchen counter.

The list started with lightbulbs, ran past brass polish, around four C batteries, and ended with a belt for the vacuum. "You should be able to get everything at Handy Harry's. Just tell Helen Irvine to put it on my account."

"Since when do we have an account there?"

"Since they opened the store. Since they're the only hardware store in town. And since they need all the business they can get." She gave me a one-arm hug, both hands full of wet, dirty paper towels.

I wanted to tell her that if the Irvines were like their

daughter, they certainly didn't need any support. In less than two weeks, she'd practically taken over the school, including Mr. Hawley, Jason, and Chaz.

"Oh," Mom went on. "Barney Wilkin called. He wants you to work the four-to-nine shift at the Sail-Inn this summer. Just weekends."

"Oh," I said in return. It wasn't an enthusiastic "oh."

"It'll add to the college fund," she said as if I needed reminding. "And don't forget—those weekend campers do leave good tips."

"Maybe Quik-Stop would have this stuff," I suggested, looking over Mom's list.

"Why would you go there?"

"I just thought we ought to use hometown people."

"Why? Aren't the Irvines hometown people now?"

"I suppose, but they're . . ."

"They're what?" Mom dropped her voice two notches. Some mothers raised their voices when they got upset. Mom always lowered hers to a half-whisper.

"Well, they're different."

"Different from . . . ?" Mom waited.

"From us." It was not the right answer. Mom's face told me that.

"Handy Harry's," Mom said. "Now scoot. I need those things."

I scooted.

On sunny days, LaMond looked like one of those small towns you see profiled on TV by somebody who lives in New York City and drives around the country

once a year looking for local color. Our town might not have a lot of history or future, but it didn't matter because we had Lake Ulmer. It was always a thrill, after we'd been down to the neighboring town of Maple Grove, to come up over a little rise, and there, stretching ahead, was the lake, tucked in between cornfields, where no lake should have been.

That was another thing about LaMond: No one used directions like south and north and east and west. Instead they went "down to" Maple Grove, "up to" Great Bend, "over to" Boyer, and "back over" to Regina. Right now, though, it was "up to" Handy Harry's.

The Irvines' store occupied the oldest building on Main Street, but they'd remodeled the front so with its big, new display window, it looked like a store at the mall, even down to the HELP WANTED sign.

As I stepped inside, I could tell it was new just by its smell. Most of the stores in town were musty, as if dampness from the lake had seeped through their walls. The Irvines' smelled of fresh paint, and cinnamon from the rack of scented candles on the wall next to the front door. I picked up one of the little plastic baskets stacked on the floor and started down Mom's list.

By the time I finished and walked back to the cash register, I had to stand in line. It didn't take long. In LaMond, two people make a line. I didn't mind because it gave me time to look at Mrs. Irvine. She wasn't as tall as I was, but then neither were most women I knew, and she was too pretty to be anybody's mother—even Sarah's.

When it was my turn, I set the basket in front of

her. "Please put these on my mom's account. Marge Sullivan."

She stopped punching prices on the cash register and looked up at me, smiling as if I were special. "You're Marti."

"Sure," I answered.

"Sarah's new friend. She's told me about you and how nice you've been—introducing her to your friends. Helping her at school."

I had trouble moving my eyes to meet hers.

"It's made a difference, you know. She misses the kids she knew in Evanston."

"I thought you came from Chicago."

"Well," she laughed a little laugh as if she were apologizing for something, "Evanston's a suburb. She tells me you're a fine basketball player." She finished ringing up the things I'd bought. "You're helping her feel at home here."

There's nothing worse than having someone think you've been nice when you haven't intended to be. "Sarah wrote a really good paper for history." It was the only thing I could think of to say. "Mr. Hawley read it to all of us."

"I know. Her dad and I were proud of her, and besides it helped us all to know more about the town and the house. You must come home with Sarah sometime and see how we've restored it."

"That would be nice," I answered.

"Come soon, then." She smiled at me. "Shalom, Marti."

"Shalom?"

"It's a lovely word, isn't it? It means 'peace,' and we use it to say hello or good-bye."

I took the slick new biodegradable bag—new in LaMond—mumbled a thank-you, and walked out of the store.

"Sarah's new friend!" I could still hear the soft pleasure in Mrs. Irvine's voice. I wondered if Sarah had lied to her mother, or if somehow, she actually believed it herself.

What do you do when you've been given a friend you don't want or need?

Personal Foul

School was finally out for the summer and we were seniors. No matter how peaceful the rest of the year was, LaMond sprang to life in the summer. Kids on bikes headed for the swimming beach. Marvia lured little kids to her story hour and enrolled them, one by one, in her Summer Reading Program with T-shirts for prizes stating, I'M PROUD TO BE A BOOKWORM. Wispy, white-haired people settled on the lake's floating dock to fish and talk. The pickup trucks on Main Street were clean and shiny.

In June, when farmers had corn and soybeans planted, the town sponsored Polka Daze at the Moose Lodge. July was really full: the Karp-Katching Kontest and then Lake Ulmer Summer Water Karnival. That included the Lake Ulmer Miss Teenage Pageant with its $500 first prize and ended with the Parade of Water Floats. August meant Basketball Camp.

Sarah with an H

It was after Polka Daze when I called Muffie to see if she wanted to bike around the lake with me. "We really ought to jog," I told her, "to get in shape for camp, but it's too hot."

"It's the tenth of July," she said. "Haven't you looked at the calendar?"

I looked. "All I see is a large ten."

"Marti, use your brain. It's just a week until the pageant and I have to get ready for it."

I thought of pointing out that she'd been in the contest for the past two years without winning, but I didn't. "How are you going to get ready? Work on your suntan?"

"Of course. And I need every bit of time to let my nails grow, and I have to practice walking and besides"— she sounded worried—"there's the talent segment and I'll have to rehearse."

In her other two tries for the title, Muffie's talent had been skipping rope to a recording of "Stars and Stripes Forever."

"Why?" I asked. "Are you going to change the music this year?"

"I'm doing something new." She took a deep breath and whispered, "You've got to swear not to tell a living soul. It's going to be a complete surprise."

I couldn't think of anyone who would be interested, but I said, "I swear. I swear."

"I'm going to do a pantomime of"—her voice got back to normal—"of being a television weather girl on the five o'clock news! I'm making charts and everything. I do it all to taped music."

I could tell she was waiting for me to gasp, so I tried, and added, "Wow."

"It may not mean anything to you, Marti. You'll be going to college, but those of us in entertainment need all the exposure we can get."

"You won't be wearing any clothes?" Muffie didn't get my joke. "Promise me one thing. When you get to be a weatherperson on national TV, don't stand in front of our state on your map and block it out. Stand in front of somebody else's state."

"I promise," she answered, "but I have to go now."

She hung up and I decided to take a bike ride anyway.

Although the lake was only three miles across, the road around it was about eight miles, mostly level and empty of traffic until later in the summer. Today there were only a few walkers, older women mostly, and the usual clumps of people fishing, their territory established by lawn chairs, picnic baskets, bait pails, and extra rods. I wondered where they'd go if Mr. Barnes got his development.

About three-quarters of the way around the lake, the road dipped closer to the shore and the State Park began. I turned off and followed the gravel lane leading through a grove of river birch to a scattering of picnic tables overlooking the lake. The only sounds came from the lapping of water on the beach, the wind stirring the high tree branches, and red-winged blackbirds calling to each other.

Someone, back toward me, sat on top of my favorite table, the one closest to the lake. When I got nearer, I

saw it was Sarah H, and wondered why out of all the places she might be, she had to be sitting on *my* table.

She heard my bike tires on the gravel and turned toward me. "Hi," she said and smiled as if we'd made plans to get together that morning and I was right on time.

I found myself smiling back and, since there was no way I could just pedal off in the other direction, I propped the bike on its kickstand and sat on the other end of the table. "Out for a run?" I asked. Her hair was damp with sweat and curled in little wisps around her face. On her, it looked good. On me, it would look messy.

"Just once around the lake. I was kind of checking it out before the Summer Karnival. Are you going on the run? We could do it together."

"No way!" She'd never seen those hundreds of people in Nikes and shorts pounding around the lake. If you stumbled and fell, they wouldn't be able to scrape you up until next week. "I'll stick to the Karp Kontest. It's safer." I watched a gull swoop across the inlet. "Is your folks' store going to have a float in the water parade?"

She shook her head. "Not this year. They didn't know about it in time and besides, we don't have a boat. How about the place your mom works? Will they?"

"Sure. The same one they have every year—Bud Newby's pontoon boat and a big sign that says DON'T JUST DROP IN, SAIL INN. It's awful, but it doesn't cost much."

"Mom said you were in the store one afternoon." Sarah glanced at me and then looked away. "Did she make a big fuss over you? I mean, she's great, but

sometimes she comes on too strong."

I knew exactly what Sarah meant. My mom could make me shrivel when she told someone about the basketball games I'd played. She always made it sound as if I were the only person on the team. "Mothers," I said and shrugged. I was glad I hadn't told Muffie and the others that, according to Mrs. Irvine, I was Sarah's best friend.

She must have picked up on what I was thinking because she said, "Mom and Dad really love it here, but they're afraid I miss my old friends."

"Do you?" I asked. I'd never been away from LaMond long enough to miss anyone.

"Of course." She frowned. "Wouldn't you if you moved away from here? Wouldn't you miss Muffie and Liz and all the others? When you move to a new place, you know who you are, but nobody else does, so you have to start being yourself all over again and nobody but you really cares."

Since the only reason I'd ever leave LaMond was to go to college, her questions didn't make a whole lot of sense. So what I said was, "I guess it takes a while to fit in."

"That's what I tell Mom."

I had never thought before what it might be like to be an outsider in LaMond. I hadn't done anything to make her feel that way, but I hadn't made it any better either. Still, I wasn't about to offer myself as buddy of the year.

I hopped off the table and got on my bike after making a big deal of looking at my watch. "I've got to go. Come over some time and we'll shoot baskets," I added,

and then because I felt something I couldn't name, I went on, "and tell your mom 'hi' from me."

I pedaled slowly down the road. I didn't have to go, but it was the best excuse I could come up with. It doesn't feel good when you discover you're really not as nice as you always thought you were. So I started thinking about something else, but there wasn't much to think about except the Karnival. What with Muffie busy rehearsing for the pageant and Sarah already checking out every step of the eight-mile run, maybe I *should* enter the Karp Kontest—again.

I'd tried my luck every year since I was big enough to hold a fishing rod, and the only prize I'd ever won was for the youngest fisherman—and I was a girl! Of course, I reasoned, as I pedaled up the hill before coasting down into town, there was no way to rehearse catching carp, but it wouldn't hurt to know more about them. Coach Carlson always said half of winning was knowing your competitor's weaknesses. Certainly carp had weaknesses, especially if one was lugging around a thousand-dollar tag on one fin!

By the next weekend, the Lake Ulmer Summer Water Karnival would transform the town. The Donald Shows from over to Boyer would set up a midway running from the post office clear down Main Street to the lakeshore park: Ferris wheel, loop-the-loop, shooting gallery, ringtoss, Guess-Your-Weight. Besides all that, there'd be the Round-the-Lake run, swimming matches, canoe races, a waterskiing competition, bingo games, and local food stands serving homemade pie and ice cream. For two whole days, LaMond would be aglow with

so many colored lights, you'd forget when day turned into night.

"Better than Broadway," Bud Newby boasted down at the Sail-Inn, although the closest he'd ever been to Broadway was when he missed a turn in Dubuque and found himself across the Mississippi headed east with no place to turn around.

The crowning event was always the Lake Ulmer Miss Teenage Pageant. The trouble was, though, that no girl from LaMond had ever won it. I knew I didn't have a chance, so I never tried.

The Karp Kontest was different. Whoever caught the tagged carp that Emil Clay secretly slipped into the lake in the morning took home a thousand dollars. I had plenty of time for what Mr. Hawley called "research." A few days before the contest, I studied up on carp in every book Marvia suggested.

"*Cyprinus carpio,*" I read, "feeds on the muddy bottom on water plants and small animal life. It hibernates in the winter and requires no food." That was interesting, but not very helpful. The stuff I'd found about bait was lots better.

"Hey, Marti! What are you up to?"

It was Sarah with an armful of books.

"Research," I said, pointing to the big C on the spine of the encyclopedia. "C is for carp, even if we spell it with a K in LaMond like we do everything about the Karnival. It's a tradition."

She sat down across from me and stacked her books on the table.

"Poetry?" I asked, looking at the cover of the one on top.

"Yes. I'm looking for a poem to memorize."

"Why do you want to memorize a poem?"

"For the Lake Ulmer Miss Teenage Pageant," she said.

"I thought you were going to enter the Round-the-Lake run."

"That's in the morning. The other thing is in the evening. It was Mom's idea—a way of getting to know more kids my age. But I think the talent part will be fun."

I wondered if I should tell her what the Kontest Kommittee had in mind when they said "talent"—tap dancing, acrobatics, baton-twirling and, once in a while, a xylophone.

"I haven't decided for sure which one, but I'm thinking of Amy Lowell's 'Patterns.'"

"I don't believe I know that one," I said, as if Amy and I were old friends.

"It has a dramatic last line, only really, it's a question." She looked up toward the ceiling and said in an angry voice, "Christ! What are patterns for?"

I was glad we were the only ones besides Marvia in the library. I could almost hear the hoots of laughter she'd get if she recited something like that, but I didn't tell her. Instead, I said, "You should get the judges' attention."

Walking home I tried to understand why I'd said that. When it came to Sarah, I couldn't figure *me* out.

I didn't think about it very long because I had a lot of things to do. I had to go to the Conservation Officer's post and get a depth map of the lake, and I needed the solunar tables out of the newspaper to check out the best

time of day for fishing. Most of all, I had to make dough balls for carp bait.

The dough balls took not only time but ingredients.

Cornmeal, dry raspberry Jell-O, olive oil, vanilla, and peanut butter—I mixed them all together and rolled them in little balls the size, one book said, would fit in a carp's mouth. Carp didn't have teeth in their mouths, just in their throats, which made size a little hard to figure. Then I biked out to Liz's farm to buy some sweet corn for bait just in case dough balls didn't work.

By Friday morning's seven o'clock starting siren, I'd be ready.

The carp weren't!

I sat, pole in hand, forefinger on the line to catch the first tremor of a carp nosing my dough ball, but nothing happened even though the solunar table said fish would bite. Morning dragged on to high noon and all I caught was a bullhead and a tiny catfish; noon drifted into afternoon. At two o'clock, I decided carp were a lot more intelligent than the people who fished for them. I reeled in my line and went home, defeated.

Sarah, though, won her class in the run around the lake. As I trudged past the platform where prizes were given, she was receiving a medal tied on a red ribbon. I kept on walking.

The Lake Ulmer Miss Teenage Pageant took place on the same temporary stage set up between the mud-volleyball arena and the Test-Your-Strength machine that came with the Donald Shows. By seven o'clock when I

got there, the lawn in front of the stage was filled with people in lawn chairs and whole families sprawling on blankets.

The first contestant was already onstage. It was some girl from down at Maple Grove who did a tap dance while twisting balloons into shapes that looked sort of like animals. She got a lot of applause from the Maple Grove people.

This year there were ten contestants and I skipped most of them by watching the audience. Jason and Chaz were leaning against a tree next to the stage and I wondered if they were there because of Sarah or because of Muffie.

When Muffie's name came over the loudspeaker, I started paying attention. For a full ten minutes of "talent time," she pulled out charts, pointed at diagrams, and ended by plastering handfuls of smiley faces that were supposed to look like sunshine all over a map of our county. All the while, the tape recorder offstage blasted out "the rockets' red glare, the bombs bursting in air" played by the LaMond High School Marching Band.

The LaMond people clapped and whistled and cheered.

I knew Sarah was next and last on the program. Part of me wanted to leave before she made an idiot of herself. Part of me was ready to laugh.

There was a little stir in the audience and a few giggles when she walked onstage wearing some kind of old-fashioned long dress that looked like it was made out

of the same material that covered Mom's fancy brocaded chair. Once Sarah opened her mouth and got started on the poem, the giggles stopped and everyone leaned forward, really listening.

It didn't sound as much like a poem as it did a story, or maybe a play. I don't know whether that was because of the poet or because of the way Sarah said the words, but for a little while, I really believed that she was a grown woman thinking about her lover as she walked through a garden, even though Sarah didn't really move much. When we found out that the man she was going to marry had been killed in some war, there was a little gasp from all of us.

After the last line—"Christ! What are patterns for?"—it was so quiet that all you could hear were sounds from the midway. When people began clapping, you could tell they really meant it, even the ones from down at Maple Grove.

Sarah was the first person from LaMond to win the title and the $500. Muffie came in second for the third time.

When I saw her the next day Muffie had things all figured out. "Anybody could win with a sexy poem like that and she even got away with swearing at the end! Of course, one of *them* wouldn't care if they took His name in vain."

I didn't ask her who "them" was. I knew what she meant.

Mr. Hawley told us once that there were signposts

marking off the great events in history, and if we learned them, we could always place the past in its proper order. After Summer Karnival, my signposts said nothing but SAIL-INN TRUCK STOP on them. Four until nine every Friday, every Saturday, and every Sunday I wore my little sailor outfit and became Marti, swabbie first-class.

It was a hot July evening. Bud Newby was sitting in his usual spot at the end of the counter next to the homemade pie display along with Muffie's dad and Rudy, our town garbage man, even though the sign on his truck said SANITATION SERVICE. In spite of the heat, they were drinking coffee. The second cup was free if you ordered either a hot beef sandwich or a piece of pie. It was pie this evening.

"Two cherries and an apple," Mom said as she served the men and refilled their coffee cups. I started clearing dirty dishes from the booths that lined the café.

"Didn't even have a float in the parade. Did you notice?" Bud slurped a loud sip of his coffee.

"They're only interested in turning a profit." Rudy attacked his pie as if he were wielding a pitchfork.

"And keeping it," Mr. Barnes added, wiping the clean fork Mom had given him with his napkin.

"Yep," Bud Newby added. "Let one in and pretty soon you got a whole Main Street full of cut rates."

"What did you think of the girl—reciting that poem and winning?" Rudy slumped low over the counter, cradling his arms around his plate.

I met Mom as I pushed my way through the swinging door that led to the kitchen. She shook her head and

muttered, "Can you believe what you're hearing?" I stopped inside to listen.

"It wasn't a poem I'd ever let my daughter recite in public," Mr. Barnes announced.

"She didn't learn any of that stuff here in our high school," Bud said as I came back through the door carrying a stack of clean coffee cups. "It's those liberals back East telling us how to run our schools. That plus the government giving all that money to those Jews in Israel. Like pounding dirt down a rat hole."

Mom was standing at the end of the counter and I could tell by the muscle twitching in her jaw that she was fighting a losing battle with her mouth.

"Yep." Rudy scraped up the last bit of pie with the side of his fork. "We don't need any of those ideas here in LaMond any more than we need kikes."

Muffie's dad folded his paper napkin as if it were pure linen and placed it beside his empty plate. "The girl memorized the whole piece. Did you notice?"

"Then why was she holding that piece of paper as if it wasn't all written down for her?" Bud laughed. "You got to get up early to beat a hebe."

Mom had moved closer to them as if their words were pulling her against her will.

"Who picked the judge and where'd she come from?"

"The wife said Marvia got her." The way Mr. Barnes said "the wife" made it sound as if Lois Barnes belonged to somebody he didn't know very well.

"It figures," grunted Bud. "Probably one of those college profs who don't have no idea what LaMond's about."

"Another member of the tribe, I bet." Rudy laid down his fork. "They stick together, you know."

Mom motioned for me to collect the empty plates and gather the cups while she added up their checks. Her face was almost white except for a bright red spot on either cheek. She slapped the checks down in from of them, pulled off her sailor hat and her name tag, dropped them on the counter, turned and yelled to the kitchen, "Barney, get the cash register. I quit."

The men sat, mouths open, staring at her until she faced them. Her voice was low. "Rudy, you are culturally deprived, and you, Bud, are culturally depraved. And you, Mr. Barnes, ought to be ashamed of yourself because I am ashamed to be in the same room with you."

She spun around and was out the door before they could move.

I was so surprised and embarrassed that I sidled into the kitchen and waited until the men left before I followed Mom home.

I didn't jog; I walked—slowly, trying to sort out what had just happened. One thing was sure: Everyone in town would know about it by noon the next day. It wasn't as if Mom had worked at the Sail-Inn for fun. Aside from the income from a few investments Dad had made before he died, Mom's salary was the only real money we had.

I guess what bothered me most was the anger I'd seen on her face. I knew she could get mad, but that was about stuff she saw on TV news or maybe something she read in the newspaper. Except for the land deal to change

the road around the lake, she'd never been upset with anything that happened in LaMond.

"Did the roof sail off the Sail-Inn?" she asked as I ambled into the kitchen. Her face was the right color again, and from her voice you couldn't tell that she'd quit the job that bought our groceries.

"Barney wasn't mad or anything," I told her. "I think he thinks you didn't really mean it. That it was just premenstrual syndrome or something." I knew I sounded hopeful, but I couldn't help it.

Mom picked up the glass of lemonade she'd been staring at when I walked in, took a sip, and made a face. "I have a syndrome all right, an antistupidity syndrome. Didn't you understand what they were saying?"

I sat down across the table from her. "Sure. It wasn't very nice, but it was just a bunch of words. Don't you remember what you used to tell me? 'Sticks and stones . . .'"

"In this case, it's not just the words, though they're unforgivable. It's the hatred behind them."

"Mom," I said as reasonably as I could, "you didn't have to quit. Not just because of the Irvines."

She shook her head very slowly, and when she spoke, her voice was soft. "Marti, you really don't understand, do you? It's not just because of the Irvines, it's because of you and me and this town we live in." She rubbed her forehead as if she were trying to erase something. "Why do you think we moved back here to live after your father died?"

Since I'd been only a baby at the time, it wasn't a case of "moving back." This was the only place I'd ever

known. "I guess because you grew up here and Grandma left you this house and because you didn't have anywhere else to go."

"Honey, we had the world to choose from. It would have been harder somewhere else, but we could have managed. We came here because LaMond is a small town, a good town where people are honest and care about each other. A town where you could grow up safely and not be touched by all the rotten things that happen every day, everywhere."

I began to get impatient. We had a major money problem, I was going to have to face Muffie and the other kids, and Mom was talking about stuff that didn't matter.

"And so?" I asked.

"And so that's probably why the Irvines chose LaMond."

It was like we were speaking two different languages. "But your job," I said. One of us had to be practical.

Mom stood up and stretched. "Marti, don't worry. It'll be okay, I promise. They always need help at The Home, or maybe the bank." She half grinned. "Well, maybe not the bank. Everything will work out. Now, let's get to bed. We'll talk some more in the morning. Remember, tomorrow's a whole new day."

We gave each other a good-night hug leaving a whole lot of things unsaid, at least on my part. That night I didn't bother to look out my window to see if there was a lighted window on the second floor of Hill House.

I knew Mom was pleased the next morning when I

told her that I too was sailing out of the Sail-Inn. I think she thought it had to do with a matter of principle. It didn't. I was so embarrassed for her that I couldn't go back and face those men ever again. She didn't waste any time discovering something else for me to do.

She called Gladys Payne and Gladys called Wanda Jenkins and Wanda called Jean Meyer at The Home and Jean called me. "My niece from over to Boyer is going on vacation. Would you like to fill in for her?" Two other girls had applied for the job, but I had it without even trying. "That's the thing about living in LaMond," Gladys said. "We take care of our own."

"What will I have to do?" I asked Mom.

"They'll probably start you with the book cart. Just help out wherever they put you and remember to smile."

A few mornings later, I wasn't smiling as I walked past Hill House on my way to work wearing the "white slacks, light-colored blouse, and happy face" the instructions from The Home insisted on. The clothes were easy. The happy face was something else.

And it was all because of the Irvines.

I stepped into the large reception room with a lounge at one end and a dining room at the other with an office between. As I waited for someone to appear, I read the motto on the desk. HOME IS WHERE THE HEART IS. If that was true, I was definitely not at home in The Home.

"May I help you?" A face smiled across the counter at me.

By lunchtime I had received all my instructions along with a tour of the entire home plus a vivid

description of each floor. "Pastel colors and lovely wall-paper in every room. Days full of activities. Plenty of room for treasures and special things. Residential suites available."

Fully instructed, I took my magazine and book cart and started down the Rosewood Wing out to the Sunshine Parlor.

"I'm Marti. Would you like a book? Or maybe you might like a magazine?" I said to the first lady I saw. She was staring out the window.

Without looking at me, she said, "No. I would not like a magazine. I would *like* to go home."

I moved on with my cart.

I was supposed to ask everyone, so I approached another sitter who wasn't doing anything. I decided on a new sales pitch. "What book would you like to read?" I asked, pulling out three books so she could choose.

"I don't know," she said in a voice that didn't sound as if it had been used recently.

"Maybe you have a favorite book or author. If I don't have it, I can get it for you from the library."

"I never had time to read. Now that I have, the words don't mean much."

At least she seemed a little interested, so I went on as my instructions had instructed. "If you could have any book you wanted, right now, what would it be?"

She closed her eyes and smiled. *"Black Beauty.* It's a lovely story about a talking horse."

"I'm afraid I don't have that one," I said.

"The horse thinks, too," she said. "It's so real."

"Maybe I could get it for you," I suggested. "I'll check the library."

I didn't get rid of any books or magazines that first run, even though I covered all the wings and the lounge as well.

"They like it better when Marvia comes up in her van and takes them down to the library. She either reads to them or has them read something they've written," the office girl informed me.

I didn't have a chance against competition like that, so I parked my cart and headed to the kitchen to help carry food trays. Food was easier to get rid of than books.

It was a few days later when I found Elva's suite. I knew it was hers because, at The Home, the residents' pictures were posted above their names next to their doorways. I guess it helped remind them which room was theirs. The door was open when I knocked, but no one answered, so I walked in anyway with the fresh towels it was my job to deliver that morning.

Her room was different from the others I'd been in. For one thing, it was in the "retirement wing," which basically meant she lived there from choice rather than necessity. She had the rooms to herself even though they were big enough for two people. The main thing, though, it wasn't stuffed full. Most people seemed to have brought with them everything they could cram into whatever space they had—overstuffed chairs, footstools, floor lamps, table lamps, tables with little

crocheted mats draped over any bare spot.

Elva's suite was something else. Two skinny leather chairs were sleek but still looked comfortable, and the rest of the furniture was made of smooth, light-colored wood. There wasn't a doily in sight, but on a wide work-table was a word processor and a printer—better than anything we had at the high school.

I did the towel switch and left before I was tempted to turn on the word processor just to see what might pop up.

It wasn't until the next day that I saw *her*. She sat by herself in the lounge reading a newspaper. I walked up and said, "Mrs. Beals, do you know who I am?"

She lowered the paper and looked at me over the top of her reading glasses. "No, my dear, but if you ask one of the nurses, perhaps she can tell you."

I didn't know whether she was being funny or being senile, and my face must have showed it because she folded the paper and leaned forward.

"Of course I know who you are, Marti. And even if I didn't recognize you, I'd have to be deaf not to have heard you're working here for a while. Word of anything different gets around fast." She chuckled and added, "Almost as fast as news gets around LaMond."

"What news?" I asked, trying to sound casual, but I could feel my face flushing. If people here knew about Mom's big scene, then so did everyone else in town.

"About your chances of being a top scorer next year. About Sarah Irvine's winning the Pageant. About the Barnes girl coming in second. Poor child." She chuckled and added, "Of course, I take credit for Sarah."

I sank down in an empty chair. "Credit for Sarah?"

"Well, perhaps not for her performance, but certainly for suggesting the right poem."

"You know Sarah?" I was starting to feel like a question mark.

"Certainly. She came to ask about LaMond for a paper she was writing and we hit it off from the start. Now she stops in to see me just to talk. She's a delightful young woman and she's very fond of you."

"We're in the same class," I began, "and she plays basketball too."

"Then you should grow to be friends. You have so much in common. It's worth the risk."

"What risk?"

"The risk of seeing oneself mirrored in new eyes." She laughed softly. "It's something that happens seldom in LaMond."

"I guess you're right about that," I said. I didn't know what she was talking about.

"It's so important to have friends. They get fewer as you grow old, you know." She looked out the window, which fronted on the parking lot. "I always knew I'd get old someday, but I didn't know it would happen so quickly."

She left space for me to say something, but all I could manage was, "Oh?"

I couldn't understand. After all, if you kept on living you were bound to grow older—something I was looking forward to.

I was trying hard to think of something else to say when Darla from the front desk walked toward us

waving an envelope and smiling. I was very glad to see her.

"Sorry to interrupt, Elva, but I knew you'd want this. It's from one of those magazines you write for and somehow it didn't get put in your box this morning. Marti, Hannah in housekeeping needs to see you for a minute."

I said good-bye to Elva and fled thinking that, even in The Home, Sarah hovered.

In spite of my being sure all of LaMond had heard of Mom's blowup, I decided I was wrong since no one mentioned it. I even stopped worrying about our immediate money problems when Mom reminded me that she hadn't taken a vacation in the last two years, so Barney owed her four full weeks with pay whether she quit or not.

The days fell into a routine that was as comfortable as it was dull. I ran every morning before breakfast, shot baskets for an hour afterward, showered, and dressed for my job. When I got home in the afternoon, Mom was waiting for me with something cold to drink and, more often than not, a plateful of freshly baked cookies.

"So what's the news from The Home?" she asked.

There was always a story to share.

"Today it was the Cronks," I said. "John and Alice. They have a room together on the third floor. They're the only married couple in The Home. They're both in wheelchairs and they were talking to each other while I straightened up their room.

"Alice must have dozed off because all of a sudden she said, 'I'm just tired out. I spent the whole morning cleaning house, baking bread, doing laundry, and working in the garden. I'm plain tuckered out.'

"I wondered what her husband would say.

"He patted her hand and said, 'Alice, you can't be tired. You haven't done all that work. Don't you remember? We're here in The Home. We haven't lived in our house for five years.'

"She shook her head and told him again how tired she was from all that work.

"He was quiet for a while but as I was leaving, he leaned over and asked her, 'Did you remember to put the cat out and turn up the thermostat this morning?'"

Mom was a great audience. I could always get a reaction from her—sometimes laughter, sometimes a sad shake of her head. I think she worried about me though because this time she said, "Marti, you're not having much fun this summer, are you? You don't do anything but run, shoot baskets, and go to work."

She was right, but I tried to make her feel better. "What's there to do? Muffie's on vacation with her folks and all the other kids have jobs. Besides, it's not long till Basketball Camp and that's always fun."

It was Camp I was thinking of on my way home the next afternoon, and fun wasn't any part of it. I had just one season left to earn an athletic scholarship that would take me through college. Last year our team had made it right up to the Regional games that led to the State Tournament before we were knocked out. I played well and my scoring brought some headlines on the sports pages and chats with coaches from two universities.

Everything depended on how well we played in the season ahead. I wasn't worried about what I could do on

the court, but how the team would play was another question.

I'd almost walked by the pickup truck parked at the curb when its horn blasted and Jason yelled at me through the open window, "Hey, Marti! Come on. Jump in. Chaz says it's time for fun and games."

"You've got a deal," I said, grinning at him. "I'm not up for any games, but some fun I could use." There were times when I could understand Muffie's obsession—Jason had a smile that could melt the ice in Lake Ulmer.

Chaz had the door open waiting for me as I hurried around the rear of the truck. I had one foot in the cab before I realized there weren't two of them, there were three.

Sarah sat between them, smiling at me.

"Come on, Marti. Crawl in." Chaz slid closer to Sarah.

"Is this legal?" I asked as I closed the door. "What about seat belts?"

"Here." Chaz pulled down a strap. "Use this one. Sarah and I'll take this." He stretched the center belt across Sarah's and his laps and tugged it into a buckle beside him.

"What's going on?" I asked Sarah.

"A delayed orientation tour," Jason answered, pulling away from the curb.

"A little something we promised our chemistry lab partner before school was over," Chaz added.

Sarah laughed as if it was her own special joke.

"See, Marti, our last project was water-testing some-thing called 'run-off' . . ."

"From a hog-confinement setup . . ." Chaz inter-rupted.

"And Sarah's background didn't include hog con-finement," Jason finished.

"So they promised to show me what one looks like. It's neat you can come with us." She sounded like she meant it.

"You're interested in hogs?" I asked.

"I don't know. I never met one." She smiled at me again. She would have fit right in working at The Home.

"It's the perfect afternoon," Chaz said to me. "Per-fect hog weather."

He was right about that. The temperature must have been in the nineties with humidity to match, and the wind was roaring in from the south. Sarah was in for a total sensory experience.

We circled the lake on the road hugging the shore until we veered off and followed gravel into farmland. We bumped along between corn and bean fields leav-ing a jet trail of dust behind us.

"I'll take us in head-on," Jason said, "so you can get the full effect." We turned off into a lane that bisected a field of alfalfa.

The air suddenly became heavy with an odor that blanketed the truck.

"We're getting close," Chaz said. "Can you tell?"

"I can't hear you." Sarah sounded as if she was

breathing through her mouth. "That smell is clogging up my ears."

I laughed. "You won't notice it after a few minutes. It sort of sinks into your skin and becomes a part of you."

Jason stopped the truck and we got out so Sarah could look around, but there wasn't much to see—just long, low buildings that held, safely out of sight if not out of smell, hundreds of pigs. The high point of our visit was Jason's showing her the big hog-waste holding pond and the machine that sucked up sludge so it could be used as fertilizer on the fields.

It was dumb—the four of us being practically suffocated in the middle of a pig lot—but Sarah seemed to love it. She had a million questions, some of which even Chaz couldn't answer, so Jason and I made up wild possibilities. I almost convinced Sarah that the sparrows flitting around the buildings were really special birds called double-breasted seersuckers and they lived only in hog lots.

We were all laughing when we got in the truck and started back to LaMond. It was easy somehow, maybe because Sarah treated the guys the same way I did—like they were buddies, not bodies. If Muffie could do that she might have a better chance with Jason. I squashed the thought in a hurry. Muffie would consider it treason.

When Jason said, "How about a Coke? Chaz will buy," Sarah and I were in complete agreement, but when Jason wheeled in front of the Sail-Inn, I could have killed myself. It was the last place in LaMond I wanted to be—especially with Sarah Irvine.

There was no way to avoid it, though, short of breaking my ankle getting out of the truck. I tried to be
inconspicuous as I followed everyone through the door,
but that's hard when you're as tall as I am. Jason slid into
a booth with Chaz next to him and Sarah and I shared
the other side. The place was empty except for Verda,
who was back from vacation and had taken over Mom's
shift, and, as always, Bud Newby in his usual spot at the
counter.

Verda didn't bother to walk over; instead she called
across to us, "What'll it be, kids?"

"Four small Cokes," Jason called back. "Chaz is buying and he's cheap."

"What's it like, working at The Home?" Sarah asked.
She made it sound as if it had been a matter of choice.

"It's okay for a while," I said, glancing at Bud Newby
from the corner of my eye. "I didn't think so at first, but
the people who live there are just like anybody else, only
maybe more so."

Sarah nodded. "Elva says that their biggest problem is
that they sometimes forget to remember what they forgot.
You must not work on Sundays. I've never seen you there."

"You go to see Elva every weekend?" I couldn't imagine what they would have to talk about.

Before she could answer, Verda was over with our
drinks. I waited for her to ask me about Mom's big exit.
Instead, she said, "Here's your order, big spender. Marti,
tell your mom I said hi."

Then Jason and Chaz began telling us about *their*
summer jobs and arguing about who got paid the most

and did the least and whose boss was dumbest. Sarah and I voted for Jason, who was working at the local popcorn company. His only responsibility was to run the lift that hoisted the man who was painting sheds. Once, he dozed off when the guy was two stories up and didn't wake until a paintbrush hit him on the head.

Our vote meant that Jason, not Chaz, paid for the Cokes.

On our way out, Bud Newby looked up from his seat at the counter and, pushing his cap back, said, "Hey, Jason. Chaz." His eyes skipped over Sarah and me as if we didn't exist.

The guys decided they had to waste their money on some scratch-off lottery tickets. Since they were underage, they stopped to talk Bud into buying them. Sarah and I went out and leaned against the truck.

"What have you been doing since the Karnival?" I probably should have complimented her on winning the contest, but I hadn't thought of it earlier and now I figured it would sound phoney.

"Helping out at the store," she said. "We've needed someone full-time because Dad's had to be gone so much. Grandma's moving into a retirement home and he's taking care of selling her house and business and everything. I've been filling in and trying to earn enough money to make a down payment on a car."

I was surprised. Sarah didn't seem like the kind of person who would have to work for something. Like, if she wanted a car all she'd have to do would be to ask for it. "So, how's it going?"

She looked as if I'd said something amazing. "It's gone," she said. "I was just there part-time and when your mom came in . . ."

"My mom?"

"Sure. She came in this morning and said she'd like the job. Not my job, the real one. The one we haven't been able to fill." She slowed down and stopped. "You haven't seen her yet, have you? I'm sorry. Can you pretend to be surprised when she tells you?"

I took a deep, slow breath. "I sure can, Sarah. I sure can."

Jason and Chaz showed up before I needed to say anything more. Jason had won five dollars, so our Cokes didn't cost him anything after all.

They dropped me off at my house and as I waved good-bye, I wondered how some family could come to town and change everything—Mom had quit one job because of the Irvines and now she'd be working for them. I wished things had stayed the way they were.

LaMond was not used to change, so when the noon whistle went off at nine o'clock one morning, everyone knew it was either a tornado, a drowning, a car accident, or a heart attack. I was just winding up my morning run when everyone in the stores downtown hurried outside and peered up and down the street. Within minutes, the County Sheriff, Boots McCook, came roaring up, siren screeching, and skidded to a stop in front of the Public Library. Jason and Chaz were already standing out front.

"What's happening?" I shouted above the noise of the crowd.

"Somebody stole the dolls," Jason said as I ran up beside him.

"The Bebe Jumeau?"

"That one and half a dozen others," Chaz explained.

"But she's worth enough . . ." I began.

"Enough for a down payment on a car." Jason shook his head. "Why didn't I think of it first?"

"Because you're too smart to do something that dumb. Who discovered it?"

"Elva Beals. She was filling in for Marvia this morning." Chaz was a genius when it came to information.

"How come you know all about it?" I challenged him.

"I asked."

Muffie appeared along with everyone else in town. I hadn't known she was back from vacation. "Can't you see us on television?" she said breathlessly. "Maybe we'll be on *Unsolved Mysteries*."

Boots McCook disappeared into the library, while Bud Newby, his sometime deputy, stretched yellow tape across the lawn, telling us all, "Step back, now. This is a crime area."

Chaz turned to me, his voice forced into falsetto. "Don't you feel safer in LaMond when the sheriff deputizes Bud?"

"Bud's never been in on a crime before," Jason said. "The only time he gets to be deputy is when McCook goes fishing up in Minnesota for a week."

Leaving his yellow tape fluttering in the breeze, Bud headed inside the library.

"What's he going to do now?" Muffie asked.

"Solve the crime!" Chaz answered, but before he could get the last word finished, Bud reappeared, leading Elva Beals down the steps. He helped her into his pickup and drove off toward City Hall.

"They're going to put her in jail!" Muffie gasped. "We'll be on television all over the state. A librarian stealing from a library!"

I thought about reminding her that bankers sometimes stole from banks.

"Elva wouldn't steal a bookmark," Jason said as he scanned the crowd. I was sure I knew who he was looking for. She wasn't there.

By nightfall, posters offered a $500 reward and prominently displayed the names of businesses that donated the money. Most gave $25. Handy Harry's put up $100.

"Show-offs," Bud Newby said to anyone who would listen as he tacked up the signs on every available post in town.

The next day the sheriff called in for questioning everybody who'd been at the library the last couple of days: Muffie, who had to get her fix of gothic romance novels; Chaz, who had to look over the latest cartoons in the *New Yorker*; Sarah, who had suddenly become interested in *Consumer Guide*; Jason, who dropped in to see if Sarah might be there; and me, who kept trying to find some books that people at The Home might be interested in reading.

Besides us there were a couple of members of Mom's Atheneum Society, who had to present a program at the

next meeting, and a bunch of little kids who attended Marvia's reading time.

It was a terrible feeling, being questioned about a crime, but the worst part were the crazy suspicions.

"It's definitely an inside job." Muffie sounded as if she belonged on a detective show.

"How do you know?" I asked her.

"No fingerprints. No broken panes on the display case."

"Why would there be?" I asked. "The case doesn't have a lock."

"It's somebody who wants money," Muffie insisted. "Someone who spends lots of time in the library."

"Like who?"

We were standing outside the mayor's office waiting for Chaz to come out from being questioned.

"I haven't decided yet, but here comes Chaz. Jason's next. Where is he?"

I turned and looked up toward Rose Road and caught a glimpse of shiny blue. The car, a convertible, cruised down the hill, turned onto Main Street, and pulled up at the curb.

"Oh!" Muffie gasped. "I can't look."

I could. Sarah was behind the wheel and beside her, Jason, who leaped out without opening the car door and came loping toward us. "Are they ready for me?" he asked as Sarah pulled away with a half-wave in our direction.

"Not really," I said. "When did Sarah get that?"

"Just this morning. Only 30 K on the odometer."

Muffie looked at me with her I-told-you-so look, her eyebrows practically disappearing into her hairline. "When does *she* get the third degree?" Muffie still avoided saying Sarah's name.

"Sarah's already had it. First thing this morning. I'm the last." I noticed Jason *always* said Sarah's name. "What all did they ask?"

He was looking at Muffie but she didn't answer, so Chaz filled in. "You just have to account for any time spent in the library the last few days—when, why, and all that."

"Easy. I was only in there once with Sarah and she's already told them."

That did it for Muffie. "I have to go."

"Where?" Jason was either innocent or dumb.

"Home. Mom said I could borrow her car this afternoon. Marti and I are going up to Marietta—shopping. Aren't we, Marti?"

"I guess so," I agreed reluctantly. Shopping was Muffie's pacifier. I knew we'd hit every clothing store in town and she'd come out with plastic bags full of stuff that I'd end up carrying.

"She sure chose a funny time to show up with a new car," Muffie said, looking straight at Jason.

"Who? Sarah? Pure chance." He stopped then and turned to the rest of us. "Hey, you're not trying to say . . . ?"

"It has to be an outsider," I broke in. "No one in LaMond would do it. Those dolls have been sitting there for years and no one has ever touched them."

Just then a woman came out of the mayor's office and

motioned Jason to come in for questioning. "Hang around, Muffie," he said. "Hold up on the shopping and we'll go to the Sail-Inn for some food. I'll even buy."

Muffie's smile looked like the happy face buttons we had to wear at The Home. Chaz looked at me and walked away. I followed.

"You know," Chaz said, running a hand through his hair, "Muffie's blood flows so fast when she sees Jason that there's none left to get to her brain."

"At least I won't have to go shopping." We turned off Main and headed down to the city park.

We walked on not saying anything, but sometimes you know when something is waiting to be said. Frowning, Chaz scuffed at a stone with the toe of his sneaker. "Can I ask you a question?"

"Sure." How else could I answer?"

"Will you tell the truth?"

"Maybe." I knew I wasn't going to like what was coming next.

"What do Muffie and you and the rest have against Sarah?"

I didn't know what to say. "What do you mean?" I stalled, trying to think up words that would explain something I didn't understand myself.

"You don't hang around with her. She's always alone."

"Maybe we don't hang out together, but we don't ignore her either. Besides, it's summer. Remember? Everybody is working or on vacation or something." It was a stupid answer and I knew it wasn't what he meant.

We sat down at one of the picnic tables. Chaz brushed

off some crumbs and a covey of ants and rested both elbows on the table.

"Besides, she's not easy to get to know," I tried again.

"Because she's Jewish?"

"I didn't say that!"

"I thought that's what I heard."

I almost got up, walked away, and left him sitting by himself. I guess I didn't because he was putting into words questions that I hadn't been able to ask myself.

"Listen," he went on. "I'm Swedish. You're Irish. Sarah's Jewish."

"I don't think that has anything to do with it," I argued. "Aren't there Polish Jews and German Jews and French and Russian? It's more a religion."

"I'm a Methodist. You're a Presbyterian. Sarah's a Jew. So what?"

Chaz could always argue me into a corner. "Well, maybe it isn't nationality or religion. Maybe it's cultural." The word came straight from Hawley's history paper assignment. "Anyway, she's different."

"Different from what?" Chaz looked as surprised as if I'd told him that I was the one who'd stolen the dolls from the library. "You mean from the rest of the people who live here? You think we're all the same? Your mother and Bud Newby are the *same?* Elva Beals and Mr. Barnes are the *same?* Get real!"

I didn't have an argument for that.

"It's not culture or religion or nationality that bothers people in this town," Chaz went on.

"What is it, then?"

"It's stupidity. And stupidity is no excuse."

"It'll be better when basketball starts. She'll make the team and everybody will forget the other stuff." It was easier to say when I didn't include myself.

"Don't count on it. That 'stuff' is all around—like pollution."

Full Court Press

The missing dolls didn't even make the next week's issue of our county newspaper. LaMond settled into its usual pattern with Boots McCook's remark summing up what everyone but Marvia and Elva felt: "It was only some dolls. What if it had been the bank?"

It had been another hot, sultry day, the kind when the air conditioners at The Home spewed out blasts of steam instead of cool breezes. I stopped at home after work long enough to change into a swimsuit and head for the beach. Even the lake water felt lukewarm as I swam out to the diving tower.

Climbing up, I saw Jason and Chaz stretched out on the raft moored across the cove. At first glance I thought it was Muffie with them. When she turned, it was Sarah in a sleek two-piece suit that wouldn't begin to cover even a part of me.

I dived in the water and swam to the raft.

"Some people work. Others play," Chaz said as he helped me up. They looked as if they'd settled in for the afternoon.

"Yeah," I agreed. "Some slave, others picnic."

"Great!" Sarah moved over so I could share her beach towel. "Marti, you're a genius! Where shall we do it?"

"Do what?" I'd just arrived and already I felt as if I were playing catch-up.

"Have a picnic." She grinned at me. "It was your idea."

Jason sat up. "Sure. Chaz and I will bring liquids and you two can bring solids."

"And we'll picnic on the battlefield," Chaz said. "On the beach right where the Save Our Shoreliners and the Development people are waging their war."

I knew from the way he was looking at me, he was daring me to say "no."

"When?" I asked.

"Tonight," the three of them said in unison.

So, that night, the four of us sat around a fire on the beach roasting hot dogs and watching the sun set behind the trees across the lake. Sarah brought marshmallows and we speared them on willow sticks and toasted them over the fire while we talked about what college might be like for Chaz and Jason, and about the chances of our basketball team making it all the way to the State Tournament.

Finally Chaz and I spread out the fire while Sarah doused the embers with lake water. It was almost dark when we headed for Sarah's car.

Chaz saw it first and grabbed my arm. "Oh, no." His voice was so angry, it sounded like a stranger's. "Who would do that?"

I looked. "Don't let Sarah see it," I whispered, but I was too late. She was peering over my shoulder at the ugly red swastika painted on the windshield of her car.

Jason touched a dribble of paint with one finger. "It's still wet."

Without saying anything, Sarah opened the door and squeezed in the driver's seat.

"You can't see to drive." I tried to rub the paint away with the sleeve of my shirt, but all it did was smear.

"I'll drive," Jason said. "We'll go back home and get some paint remover. I can drive there with my eyes shut."

In silence, with Jason peering through one leg of the swastika, we made it out to his farm.

"Do you want to call the sheriff before we clean it off?" Chaz asked as we got out of the car.

"No." Sarah's answer sounded automatic. "It wouldn't make any difference."

We watched as Jason came out of the shed carrying a can and a couple of rags. He and Chaz worked until the window was spotless. "I know what we'll do," Jason said when they finished. "We'll go back to LaMond and drive around until we're sure everyone sees us."

"And we'll wave at everyone," Chaz added. "It won't change what happened, but it'll make me feel a whole lot better."

Later, when Sarah dropped me off at my house, I deliberately lied to her for the first time. "None of us

would do it," I said. "It must have been someone from down at Maple Grove or somewhere." I even tried to believe my own words.

"It doesn't matter, Marti," she said. "I know it wasn't you or Chaz or Jason, and that's all that's important. You're my friends."

After that it was Basketball Camp with all of us thinking of the season ahead. From now on, it would be hoops over books at LaMond High until March when the season ended.

"Ever hear of anyone making headlines in the *State Herald* by reading a book?" Bud Newby said every year. "It's the game of basketball that puts *us* on the map."

There was no chance of our getting on the map the way things went during the first part of Camp. It was more like a war than a game and there was no place for friendship.

The battle began when the coaches divided us into scrimmage teams after two long days of drilling on rules and fundamentals of the five-girl game.

"Did you see the list?" Muffie's face turned crimson. "There are six teams and only one of them has a captain from LaMond."

"Who?" I asked. "Liz?"

"No!" Her neck was even redder than her face. "The Princess."

"She's only been here since May and she's taking over everything." Angie was so mad, she was almost in tears.

"Is anyone we know on her team?" I wasn't sure if I wanted to find out whether or not I was.

"Me!" Muffie snapped. "I feel like going right up to Coach and telling her I'm quitting basketball. It was bad enough when she won the pageant. . . ."

"She was smart, though," Angie said. "Picking that poem."

"They all are." Muffie leaned closer. "And they all stick together. The Irvines don't even go to church here. They drive ninety miles clear over to Ute City on Saturdays to be with the rest of them."

"And, of course, she looks Jewish." Angie sounded almost happy.

"How do Jews look?" I wondered where she'd ever seen any.

"Don't you know? Like the Irvines."

Mr. Irvine was tall and blond and blue-eyed. Sarah's mom was small and dark-haired like Sarah, and like Angie, for that matter.

"Well, maybe they won't be around very long." Muffie looked serious. "Dad says they'll probably stay just long enough to make money and then there'll be a fire and they'll collect insurance and leave town."

I didn't tell anyone, but I sort of thought Coach might have chosen me as a team captain, even though Sarah had played five-girl before and from watching her in practice, I knew how good she was. It wasn't a big surprise that her team beat the Reeboks off everyone they played before the Scorpions, as they called themselves, met my team. We didn't have a clever name. We were just the Blues.

By the end of one quarter of play with the Scorpions, we were black and blues.

By the beginning of the fourth quarter, I was purple—partly because I was embarrassed by the way our team was playing, partly mad at myself because with Sarah guarding me, I was scoring about half the points I usually made. But Muffie looked like a potential All-Stater with her cross-court, bullet pass to Sarah, who kept flipping in three-pointers.

We called for a time-out about five minutes into the quarter to try to get our nonexistent game back together. We'd lost it somewhere when the Scorpions scorped to a six-point lead that we'd never caught up to.

Ann, our captain, who came from down at Maple Grove but was okay in spite of it, shook the sweat from her face and said, "If this was six-girl, we'd wipe them off the court."

"Well," I said, "it isn't and they're doing the wiping."

"What do you Blues think you're playing here? Croquet?" One of the coaches trotted across the floor. "Tiddledywinks, for Pete's sake? Let's see a little aggression. You!" He pointed at me. "You're supposed to be a forward. You know what that means? It means you go FORWARD! You see that guard ready to stop you?"

I looked at Sarah, who was ready to mess up another of my shots.

"She's the enemy. You're going to out-move her, out-fake her, out-muscle her, and shove your way up to that goal up there. See it? Nothing's going to stop you. Now I want to see some concentration when you get the ball. Understand?"

"Yeah." I glared at Sarah. She was standing near the

center line, waiting for the time-out to end and looking unruffled and confident. I concentrated on my enemy.

Ann took the ball out-of-bounds and lobbed a pass to me. I dribbled toward the bucket and ducked around Muffie, who had her hands fluttering over her head as if she were signaling a kind of alarm. Sarah stepped in front of me. I switched the ball to my other hand, made a quick pivot, and felt my free elbow catch her hard just below her ribs. No whistle blew as I slipped in a layup with my left hand.

Amid cheers from my team, I turned and raced back down the floor, but I couldn't resist smiling at Sarah— not in friendship, but in triumph.

We didn't win, but we tied the Scorpions with my last shot.

"That's more like it," the coach shouted. "We won't play off ties. It's only a practice game."

I walked down through the city park and followed the familiar shoreline to our house. I guess sometimes you have to be alone to face the person you really are, and I was not liking the person I saw.

I wanted to believe that elbowing Sarah out of the way was just good, aggressive basketball hustle, but another part of my brain told me that for a minute or two she really had been my enemy.

I decided as I walked up to the back door that I'd ask Mom about it. She was funny that way—sometimes she had answers for questions I hadn't even thought of. I didn't have a chance to ask.

Seated around the dining room table, looking like an

assembly line, were Marvia, Elva, Sarah's mother, and Mom. Marvia folded a page from a stack of paper at her side, handed it to Elva, who slipped it into an envelope and passed it on to Mrs. Irvine, who sealed and stamped it. Mom finished off by writing an address on the envelope and dropping it into a box on the floor.

Without lifting her pen, Mom said, "Marti, you can alphabetize these by towns and recheck the zip codes."

"What's it for?" I asked, marveling how quickly my problems with basketball and Sarah could evaporate under Mom's orders.

"SOS—Save Our Shoreline," Elva announced as if she really *was* the mayor of LaMond. "It's to stop the Development people from stealing lakeshore from the citizens and turning it into rows of Bud Newby's corncrib houses."

"We're appealing for money for a lawsuit," Marvia added as she folded another paper in a split second and added it to the pile beside Elva.

"Marvia did a title search on the shoreline." Elva smiled. "She discovered a bit of a 'glitch,' you might say, in the recording of the deed. That's our secret weapon. Of course, everyone who invested money in the Development seems to think it's a . . . what did you call it, Marvia?"

"A done deal!"

"So we're undoing the done." Helen Irvine laughed. "I'll have Sarah mail these tomorrow on the way to work, Marge."

My head jerked up at the sound of Sarah's name.

"Where's Sarah working?"

Mom glanced up at me. "She's been helping out at the library. How long now, Marvia?"

"A couple of weeks."

My elbow throbbed. How was Sarah able to get a summer job like that? I would have given plenty to spend all day behind the checkout desk and reading instead of pushing book carts and hauling food trays at The Home. No wonder Elva never took any books from my cart. She probably had Sarah bring them up from the library as soon as new publications came out.

I looked up. Elva was watching me and I had the feeling she'd heard what I'd been thinking. I went back to my zip codes and stayed there till everyone was finished for the afternoon. One by one, sweating with every step, I hauled the boxes of envelopes out and stowed them in the Irvines' car. As usual, everything came easily to Sarah—even what had to be dropped off at the post office.

I never did get around to asking Mom anything because when she wasn't working at Handy Harry's Hardware, she was meeting with the SOS women who, I learned, consisted of more than Mom and Elva and Marvia and Helen Irvine. Mom wrote letters to editors of every paper in the county and distributed leaflets to every store that would take them. My mixed feelings about Sarah were easy to ignore.

I rebounded and tipped in my last shot. It wasn't

difficult since I was alone in the driveway finishing two hours of working on getting the ball through the hoop. You'd think that after two hours almost every day for five years, I couldn't miss.

"Keep your eyes on the basket! Follow through! Hook shot. Layup. Free throw. It doesn't matter. Learn the pattern. Make it a part of you. Learn it so well you don't think. Let your muscles act!" Coach had said the same thing over and over and I knew she was right.

I pivoted, looped the ball cleanly toward the basket, and missed.

"Nice try." Muffie hopped off her bike and propped it against the garage.

"You're supposed to say it like you mean it," I said. "How was volleyball practice?"

"Boring, as usual."

"If you don't like it, how come you go out for it?"

"You've got to be kidding. Coach likes enthusiasm. Coach likes school spirit. She coaches volleyball *and* basketball. Next question."

"Want something to drink? Come on in the kitchen."

"The Princess was there, kissing up like always," she said, following me into the house. "Wouldn't you think she could do something human—like miss practice once in a while? No. Sarah-with-an-H gets there early and stays late. And she doesn't even have to. She's got a starting guard spot sewed up and basketball hasn't even started yet." Muffie perched on a corner of the kitchen table while I pulled cans of soda from the refrigerator.

"Think team," I imitated Coach's voice. "Individuals don't exist. Only the team. You're not five people. You're one person with five bodies. That's what a team is—sharing."

"When Liz plays, it's more like six bodies." Muffie giggled until she remembered what she'd been talking about. "And how can you share anything with Sarah? She has everything."

"So—pretend. You want to be an actress, don't you?"

"Weather personality," she answered. "Of course I pretend, at least when Coach is around. And that's because . . ." She paused as if someone might be hiding behind the refrigerator. "I've set two personal goals for this year."

She meant what she was saying. Whenever Muffie got serious, her eyes sort of glazed over like she was in shock.

I must have looked interested because she didn't wait for me to ask anything.

"I just read this magazine article about something called 'empowerment.' That basically means getting what you want. And it said you have to set personal goals and then use your psychic and emotional power to achieve them."

I wondered if psychic power could guide a basketball through the hoop, so I nodded.

"Well, my goal is a permanent starting guard position this season." I must have looked doubtful but she went on. "I know, I know. I can't beat out

Sarah, but Angie is going to be dead meat."

"You two are friends," I said. "And you never cared that much before about starting."

"Jason's in college this year," she said as if that explained everything.

"What's that got to do with basketball?" I was lost in her logic.

"Jason is my other goal. Actually, he's the first one. It's my last year in school and it's *my* last chance. If he likes college too much, he'll never come back."

"So?"

"So he'll be home some weekends and he'll come to all the basketball games. I want him to realize how much we have in common. I think—I mean I'm sure that's why he hangs out with you-know-who sometimes. Right? Not because he's really interested or anything. There could be more to his life than her." She stared at her can of soda as if it were a crystal ball. "There could be me."

"Sure," I agreed, "only don't forget that you were here first and you'll be here after she's gone. He belongs to LaMond."

"I never thought of it that way."

If Muffie's plan to capture Jason would turn her into a better guard, I was all for it. We were heading into a long, tough season.

I took away her empty can and patted her head. "Well, it's only September so you have a whole two months to get empowered, but practice starts soon so you'd better get yourself in gear."

When she finally left, I wondered if I should warn

Jason that he was about to become the focus of all Muffie's energy. It was silly, though. He'd been exposed to her for twelve years. He ought to be immune by now.

After a few weeks in college, Jason came home for a weekend. He cruised by the high school in his pickup. We waved. He waved, but he didn't stop.

"I have to get home, Marti." Muffie took off running down the walk toward her place. "He'll be calling me and I want to be there."

He didn't call Muffie that Friday night. He didn't call Saturday morning, either, but he stopped by that afternoon. He didn't ask her out that night. Muffie told me the whole sad story of the weekend on Monday as we ate lunch together off in one corner by ourselves.

"Angie said she saw him with Sarah on Saturday night," she confided between gulps of a cheese sandwich. "Marti, I'm telling you. All men are alike. Only their faces are different."

"Don't say that, Muffie. Maybe he was having trouble in college chemistry or something. You know Sarah is a genius when it comes to math and science."

"How could she help him when they were riding around together? Angie saw them."

"It's not the end of the world. There are other fish in the lake." I sounded like my mother! "Why don't you give Scooter Boyd a chance? All you'd have to do is look at him twice and he'd be hooked."

"You don't understand. This is serious."

I gave up. Muffie was making it sound like a soap

opera and she was the jilted wife. "You'll get over it in a day or two, Muffie. Just consider it a bad hair day and think of volleyball or basketball or even homework."

Sometimes I wondered if we were friends because we liked each other or because we'd known each other all our lives. Mostly, I guess, it was comfortable—the same as living in LaMond. There were no big surprises.

A surprise did come when I got a call one Saturday. Mom had given me a phone on my last birthday even though I didn't really need it, especially at seven-thirty in the morning.

I recognized Sarah's voice right away although she'd never called me before, and, I'd never had any reason to call her.

"Marti, I'm sorry it's so early, but Elva phoned. She wants to see us this morning as soon as we can come."

"What for?" I wasn't feeling like half of an "us."

"Something about the dolls and she said it's important. I'll pick you up in ten minutes if that's okay."

I could have said no to Sarah, but no one said no to Elva. Muffie said Elva was the perfect example of empowerment. When we walked into The Home, she was sitting in the Morning Room and motioned to a table in the far corner.

"Thank you for coming," she said as she pulled her chair closer. "I know you two are busy, but I need your help. I don't think we can wait any longer."

I looked at Sarah. Sarah looked at me.

Elva leaned across the table. "I know what happened to the dolls."

"You've got to be kidding," I said.

"I believe that is what mother goats do, Marti."

Sarah laughed, but I didn't get it for a minute so I asked, "How did you figure it out?"

Elva's lips tightened. "By using my brain at long last. I can't imagine why I didn't think of it sooner. In April I published an article in *Antiques Today* about the doll collection featuring Bebe Jumeau, describing her in detail and suggesting how valuable she is."

"And someone who read the article came to LaMond and stole the dolls," Sarah added.

"How does that help?" I asked.

"Because whoever took them will have tried to resell them," Elva said patiently. "And we will find them."

"We?"

Elva looked at me over her glasses. "I need transportation. Sarah has a car. I could have asked Marvia, but who would take care of the library? We'll go on a weekend. When I asked Sarah if she had a friend who might like to come along, she suggested you."

I looked at Sarah. She didn't look back.

"Besides," Elva pulled her chair closer, "I couldn't think of anyone else in LaMond who really cares enough for the dolls to bother. The sheriff gave up long ago. He couldn't take the jokes about his 'lost dollies.' And think of how much fun we can have."

"When are we going?" Sarah sounded as if Elva had suggested a trip to the Sail-Inn.

"*Where* are we going?" I asked.

"We are going antique shopping. I'll talk to your mothers and we'll set the day. In the article I mentioned

a few shops that specialize in antique dolls. They're just across the river. It will be a lovely trip. The trees will be in full color then. We can combine business with pleasure."

"What will we do if we find the dolls?"

"We'll play it by ear," she assured me.

Neither her business nor pleasure appealed to my ear, but I agreed to go along.

Early on a bright blue October morning we started out to prove Elva's theory. We stopped for breakfast at the Amana Colonies, where Elva, between bites of a mammoth cinnamon roll, filled us in with all the history of the "Community of True Inspiration" as the seven villages were once called.

"Everything was held in common—land, kitchens, dining rooms, crops. It's all changed now, of course. These villages are what is left of someone's dream."

Sarah was enchanted with the history. I'd heard it all before in seventh-grade history.

With Sarah at the wheel and Elva with the map and me in the backseat, we played "Guess where this quotation comes from" at Elva's insistence as we drove across the state.

I got the easy ones like "Call me Ishmael" and "It was the best of times" and, of course, "You don't know about me without you have read a book . . ." Sarah missed only one.

We had a contest to see who could find the oddest name for a town. Ladora was Elva's choice. She said it was named when the founder heard his daughter

practicing vocal exercises. "La, do, re" became Ladora.

I thought What Cheer was funnier. Sarah said that Ulmer, though not a town, was a ridiculous name for a lake even if it *was* named after somebody.

Elva folded her map and put it in the glove compartment. "I'll have to admit it's different, but if you grew up in LaMond and all you ever heard was 'beautiful Lake Ulmer,' you'd think it was a lovely word."

"Maybe it just takes time," Sarah said.

"Perhaps a lifetime," Elva agreed. "Do you suppose what we call beauty is only the familiar?"

Neither Sarah nor I tried to answer her question.

Our first targeted shop tested Sarah's driving because it was up a nearly vertical one-way street and tucked into a bluff that overlooked the river. Elva hung on to the armrest with one hand and clutched the dashboard with the other as we maneuvered a sharp turn and pulled into a narrow parking space. There had to be *something* Sarah couldn't do well.

"May I help you?" A bearded, suspendered man struggled out of his chair and strolled over to greet us as we walked in the store.

"We're just browsing," Elva replied with a soft smile.

"Anything in particular?"

"Oh, just something for my girls. A little remembrance of our trip."

"I see. The jewelry is here in the case. Collectibles over there. Dolls and toys in the back."

We strolled along, pretending not to be too interested. There were Kewpie dolls made of celluloid with

topknots and flirtatious smiles. There was a Shirley Temple doll with lifelike curls, and stacks of Barbie dolls and Cabbage Patch Kids, but no Bebe Jumeau.

"Have you girls decided on anything?" Elva asked as we moved toward the cash register. Hanging nearby on a rack were coffee mugs printed with names. "See if you can find yours," she suggested, opening her purse.

Sarah found a mug with her name missing the H. I found one with my name spelled with a Y.

"Close enough," Elva said as we walked back to the car. "After all, we had to buy something."

We spent most of the afternoon browsing through antique shops: Grandma's Attic, Memories and Keepsakes, Carrie's Collectibles, Used and Reused.

Nothing compared to what faced us as we wheeled in a parking lot and saw the sign on a sprawling building: RENE'S TREASURES.

We pushed open the glass door and were greeted by the smell of lavender mixed with the scent of cedar chips. A sign warned us to leave our shopping bags at the main desk. Although the tourist season was past, Rene's didn't seem to realize it. There were a lot of "lookers" as well as a line of "buyers" standing at the counter.

The store consisted of a large main aisle with rooms branching off in both directions. Elva led the way, and we started our search. There was a clock room, a china room, a pottery room, a glass room, an antique furniture room, a lamp room, a jewelry room—and a toy room.

Elva and Sarah found some old iron banks cast in

shapes like buildings and animals. I couldn't get interested so I moved on to the next room. I stopped in the doorway as hundreds of dolls stared down at me from the shelves that covered the walls. I stood still, moving just my eyes, scanning the rows and rows of smiling faces.

Two ladies brushed past me "oohing" and "aahing" at the display. I slowly walked into the room. Then, from high on a very top shelf, two lifelike glass eyes stared straight down at me. I shivered as if I were still the frightened kindergartner seeing the Bebe Jumeau for the first time.

Where were Elva and Sarah? A young mother, firmly holding the hand of a squirming little girl, walked in, warning the kid, "Now don't touch. Just look." I moved away and stared at a display of pincushion dolls until Sarah and Elva finally showed up.

I watched Elva, her head turning back and forth like a mechanical doll, scanning the shelves row by row. I was sure she saw the Bebe Jumeau because her mouth tightened and she leaned forward, then glanced away and looked again. She glanced to the right and left, her lips moving, and I thought maybe she was locating the other dolls.

Elva had named each of them and I still remembered some: Norah, Madame Alexander, Jack Tar, Celestine. Jack Tar was the only one I liked.

Sarah walked up to me and said, "Elva thinks it's time to leave."

For a minute I thought I'd been mistaken about the Bebe. Sometimes you want so much for something to be that you imagine it's happened.

We didn't buy anything at Rene's Treasures. When we

got to the car, Elva said triumphantly, "We need to find a telephone."

"You saw her? Bebe Jumeau?" I asked.

"Of course, didn't you?"

"I thought so, but I wasn't sure." I wanted to tell them how scared I'd been as a kid of the doll, but I was afraid Sarah would laugh at me. I couldn't imagine her ever having been frightened by anything.

"Who are you going to call?" Sarah asked.

"Sheriff McCook. I'm sure we passed a phone booth at the public park. Let's go back there."

We stayed in the car while Elva called the sheriff.

"You saw the doll first, didn't you, Marti?" Sarah asked. "Why didn't you tell me?"

"I was going to, but . . ." I didn't finish. I wasn't sure myself.

Sarah looked out at the river and ran her fingers through her hair, silky short hair with a natural curl that fell into place no matter what the weather. Muffie and Angie had hair that looked like coils of snarls sprouting in furry worms from their scalps. It took them hours to make it look that way.

When I didn't say any more, she went on. "Is this the first time you've seen the Mississippi?"

You can tell when people are struggling to make conversation. They always ask questions so you have to hurry and think of something to fill in the blank.

"Yes," I admitted. "It's not as pretty as Like Ulmer, though."

"I like rivers. Rivers go places. Lakes sit and wait for waves to happen."

"You like LaMond, though, don't you? It's comfortable. Friendly." It was a stupid thing for me to say. I hoped Sarah had forgotten that stuff on her windshield. "People always wave when they drive by. At least they lift a finger off the steering wheel."

"You've lived there all your life." She was watching a barge make its way up the river. "It's not like that for everyone."

I knew she hadn't forgotten anything. "There aren't many changes in town, so when something new happens it takes a little while for people to get used to it."

She looked at me. "How long does it take?"

"Until it stops bothering them." I thought of the men at the Sail-Inn.

"Who's them?"

"Whoever's not us?"

We were two question marks without an answer.

I was more than glad when Elva finally came back from the phone booth. "Sheriff McCook will meet us first thing in the morning. That means, he informed me, that we will have to spend the night here, which will entail getting a motel room." She shook her head. "That man has an instinctive grasp of the obvious."

Sarah laughed and I joined her even if I wasn't sure what was funny.

We didn't stay in a motel; we stayed at a bed-and-breakfast named Bide-a-Wee.

"It's not so commercial," Elva said. "More like visiting someone's home."

We each had our own room. I felt like I was sleeping between the pages of a history book. There was an old

wood dresser with tiny drawers on each side of a mirror. The top was filled with a rose-colored vase full of old-fashioned hat pins, a silver-coated vanity set of comb, brush, hand mirror, two teddy bears, and a straw basket of dried flowers. My bed had a headboard that reached the ceiling. I finally fell asleep hoping that breakfast would be better than bed.

It was.

"The sheriff should be here soon," Elva told us over omelets and freshly baked muffins. "I talked to him last night and I assume he'll follow my advice. We'll all drive over in your car, Sarah. I insisted he not wear his uniform or bring his gun. The four of us will walk in like an ordinary family." Elva took a last sip of coffee. "Now let's go out on the porch and wait for him."

He finally arrived, not in his police car, but in Bud Newby's pickup truck with Bud behind the wheel.

"Brought my deputy along just in case things get nasty."

"Did some checking after your call, Elva." Bud climbed out of the cab and walked up to us. "Found out who owns this store. Fella named Levi . . . something. He's a . . ."

"Never mind, Bud." Elva's voice was firm. "It's the dolls that concern us."

We crawled into Sarah's car, the men in front and the three of us in back.

"You do have your badge, don't you?" Elva tapped the sheriff on the shoulder.

"Yep."

"And you left your gun at home?"

"Did just what you said, Elva."

"Good." She sat back scanning the street as if she were driving.

We reached Rene's Treasures as the shop was opening for the day. Sheriff McCook helped Elva out of the car and the rest of us followed. Bud pulled open the glass door and stood like an attentive sentry as we filed through.

"Elva, you and Bud go to the room where you saw the dolls and wait there."

"Shall I tape off the place? I brought my ribbon." Bud sounded eager.

"Not yet. You girls"—Boots looked as if he didn't know what to do with us— "just keep out of the way." He walked toward the woman who sat behind a counter near the cash register. She looked exactly like Miss Fordham, my sixth-grade teacher, who'd kept me trembling for a whole school year fearing I might break one of her many rules.

"Good morning," Boots said, resting an elbow on the counter. "Are you in charge here?"

"My husband and I are," she said, and smiled at him.

"You own the shop?"

"At least part of it. Us and the local bank." Her voice was friendly. "May I help you with something?"

"Perhaps. I understand you have a fine collection of antique dolls. Porcelains. Bisques."

I looked at Sarah in amazement. The sheriff actually knew the right words.

"Yes, we do. My husband's the expert. Would you like him to show them to you?"

"If it's not too much trouble."

She moved out from behind the counter looking less like Miss Fordham every minute. "I'll have him here in a jiffy."

The sheriff looked over at us and winked. "Don't think we'll have a bit of trouble. We'll see."

The woman returned followed by a grandfather-type man in suit, white shirt, and tie. His eyes moved over Sarah and me and the sheriff in one quick glance.

"You're a doll lover, I assume. Or are you looking for something for the girls here?"

"Just lately I've become interested in collecting dolls—French dolls." He sounded so natural that I could have believed him.

"You've come to the right place. I lately acquired something quite rare. A Bebe Jumeau. Would you like to see it?"

"Very much, if you have the time."

I tried to keep from laughing. It was a good thing Elva was with us. Boots McCook wouldn't know a Bebe Jumeau from a Raggedy Ann.

Sarah and I followed the two men to the room in the back of the store where Bud and Elva were waiting.

"My friend here," Boots gestured toward Elva, "was in your shop yesterday and said your collection was unusual."

"You have excellent taste, ma'am," the owner said. "I was lucky to be able to obtain them."

"Did they come from an estate sale?" Elva asked. "They certainly look authentic."

"Oh, they are. I examined them carefully. The woman I bought them from, a lovely lady, told me they originally belonged to her grandmother. She hated to give them up, but she was retiring. Moving to Arizona."

Elva smiled. "May we see one? Perhaps the Bebe Jumeau."

The man pulled out a step stool and, balancing carefully, lifted the doll from its shelf and handed it to her.

She held the doll, its human hair barely mussed, and inspected each feature, pulling strings, maneuvering legs.

"Yes," she said to Boots. "This is the doll."

The sheriff reached in his jacket pocket, brought out his badge, and showed it to the man. "I'm afraid this doll has been stolen along with some of those others. I'm Sheriff McCook, and these"—he waved his hand—"were taken from the LaMond Public Library. Ms. Beals here can identify them."

The shop owner stared at him for a minute and then slowly nodded his head. "I should have guessed. I should have been suspicious. The missus"—he thumbed toward the front of the store—"said the price we paid was too cheap."

"Here's a list and description of the missing dolls." Elva pulled a paper from her pocketbook. "I think you'll find they match perfectly."

In less than an hour, the missing dolls were carefully packed for their trip back to LaMond, all of what the sheriff called "official paperwork" had been done, and Elva and the owners of Rene's had exchanged phone numbers and addresses. When we finally left, they were busy filling out insurance claims.

The week after our trip, a picture of the three of us appeared in the county newspaper. We even got a head-line: "Retired Librarian and Local Girls Solve Theft."

Sarah phoned me when the paper came out. The only thing I remember her saying was, "They called me a local girl!"

I couldn't understand why that was such a big deal.

There wasn't time to think about it anyway. Volleyball was over and basketball practice began. Right away I could see that Muffie had meant what she said about earning a starting position. If she could keep it up, and with Sarah playing point guard, our prospects were great.

At least they seemed that way until one Saturday when Mom came home for lunch looking like *she'd* been through a workout.

"What's wrong?" I asked. "Did you close down the store?" Mom usually ran the place on Saturdays when the Irvines drove the many miles to what they called "Temple."

"Helen's still at the store. She's upset and so am I. She caught Muffie shoplifting."

"Shoplifting what?" I couldn't imagine anything in

Handy Harry's that she'd want. They didn't sell clothes or jewelry or cosmetics.

"That's what's so strange." Mom sat down at the table and rested her head in both hands. "She had some candles, a couple of greeting cards, and earphones for a radio."

"The dork! What did Mrs. Irvine do?"

"I don't know. Helen wanted to talk to her alone. Thank goodness there was no one else in the store or it would be all over town by now."

"Do you think they'll report it?"

"That's up to the Irvines. Even if they do, the law is lenient with first offenders."

First offender! I avoided Mom's eyes. Most of us knew Muffie ripped off a candy bar or a package of gum now and then, but now she'd done something like that right where we lived. At one of the malls, maybe, but not in LaMond.

Mom took a deep breath that turned into a sigh. "Poor Muffie!"

"Poor!" Muffie had an allowance that made my wage from The Home look like a Bud Newby tip.

"She must feel so pressured."

"How?" I had to admit sometimes I thought Muffie's brain was made of butter, but pressured?

"She tries so hard to be what her parents think she should be that she's never had time to be herself. They named her Mildred, after her grandmother, and then turned her into a 'Muffie.' A mixed-up one at that."

"Is there anything we can do?" If Coach ever found out, Muffie would be off the team and our chances of

getting to the State Tournament would drop.

"Not that I can think of right now. Later, maybe." She didn't sound hopeful. "But she depends on you, Marti. Maybe you can keep her out of the stores."

"Me as a parole officer? No, thanks!"

I went outside and sat on the steps trying to sort things out. I wasn't as surprised as Mom about Muffie's sticky fingers. My first thought was to let her figure it out herself, the dumb twink. I remembered all the packages I'd carried out of stores for her. If she'd been stealing stuff, I could have been picked up for shoplifting! But still . . . stupid as Muffie was, she was one of us.

I gave up thinking. It was too late to change what had happened and I didn't know how to fix it. Instead, I jogged down the shoreline, through the park, up Main, as far as Muffie's corner. Then my brain clicked in. Sarah! It was her folks' store, wasn't it? And she was part of the team, wasn't she?

When I rang the bell at Hill House, she answered the door.

"We have a problem," I said, hoping she believed the "we." "We have to do something."

"Muffie." It wasn't a question. "Want to come in? Or go for a walk?"

"Yeah, let's walk," I agreed. "I think my brain needs air. But how did you find out?"

"I stopped at the store after it was all over. Mom told me. I feel sorry for her. Don't you?"

We headed down the hill back toward the park. "Not today," I said. "Right now I could strangle her, if her mother hasn't already done it."

"I don't think her mother knows."

"If I know Muffie, she won't tell her either." I considered myself an expert on Muffie. She didn't exactly lie to her mom, she omitted. "If the coach finds out about this . . ."

"Muffie's out for the season? But if everyone ignores it, she'll probably try again."

"Let's sit down." I pointed at a bench that looked out over the lake, where a breeze was churning the water into whitecaps. "I don't understand it. She was just getting things together, setting goals—like being a starting guard."

"What else does she want?"

"I don't remember." I skipped the Jason goal. "How do we keep her out of jail?"

Sarah looked startled. I wasn't sure whether it was the "jail" part or the "we" part.

"There's no jail involved." She pulled her jacket around her shoulders as a cool breeze gusted off the lake. "The only people who know, besides Muffie, are Mom and me and you and your mother. And Mom wants to help Muffie, not punish her."

I relaxed a little bit. At least Muffie's name wouldn't be in the paper as part of the police blotter. "You mean your mother just let her walk out?" It was too good to be true.

"Not exactly. She had Muffie put together all the stuff she'd taken and make a little display of it in the front window, and then made her write out a card that said, "This is what I tried to steal" and sign it. If she ever does anything like that again and Mom hears about it, the card goes in the window, too."

"She must be in shock," I said.

"For right now, maybe, but that doesn't mean it will work, especially if this isn't the first time."

"So why did she do it, anyway?"

"Why? I'm not sure, I don't really know her that well, but maybe . . ." Sarah stared at the lake, frowning. "Maybe she doesn't feel as if she's really good at anything. And taking stuff is something she can do and succeed at. Does that sound crazy?"

"No. It sounds possible. She hardly ever gets an A on anything, she's never won the Karnival contest, she doesn't play basketball as well as she could, and Jason . . ." I stopped. I'd almost forgotten I was talking to Sarah.

"Oh, Jason." Sarah laughed. "If she relaxes and stops chasing him, she'll have him for the rest of her life. He just wants to think it's his idea. And maybe she would relax if she knew that she really does count as a person, as somebody special, not because she's the banker's daughter."

What she was saying made sense and I wondered why I'd never thought about it before. Could an outsider see things I'd been too close to notice? "So what can *we* do?"

"You could help make sure she gives up the malls. If she stays out of the stores, she won't be tempted."

"That's funny." Muffie's trouble was making me talk to myself.

"What is?"

"That's what Mom suggested."

"You might help her with homework, study together or something. And," she hesitated. "Maybe we could spend extra time in the gym on weekends, working on her guarding."

"You mean we keep Muffie so busy, she won't have time to get into trouble?"

"Maybe you could help her be who she wants to be. Show her that you really *like* her."

"Right. Sure," I said and stood up. I was supposed to show Muffie I liked her. Muffie knew I liked her . . . I think.

I started to jog away, then turned back. "Thanks a lot. We might make it through the season after all."

She smiled. I left her sitting in the park. That was one thing about Sarah—she smiled a lot, but I didn't think she was all that happy.

When I saw Muffie, I said nothing about what had happened at Handy Harry's and neither did she. Instead we talked about Jason—he'd actually written her a letter. I suggested she play it cool and not answer with a nine-pager by return mail.

She was worried about an English assignment for the first time I knew of, probably because she had to keep up her grades for the team. We were supposed to write a review of a TV show, and I told her we should do it together, like Siskel and Ebert. We each got an A.

One day at the end of practice when we were alone in the locker room with Muffie, Sarah asked, almost shyly, "Would the two of you ever have time—maybe on

Sunday afternoon—for extra practice? I could really use it."

I was so enthusiastic Muffie didn't have a chance, and before she knew it, we were inseparable, at least for a couple of hours every weekend.

Sarah didn't try to teach Muffie anything. She just showed her over and over and step by step what makes an All-State guard. It was clear that Muffie would never be as good as Sarah, but she'd be a real threat to any team we played.

Once, on our way out of the gym after Muffie had left, I told Sarah, "It's working. I don't think she has the energy to even walk into a store."

"It's not that," Sarah said. "She's learning to be happier with herself. She couldn't have done it without a friend like you."

As I left, I wondered if I was doing all the "helping stuff" for Muffie or if I was doing it for a winning season.

Christmas in Lake Ulmer began in early November right along with basketball season with the town crew working overtime to get colored lights strung over Main Street before the crew up at Juliet could get theirs in place. This Christmas was even more interesting. People couldn't wait to see what the Irvines would use for decorations in their store window.

"They don't believe in Christmas!" Muffie had told us. "They have something called Canoeka or something like that. It's Indian, I think. Anyway, they do candles instead of trees and there's no baby Jesus or carols or presents or anything."

As it turned out, the Irvines' store was no different from any of the others on Main Street that year with its tree covered with artificial snow, Santa and his elves, and Rudolph with his nose blinking red. The Sail-Inn was the place with candles, electric ones, in every window blinking on and off so you could hardly read the menu printed on the blackboard above the refrigerator.

The event of the season for Mom was the Atheneum Christmas party held at Lois Barnes', mostly because she had a fireplace and the largest display of a village Christmas. Everyone chipped in for the holiday refreshments, though Mom always fixed the same thing—divinity candy. She could whip up a batch of egg whites, sugar, vanilla, and syrup into white pieces of melt-in-your-mouth, rot-your-teeth sweetness, each uniformly cone-shaped with identical little curlycues on top.

Mom had taken special care for this meeting because the Atheneums were going to vote on a new member. Grace, the Methodist minister's wife, had moved away with her husband to a bigger, richer congregation, leaving a definite vacancy in the Atheneum membership. As president, Lois Barnes insisted the membership remain at no more than sixteen. "That's four bridge tables, you know. After all, we have to be selective. Everyone and her sister wants in."

The thing that made this Christmas meeting so important was that Helen Irvine's name had been proposed to take Grace's place. Mom had planned a surprise

get-together to celebrate at our place after the meeting.

"It'll just be Elva, Marvia, and Gladys Jenkins. And Helen, of course," Mom explained and handed me a dust cloth. "Here, maybe you could help me out."

Mom seldom told me I had to do anything, but her suggestions were nonrefusable.

"Who suggested her name?" I asked as I swished the cloth over furniture. Who could see dust anyway?

"I did." She turned the mixer to full power in a bowl of whiteness that would soon turn into her divinity.

"Why?"

"Why not?"

"Well, you know . . . because." I couldn't find the right words.

Mom dipped a spoon in the bowl and tasted. "Because Helen is a breath of fresh air and LaMond could use some ventilation now and then. And we need it more now than then."

"Anything else I can do?" I put the dust cloth away.

"While I'm gone, you can blow up the balloons and tie one to the back of each of the chairs. We'll be back around eight. It's a dinner meeting and we have only one piece of business."

If Mom was beaming when she left, she was steaming when she stomped through the kitchen door and slammed her plate of divinity on the table. I figured something was wrong—either with her divinity or her club.

"Where are the others?" I asked.

"The party's canceled."

"Didn't anybody like the candy?" I asked, lifting the aluminum foil.

"Nobody tasted it. I didn't give them a chance. Somebody blackballed Helen Irvine!" She started down the hall, removing her best pair of earrings as she went.

"Who did it?" It was a dumb question. Until I asked, I'd forgotten the Atheneum ritual. They actually had a bunch of black and white balls the size of marbles. When they wanted to vote on something important, they dropped a ball into a purple velvet bag that Mom, as secretary, was in charge of. White for yes. Black for no.

"Who knows?" she called from her bedroom.

"Why?"

"Why do you think? It's the same old pattern."

"What pattern?"

She walked back and stuck her head around the kitchen door. "Marti! Use your brain. Anyone else would just be Helen, who, with her family, moved into the old LaMond house and opened a hardware store. But, no! She's Mrs. Irvine *and* she's Jewish *and* she's involved with Save Our Shores." She disappeared again.

"May I have a piece of divinity?" I shouted after her.

"Help yourself," she replied.

When she came back, she'd changed into her usual jeans and sweatshirt.

"Your Atheneums don't know what they're missing," I said, reaching for another piece of candy.

"How right you are, Marti," she said patting my hand and rescuing the plate of divinity.

"Who's going to tell her?"

"I am." She put on her hooded coat and picked up the candy. "I'm going to walk up to Hill House, offer her my candy, and apologize for Atheneum. To think the club was supposed to be a literary society that seeks wisdom!"

I didn't wait up for Mom. I think it was past midnight before she got home. The next morning I asked her how it went.

"She loved my candy," was all Mom would say.

Turnover

After Christmas most of LaMond seemed to forget the Irvines. Once in a while you'd hear someone call Handy Harry's "the Jew store," and there was a rumor that they did all their "real" banking in the town where they went to church on Saturdays, but they'd stopped being the main topic of interest. Bud Newby was almost the only one who still believed Sarah's dad carried a roll of money "big enough to choke a horse."

Instead, as basketball season got underway and our team started winning, the only thing everyone talked about was the prospect of the Tigerettes making it all the way to the State Tournament. Not Coach, though.

The first thing she did was convince us to change our name. "You're not a bunch of 'ettes,' and if you're going to win, you're going to have to play like tigers." The whole school voted and it was unanimous. We became the Tigers.

Even though by mid-January we'd sailed past all the teams we'd played, every practice was just as hard as if we were at the bottom of our league.

"Marti, you have to attack the basket."

"Muffie, don't take that extra dribble! Pass! Pass! Pass!"

"Don't pass, Sarah, take the shot! You can hit it from outside!"

"Move it or lose it, Liz! It's not a half-court game anymore!"

"Angie, keep those passes hard and straight. Don't toss the ball!"

Over and over, we sweated through the basics: footwork, passing, dribbling, shooting, rebounding. Over and over, Coach's voice: "Make the play! Stick to the pattern! Don't think! Let your muscles remember!"

And the patterns and our muscle memory paid off with win after win. The biggest newspaper in the state sent a photographer and reporter when we played Maple Grove, the only real threat to our record. They picked the right game.

The gym was packed full and when we ran onto the court to warm up, between the noise of the crowd and the music of the pep band and the screaming of the cheerleaders, we could barely hear the thud of our own basketballs. By the fourth quarter, the lead had switched back and forth so many times, I lost track.

Muffie's mother, who usually spoke and acted like the Queen of LaMond, was in her usual seat just behind the bench, screaming directions to Muffie, yelling at the referees whenever a call went against us, and insulting

every Maple Grove Rangerette who got near our side of the court. The only person in the gym louder was Bud Newby, whose constant refrain of, "Move it, Sarah!" and, "Get the lead out, Marti!" drowned out even Mrs. Barnes.

With just a few minutes left, it was Sarah who opened up the game for us on a fast break after she picked off a rebound, brought the ball all the way down the court, and passed it to me for an easy, undefended basket. That put us two points ahead, and Coach called time out.

She didn't waste words on compliments, just swatted Sarah on the shoulder and nodded at me. "Muffie, get the ball out-of-bounds. Sarah, Marti, it's give and go whoever's free to start it. Pattern!"

The pattern worked. Muffie forced the Maple Grove girl into a turnover, took the ball out-of-bounds, fired it in to Sarah, who passed to me, and then cut toward the basket. I faked a move in the same direction and Sarah's guard dropped her to double cover me.

It was a perfect setup. I got the ball to Sarah, whose layup was so soft it kissed the glass. We had a four-point lead at the buzzer.

Once again, Sarah and I shared a picture in the paper, not as "local girls," but as the "Twin Tigers," a name that stuck for the rest of the season.

On the court, at practice or in a game, the Tigers were a tight team: Sarah and Muffie at guard; Angie and Liz playing forward positions; and me at center. The sports writers gave us more nicknames—The Fabulous Five and the Terrible Tigers pleased us most.

Off court was different. We ate together in the

cafeteria, all of us except Sarah, who always, even in rotten weather, walked home for lunch.

"They eat different food from us," Muffie explained one day. "Like they can't eat pork, for example. It's an allergy or something."

Liz looked shocked—maybe because she couldn't imagine anything that couldn't be eaten or because her older sister had once been the County Pork Queen.

I didn't bother to mention the pork tenderloin sandwiches Sarah had scarfed down on our trip with Elva.

Since both Liz and Angie lived way out in the country, they didn't hang around after practice, and Sarah disappeared almost as quickly, to plunge into homework, I was positive. Since we were in most of the same classes, it was impossible not to be aware that she was always prepared for anything the teachers could dream up to throw at us. I also had a sneaky hunch that her grades on papers were higher than mine.

That left Muffie and me to bump along together as we always had. She'd mellowed out a little bit about Sarah, at least most of the time. Maybe it was because Jason was gone for his first year of college or because her parents had finally given her a car of her own. Or maybe she felt guilty about what everybody in town assumed her mother, Mrs. Barnes, had done to Sarah's mother . . . blackballed her.

When four of us Tigers discovered we'd each received an invitation to a surprise party for Sarah's birthday, we were the ones who were amazed.

"I didn't know they did birthdays," Muffie said as we

slid into our usual places at the lunch table. "But did you notice the writing? That's real calligraphy!"

"Cal . . . what?" Angie asked.

"It means very fancy penmanship," I said.

"That and the paper and the envelope! Did you feel them? I'll bet they cost a lot."

Muffie had a real eye for money.

"Who else do you think was invited?" Angie stopped in mid-chew and stared across the lunchroom.

"Who knows? The point is, what are we going to do?" Liz was about as subtle as a baseball bat, but she put into words what we were all thinking.

"Either way we'll all have to RSVP." Muffie looked over at me as if she'd sunk a three-pointer.

"What do you mean?" Liz leaned forward.

"Oh," Muffie explained. "It's Spanish or French or something. It means you have to tell whether you're going to come or not."

"I know you have to tell them if you're coming or not, but I never heard what it stands for . . . have you?" Liz licked her fingers and retrieved the last crumb of her brownie.

"Well, have you ever heard of a mother giving a surprise party either?" Muffie snapped.

"Maybe we could write one letter and everybody could sign it," Angie suggested.

"It says dinner." Muffie pulled the invitation from her book bag. "We can't not go. We'll get to see the inside of Hill House. Bud Newby told my dad they spent a fortune on it."

"Then, I mean, are we actually going?" Angie looked worried. "Of course, my dad says never to pass up a free lunch."

The silence at the table lasted almost a second too long before the rest of us answered. "Of course, sure, you bet."

"Well, then," Muffie said, "shall we chip in for a present or buy separate ones?"

"The invitation said, 'No presents, thank you.'" I said.

"Well, that's not the way we do it in LaMond," Muffie said. "I mean, what good is a birthday without a present? Besides, Sarah will expect one and we don't want to look like . . ." I knew she changed the word she was going to use. "Like pikers, do we?"

"She doesn't know about the party," I reminded her. "So how could she expect a present?"

"Oh, whatever." Muffie closed her eyes, did little figuring motions with her fingers. "Five dollars each," she announced. "Marti and I will be the gift committee. We'll go to the mall tomorrow and prowl."

"What will we wear to the party?" Angie sounded like a kid going to her first day of school. "I mean, it said 'dinner,' not 'supper,' and 'entertainment afterward.'"

We all looked at Muffie as if she were LaMond's answer to Miss Manners.

"We'll dress up, of course. It'll probably be a formal dinner and we don't want to look like a bunch of hicks."

As we left the table, Muffie grabbed my arm. "Pick you up at ten. Start thinking present."

Mom had a few words for me as we waited for Muffie

to pick me up the next day. "Keep her in sight and be careful. Don't let her carry that big tote bag of hers. It'll be a real test for her."

"You knew all about the party, didn't you?" I leaned against the kitchen door.

She grinned at me. "Who do you think made the invitations?"

"You're kidding! I didn't know you could do stuff like that."

"Another hidden talent. I haven't tried it for years. They looked good, didn't they?"

She looked so pleased with herself that I told her, "Muffie thought a professional did them. Who else is invited?"

"The Terrible Tigers, of course."

"The whole team or just the starters?"

"All of you. Leaving anyone out wouldn't exactly boost team spirit, would it?"

"Great," I said. "That'll make it lots easier."

"Easier? It's a party, not a ball game."

"Yeah, I know, but this way we don't have to worry about running out of things to talk about." I heard Muffie's car pull in the drive.

Mom frowned. "Since when has Muffie ever had trouble talking?"

"Never," I said and laughed, but I hadn't been thinking of Muffie; I'd been thinking about me.

Muffie and I thought "present" all the way down to Sioux Point and most of the afternoon as we covered practically every store in the East Mall and continued

searching at the West Mall. I hovered over her like a shadow.

"It's hard to shop with just twenty dollars," Muffie complained. "Especially when we don't know what we're looking for. It ought to be something cheap that screams 'money.'"

We stopped in a little jewelry shop where Muffie slipped a gold chain from a display carousel. "How about this? It's only nineteen dollars." At the end of the chain hung a gold cross.

I looked at her and shook my head.

"Well, maybe we can find one with a guardian angel or something." Muffie put the necklace back and I took a deep breath. Mrs. Irvine could get rid of the evidence in Handy Harry's window.

"Let's try over there." I guided her to another counter.

We found a plain gold chain but it was marked $24.50.

"Maybe we could jew them down," Muffie said. Sometimes Muffie's brain wasn't connected to her mouth.

"Muffie!" I tried to keep my voice down, but her name came out so loudly that the clerk at the next counter looked at us. "You shouldn't say that—especially when we're buying a present for Sarah."

"Say what?" Sometimes Muffie could be just plain stupid. Sometimes she pretended she was stupid. Most of the time I couldn't tell the difference.

"'Jew them down,'" I whispered. "Like you shouldn't say 'welsh' on someone."

"Why not?"

"Because . . ." I searched for an explanation. "Because some people *are* Welsh."

Muffie wasn't interested. "Okay, whatever," she said. "Let's get the necklace. You and I can split the difference."

We split the cost of a birthday card too. It was sappy but cheap:

> *A cheerful birthday message*
> *we're sending your way.*
> *May you remember*
> *This happy, happy day!*

There were some really funny, nasty, insulting cards, but they were the kinds you could send only to a best friend.

The first surprise of Sarah's party for the team was when Mom, not Mrs. Irvine, opened the door of Hill House and invited us in. Maybe it was better that way because all fifteen of us managed to arrive at the same time and since everybody had known Mom forever, it wasn't so much like going into a strange house. She explained that Sarah and Mrs. Irvine were on their way back from driving Sarah's dad to the airport to catch a plane, and that helped too. It allowed everyone a chance to take a good look around without having to be polite.

I checked out the four of us and then glanced at the rest of the kids. "We're way too dressed up," I told Muffie. Everyone else looked like they were going to spend an evening hanging out with friends on a lazy

Saturday night. We were the only ones dressed for going to a graduation reception.

"We show good taste," Muffie muttered back. "Forget it."

Liz was excited about the parquet floor in the entryway. She punched Angie in the arm. "Would you look at this? It'd be perfect to practice dancing." She and Angie had just gotten hooked on learning the western line dances, probably because Liz could finally fit into a pair of tight jeans.

Mom directed us into the den where a fire was blazing in the fireplace, and music spun down from speakers mounted on the wall. Cans of pop in an ice-filled cooler and enough junk food for the whole school were laid out on a table at the end of the room.

Muffie was busy scoping out the furniture while everyone else was munching and rehashing whatever happened during the day. It was like being in the hallway at school when you say, "How's it going?" to someone you talked to before the last class. Mom had been right—no one had any trouble talking.

The noise level was rising when Mom stuck her head through the doorway. "They just drove in. Get ready!"

For a little while, we'd all forgotten about the reason we were there. Anyway, we stopped talking and waited, grinning at each other as if we, and not Sarah's mom, had dreamed up the whole idea. I don't think any of us had been given a birthday party since we were little kids. And it never had been a surprise.

We heard the front door open and Mrs. Irvine's voice

saying, "Honey, just take those books to the den and put them on the desk, will you?"

As Sarah walked into the room, we jumped to our feet, screaming, "Surprise! Surprise!"

Then she did something with the books she was carrying that she'd never done with a basketball. She dropped them. The kids went crazy. "Turnover! Turnover!" they shouted. "You lost the ball!"

They were watching her hands. I was watching her face.

She looked at me, her eyebrows arched, her mouth hesitating between a gasp and a smile. It was as if we were on the court in the middle of a tight game and she was looking for some kind of signal that she could understand and the opposition couldn't see. For that instant I was sure I knew what she felt, so I shrugged and grinned and opened my arms in a wide gesture.

Sarah's response was immediate as she imitated me. "Oh! Wow!" she said. "I don't believe it!"

Then everyone yelled "Happy Birthday" and rushed around her to give the kind of team hug we ended every game with. I was on the outside of the circle, but for a little while, I felt as if I'd thrown her the perfect pass that allowed her to make the perfect basket that won the most important game of the season.

By the time the party ended, we'd demolished a tableful of pizzas, a five-foot-long submarine sandwich, and almost all of the pop. We were roasting marshmallows in the fireplace and making our own S'mores when Sarah's mother brought in a small gift-wrapped box.

"Happy birthday, honey," she said and hugged Sarah, then turned to us. "I was going to save this for later, but then I thought since you're all Sarah's friends, she might like to share it with you."

Muffie looked at me and winked. I pretended not to notice and watched Sarah unwrap the present.

She looked puzzled. "It's a videotape," she said, "but there's no title."

"Put it in the VCR," Liz said. "Maybe it's highlights of the Tigers' winning season."

"Or an up-close profile of Tom Hanks!" Angie suggested.

"Or how about a film of guys pumping iron?" somebody added.

"That's the biggest screen I've ever seen in my life," Liz whispered as Sarah adjusted the set.

"They probably got it wholesale," Muffie muttered back.

When the screen came alive, there was no picture at first, just some soft music and a man's voice. "Sarah, you've given us seventeen years of joy, and your mother and I hope that these few minutes of film will give you the same pleasure. For us, always, you will be exactly what your name means—a princess."

The music came up and a title came on, just like a real movie: *The Princess, starring Sarah Irvine.* You could hear a little gasp from the kids as if they'd never seen a video before.

The tape lasted about half an hour, but it wasn't like watching someone's boring home movies. It was all

about Sarah, of course, but someone had taken photographs and videotapes with her in them and put them together like something you'd see on public television with really neat music and Mr. Irvine telling the story of Sarah's life.

It was weird to watch Sarah on the screen and the real Sarah at the same time. She really had been a baby once, grabbing a chunk of her first birthday cake and smearing icing all over her face. Growing up, except that it was in some other place, she didn't seem different from any of us.

It could have been LaMond except for one time when there were pictures of her at a party that the voice said was a bat-mitzvah and Sarah was in the middle of a whole bunch of people and she was answering questions and making a speech in a language I'd never heard before.

The very last pictures on the screen were the photographs of Sarah and me, first with Elva and then in our basketball uniforms. When it was over, the kids clapped and yelled like they'd been watching an Academy Award winner.

Sarah looked up at her mother. "That's the best present I've ever had in my life. Thank you."

Maybe, for a minute, I felt a little jealous. I knew Mom loved me just as much as Sarah's parents loved her, but pictures of me had ended with one of my leaving for my first day of kindergarten. I had been crying, my nose was running, and I did not look at all like a princess.

Mom stayed to help clean up, so after we said good-bye to Sarah, Muffie and I walked home together.

"I think she really liked the necklace," I said.

"Oh, who knows?" Muffie answered. "She's always so polite you can't tell what she's thinking. And did you see the stack of presents she got at that religious party? That bat whatever? I didn't know she could speak Jewish. Do you suppose they talk that way at home? It sounds so . . . foreign."

"I think it's called Hebrew," I said. I didn't want to talk because I was thinking of how Sarah's and my face had looked on the TV screen. If you didn't know better, you would have sworn we were the best friends in the world.

January and February disappeared in a blur of basketball: long, noisy bus rides through snow and ice to dozens of different high-school gyms that all smelled and sounded the same. Mom and the Irvines made it to most of the games, but Mrs. Barnes and Bud were always there with lots of advice for Coach that she didn't need. The whole town was behind us.

The united front came unglued, though, the night we played Beaconsfield. Word came over the Maple Grove radio station that the judge had ruled in favor of Elva and her SOSers. Mr. Barnes and Bud Newby and the rest of the developers had lost out.

That night, just before tip-off, the Barneses, Bud, and a whole bunch of their friends marched into the gym and sat down at the west end of the bleachers, leaving no

space for anyone else. When Mom, Elva, Helen, Marvia, and *their* bunch came, they sat at the east end.

Whenever we made a basket we were caught in the middle of stereophonic sound.

I wasn't sure whether we won the game because Sarah out-shot the Beaconettes with her dead-eye three-pointers or if we won because the "divided" town of LaMond tried to out-shout each other.

When I got home, Mom and the rest of them were sitting around our dining room table.

"It's a rift that may never heal," Marvia was saying. "You know how long it took for people to get over my buying a computer for the library."

I sat down on the stairway and listened.

"Quentin Barnes has always been a poor loser." Elva lowered her voice as if he were close enough to hear her.

"The town will survive and we'll probably live to hear them take credit for protecting the shoreline." Mom laughed.

"And the best fishing spot on the lake," Marvia added.

Mom turned to Sarah's mother. "There's one thing to be said for LaMond, Helen. We may not use the same hymnals, but sooner or later we remember we're all in the same choir."

"Quentin might join the choir faster if we all pulled our money from his bank." Marvia sounded serious.

"I'm not sure." Elva pushed herself away from the table. "Winners forget in time. Losers remember."

"I have an idea." Everyone looked at Mrs. Irvine. "We

could reorganize SOS into BOS—Beautify-Our-Shores—and make a park on that stretch of shoreline."

"What a wonderful thought!" Elva almost shouted.

Mom joined in. "Elva, you could talk to Quentin Barnes and see if he wouldn't like to be the first contributor."

"I know just how to do it. Tell him that if he'll make a substantial donation, we'll see the park is named after him. That man always was in love with his own name." She paused for a minute. "And we could see that Bud Newby gets to build a gazebo and tables and benches."

They were deep into their plans when I went to bed.

By the time we got through the district and regional games, I was one of the top scorers in the state and Sarah was gathering honors for rebounding and free-throw shooting. Without Sarah around, I would have been shooting more, but with no Sarah, the other teams' scoring might have been out of control.

March Madness! The Sweet Sixteen! We were undefeated in conference play, undefeated in district and regional tournaments, and headed for the capital city and Girls' State Basketball Tournament. Whenever we'd be playing that week, the whole town of LaMond would close down. There'd be chartered buses and caravans of cars all headed past Lake Ulmer for the game.

On the bus, we crept through city traffic and finally pulled up in front of the President's Hotel, the school bus plastered on both sides with big orange and black signs:

LaMond Tigers Number One! Wearing our team jackets with the tiger face on the back, we hurried out of the bus.

"We stayed in a place like this last summer," Muffie said. "Wait until you see the pool and hot tub and, besides that, there's a whole room full of video games."

I had never stayed in a hotel before. I didn't think the other kids had either, except for Sarah, so I followed her and tried to act cool.

"Would you look!" Liz stood on the curb staring up at the building. "It's got fifteen stories. I counted them."

"We're not here to count stories," Coach ordered. "Pick up your luggage and bring it into the lobby while I sort out room assignments."

The air was full of strange smells, stale and heavy, not clean and fresh like at home, and there was a constant roar of cars whizzing by, horns honking, and tires screeching. My stomach felt funny, but maybe it was from having been on the bus for so long.

The five of us starters shared one big room and the rest of the team were in rooms along the same hallway.

We were unpacking, but Liz couldn't pull herself away from the window. "Imagine being this high up. People sure look funny down there."

Muffie had brought enough clothes to last a month and she was hogging most of the hangers.

"We have to eat here in the hotel tonight," she announced, "but tomorrow after practice, we get to go shopping and we can eat lunch wherever we want to."

"Shopping for what?" Angie asked.

"I'm going to look for a prom dress. Mom says there's a great store here."

"I'm not thinking about proms." Liz finally turned away from the window. "I'm worried about how it will feel out on the court of the auditorium. You know how it looks on TV—enormous!"

We didn't talk much after that. Maybe we were all wondering the same things: Were we as good as LaMond thought we were? What if we lost our first game?

For almost as long as I could remember, I'd listened to radio broadcasts of the State Tournament or watched the finals on television, but nothing had prepared me for what it was like to walk into the auditorium. No wonder the players, most of them from small towns like ours, called it "the Big Barn."

I'd heard stories about "tournament jitters" and I had a first-class case of them. Sitting behind the basket at one end and looking down the floor was like trying to see the goalposts at the end of a football field. Everything seemed strange, the players tiny and the baskets high and completely out of range.

What I felt must have shown on my face, but only Sarah noticed. Maybe the rest of the team was as awestruck as I was.

"Hey," I heard her voice close to my ear, "do you think Bud Newby's got a voice loud enough for this place?"

The idea made me laugh. "Maybe not," I whispered back, "but Muffie's mom does."

And just that fast the jitters faded and I began looking forward to our first game.

The whole week was like living inside a dream where things moved faster or slower than they should and nothing stayed quite in proportion. Tasting the first bite of pizza in our hotel room was more exciting than watching the last seconds of a game that knocked out one of our biggest potential rivals. I wondered if anyone else felt the way I did—maybe Sarah. I didn't ask though, because it would sound crazy, and as team captain, I was supposed to be totally in control.

Our first-round game was with the Hawkettes, a team from up in the northwest corner of the state. We had the game won in the first quarter and they never came close to catching us after that. The next afternoon we faced some Rockettes from down on the state line. They had us beat until their star forward fouled out along with their tallest guard. In the last few minutes of the last quarter we began to take over and we sneaked by with a three-point victory. That left us taking on the Elfs from Elfton in the championship game of the tournament.

Elfton was even smaller than LaMond and as long as I could remember they'd managed to send a team to State. Given a choice I would have picked almost any other team, even from one of the bigger schools, to meet in the final round. Bud Newby always said they didn't raise anything down in Elfton except girl basketball players and corn.

We'd watched them play a couple of days earlier when they destroyed the Zephyrettes, last year's champs. In our hotel room, after the game, we rehashed the disaster.

"Those were the biggest elfs I ever saw," Sarah said. "Those guards must be almost six feet tall!"

"And that's *without* shoes," Liz moaned. "I think they're clones."

"Cousins," I told her. "Haven't you noticed? Year after year the last names never change."

"Ditka, Dykstra, Dawson," Angie chanted. "And about every other year a Fresson and a Felson."

"And the one who plays post," Muffie said. "Dinah Dawson! She's as tall as you, Marti, and twice as big around. She just runs over whoever's guarding her and never gets called for charging."

"Yeah, and did you notice in the papers the writers keep calling them the team from tiny Elfton? Like they're always underdogs or something. They're not underdogs, they're practically an industry."

"And their cheerleaders are so tacky!" It was Angie's turn. "They're not even original. They just copy everybody else's yells."

"What bothers me," Sarah began and we all leaned forward to listen because none of us thought anything ever bothered Sarah. "That little girl in the green outfit and the shoes with pointy, curled-up toes."

"The mascot," I agreed. "I'll bet she's three years old and the coach's daughter. Somebody should step on her and put her out of her misery."

"If they don't stop shoving popcorn and candy in her mouth, she'll never make it to kindergarten." Liz looked happy with the idea.

"Lights out, girls!" Coach said as she opened our door. "To bed!"

I think we were glad to stop talking about the Elfs, but I'll bet all of us dreamed about them that night.

The dream turned into a nightmare when we met them on the court.

Not at first, of course. After surviving earlier games, we'd adjusted pretty well to the huge arena. We knew the court was ten feet longer than anything we'd been used to, but after the first game, it didn't seem like much of a problem. The real hang-up had been the freestanding baskets.

Everywhere else we'd played, the baskets stuck out from a wall. Even though the backboards were see-through plastic, there was nothing behind them to see except for a gym wall. No bleachers, no shouting fans, just a blank wall.

Here, the baskets hung from the ceiling and looked like they were suspended in space while beyond them, row after row of fans screamed and waved. It was bad enough for me lurking around the free-throw lane in the post position, but for the guards, if they wanted to make a long shot, they must have felt like they were looking through the wrong end of a telescope. The most we hoped for was that every team felt as disoriented as we did.

The nightmare had nothing to do with the people

watching: whole high schools, mothers, fathers, aunts, uncles, and townfuls of hopeful enthusiasts including half-naked boys, their faces and torsos painted in team colors. There were cameras everywhere, not just the ones hometown newspapers used, but television cameras that you knew were tracking every move, showing every mistake.

The nightmare began when, halfway through the first quarter, the score was Elfs 16–Tigers 8. We were being eaten up by a bunch of giant gnomes.

I was cold. Stone cold. Nothing I touched would drop through that magic hoop. Muffie, Angie, and Liz kept us on the scoreboard. Sarah hadn't even tried a shot. If our defense hadn't worked, more or less, we could have been twenty points behind. It was so pathetic that even Bud Newby wasn't yelling.

At our first time-out, Coach didn't waste words. "Defense, attack the ball. Make them change their game. Sarah, until Marti gets her touch, set up for the others, but if you have the chance, shoot from the outside. Don't push it, but give them something to think about. Now, go do it! There's a whole game left to play!"

It wasn't pretty, but we gutted our way through the rest of the quarter and ended trailing by four points. I couldn't figure out what was going so wrong. The Elfs were good, but not that good. Something was wrong with us. It was easier to think "us" than "me."

The second quarter wasn't much better. We'd manage a rebound and they'd steal the ball on our way back down the court. Angie turned the ball over twice and I

got a charging foul. They couldn't miss a free throw and Muffie muffed two easy layups. We were lucky to go into the half only six points down.

We huddled, lumped together in the locker room, not looking at each other. I stared at the floor and remembered how impressed I'd been to find it covered with carpet instead of bare cement. Right then, broken glass would have been more appropriate.

We all expected Coach to take each one of us apart, piece by piece, to stomp around and yell and somehow, just by sheer noise, to put us back together as a team. She'd tried almost everything else—giving us new plays at time-outs, sending in more substitutes than she'd done all season.

Instead, she looked at us as if she'd been dropped in the wrong room at the wrong time. "You're twice the team they are," she said very quietly. "Go figure." And then she left.

We sat, sweating and silent, as the locker room door closed behind her. Then everyone was looking at me and waiting. As captain, I knew I should say something, anything.

Instead, it was Sarah who spoke. "She's right. We *are* better and we can win this walking away." It wasn't like a pep talk, it was more as if she was talking to herself, and we all listened hard. "We're not playing together, we're playing separately. We're not acting, we're reacting. We're letting them run our game plan."

"Sarah's right," Liz said, toweling her face. "Our rebounding is fine, but we're letting them make the

shots. We've got to stop them before they shoot. And *we've* got to move the ball to the basket instead of standing out there playing catch with each other."

"So what do we do?" Angie asked. "I mean how do we start?"

I finally found my voice. "We get serious on defense. Stay in their faces till they cough up the ball." I turned to Sarah. "You've got to start shooting from outside." I waited a minute and added out loud what I'd been thinking since the game began. "And I've got to start scoring."

"We're not getting the ball to you enough," Muffie said to me, but she was looking at Sarah. "And they've been double-teaming you the whole half. They're trying to stop you from a tournament scoring record."

"It's not a record that's important," I said, almost meaning it. "It's winning that counts."

Coach came back in time to hear what I was saying. She leaned against the lockers and looked at us, smiling for the first time since the game started. "Sounds like you *did* go and figure. Now let's get out there and win!"

We didn't dominate the third quarter, we devoured it. Everything we'd been working on all year came together and we were a team again. We held them to ten points and made them fight for every basket. Sarah put on an exhibition of three-point shooting that brought the audience to its feet and pulled one of the guards off me.

For whatever reason, besides all those hours of practice, I found the basket again.

Just when it looked as if the fourth quarter would

belong to us too, they began to climb back—at first matching us basket for basket, then, despite our defense, going on a scoring run of their own that left them a point ahead with less than a minute to play.

Liz and Angie had fouled out and the two sophomores who came in for them were trying hard but weren't able to score.

After the Elf's go-ahead basket, Sarah, dribbling at top speed, brought the ball back past center court with a guard matching her step for step until their legs tangled and both of them crashed to the floor, the ball squirting out-of-bounds. It should have been a foul because it was a deliberate trip, but nobody called it. All we got was the ball back. At least the clock had stopped and we were nearer the basket.

Coach called a time-out and we huddled around trying to hear her voice over the roar that came from the thirty thousand fans who filled the auditorium.

"Sarah, get the ball inbounds to Muffie. They'll expect you to throw it to Marti. Marti, set up next to the basket. Sarah, when you get the ball back, fake to one of the forwards, then shoot. Marti will be in position for the rebound if the shot misses and the ball will be in the air before the buzzer sounds. Whatever you do, don't foul."

Time-out ended and we were back on the floor. Sarah lobbed the ball to Muffie over the upraised arms of the Elfs, and dashed back on the court. Muffie got the ball back to her with a crisp bounce pass, and Sarah faked a pass to me, only it wasn't a fake!

The ball came like a baseball, hard and fast and

straight. I caught it chest high, pivoted, and shot just one second too late. The final buzzer went off before the ball left my hands.

"Why?" I asked Sarah, letting all my anger show, as we stumbled back to the bench. "Why did you break the play?" I knew she could hear me even over the celebration that had exploded at the far end of the court. "Did you *want* us to lose?"

She looked at me for a minute, wordless, turned, and headed toward the locker room.

"Jew!"

I didn't know where in me the word came from or why I made it sound like something dirty. I didn't think she heard me, but *I* heard myself and the ugliness made me feel sick.

We were all in the locker room, still trying to believe the game had slipped away from us, when Coach's voice cut through our misery.

"Why didn't you tell me?" she almost shouted at Sarah. We all stared in the direction Coach was looking.

The thumb on Sarah's right hand, her shooting hand, stuck out at an odd angle and was swollen double its normal size.

It was very late and everyone else in the hotel room, except for Sarah and me, had finally fallen asleep. In only a few more hours we'd be back on the bus riding to LaMond for the celebration of being runners-up in the State Tournament.

"Does it hurt?" I whispered.

We stood next to each other at the window, looking out at the city streets where only a few cars moved, but neon signs still glowed from the empty auditorium a couple of blocks away.

"Not much." Her voice was as hushed as mine. "The doctor gave me a pain pill." She was quiet for a moment. "What really hurts is my making us lose. I should have pulled out of the game."

"If you'd pulled out we would have lost for sure. This way there was a chance." I pressed my forehead against the coolness of the windowpane.

"I was supposed to take the shot," she said as if she'd repeated the words to herself many, many times. "The play was set. The pattern was there. I broke the pattern and you weren't expecting the pass."

"So you broke the pattern. But I made the basket," I reminded her, "even if it didn't count. And we're both on All-Tournament Team."

We didn't talk anymore. Sarah went to bed, but I wasn't sleepy. I listened to a police siren break the stillness of the city streets.

If I'd just reacted faster those last few seconds of the game . . . but she was supposed to take the shot, not me. It wasn't my fault. Even that didn't help.

I stayed awake trying to figure out why I'd said "Jew" instead of "bitch" or "dork" or "scumbag," or any one of a hundred other words. I'd said it automatically.

Where had the hatred come from?

The next day, I slumped in the rear of the bus, the

TIGERS NUMBER ONE sign crumpled beneath my seat. Muffie was up front surrounded by shopping bags. Sarah sat alone in a double seat.

Just a few steps and one word separated us. I scrabbled for a way out. If she hadn't heard what I'd called her, I'd have to say the same thing again, explain, and I didn't have an explanation. If she *had* heard . . . but she must not have or she would have said something last night at the hotel.

I gave up. Either way I was worse than whoever painted the swastika on Sarah's windshield or the person who blackballed Helen Irvine. I'd let what *they* thought creep into me.

It was a long ride back to LaMond.

As we rounded Five-Mile Corner outside of town, the sheriff's car, red light flashing, pulled out to escort us home. Behind our bus, a whole convoy of cars, horns honking, followed us to the high school.

As the bus lurched to a stop, I stood up and walked slowly up the aisle. Maybe we could start over again.

I stopped beside Sarah, who was making no move to join the cheering crowd outside. Touching her on the shoulder, I took a deep breath, leaned over, and whispered the only Jewish word I knew. "Shalom. Your mom said it means 'peace.'"

Sarah looked up at me. "Was there a fight?"

I breathed out in relief. Sarah hadn't heard what I'd called her at the end of the game!

Or had she?